TRESPASSING IN GOD'S COUNTRY
Sixty Years of Flying in Northern Canada

by
George Theriault

edited by
Elizabeth Theriault Pasco

TRESPASSING IN GOD'S COUNTRY
Sixty Years of Flying in Northern Canada
by George Theriault
edited by Elizabeth Theriault Pasco

Treeline Publishing,
a division of Theriault Air Services Ltd.
P.O. Box 269
Chapleau, Ontario P0M 1K0
©1994 Elizabeth Theriault Pasco

Notice of Liability
The maps displayed in this book are not to scale. They are to be used as reference only, not for navigation purposes.

Editor's Note
The stories have been written based on my father's personal memory of incidents in his life. There may be some slight inaccuracies of dates and names.

ISBN 1-887472-46-0

CONTENTS

THE EARLY YEARS

J-3 Cub at Makobe Lake, 1946

As a youngster, growing up in the small mining town of Timmins, I first learned to fish for pike and walleye (doré as we French Canadians called them because of their golden colour) with a bamboo pole, a strong line, a hook and a sinker. When casting rods became the fashion, my brothers and I eagerly followed the trend. And when my father bought a square-stern canoe and a motor, we began to travel further and further down the Mattagami River. As the town of Timmins expanded, the fish were more difficult to catch so we pushed deeper into the bush travelling the creeks, portages and lakes where the fishing was still virgin. We left home around the first of July when the black fly season was over and, except for one brief trip home for supplies, we spent the entire summer fishing and exploring in the wilderness.

DISCOVERING GOLD AND BUSH FLYING

In the early 1900s, gold was discovered in the hills around Timmins. All kinds of fortune hunters headed north where mining claims were staked by hundreds of prospectors. People say that Ben Hollinger was travelling between Porcupine Lake and the landing at the Mattagami River when he stopped for lunch and accidentally discovered a gold outcrop that later became the largest producer of gold in Canadian history.

My father, who was a reputable tailor with his own general store, made the move to Timmins when he heard that several of his friends had struck it rich. His family, the Theriaults, had grown up side-by-side with the Timmins family in the small community of Bonfield, just south of North Bay. He had apprenticed as a tailor in his father's general store and was accomplished in his trade but his real pursuit was prospecting for gold. His search

had taken him first to Cobalt then to Michipicoten Harbour (Wawa) and finally to Timmins.

By the time my dad arrived in Timmins to seek his fortune, Noah Timmins had already bought Benny Hollinger's claims and the mines were just getting underway. Another prospector, Sandy McIntyre, had sold his claims for a reported sum of $25,000 cash to the Bannermans! My dad was determined to find a place among his fortunate friends who had become rich and famous. In order to survive until he too hit the jackpot, he opened a tailor shop, hired stakers and took options on several mining claims. Some of these claims later became gold producers. But, unfortunately, my dad's timing was never quite right and his hopes of establishing a prosperous mine never came to fruition. Long after he had retired from his trade and lost his eyesight,

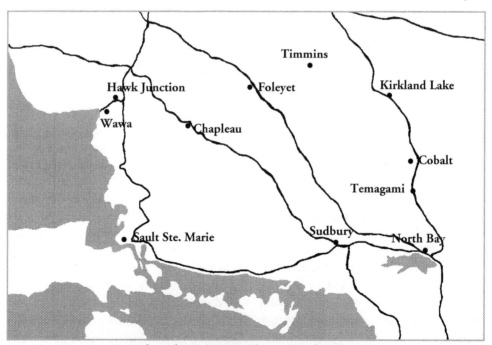

A section of northern Ontario showing railroad connections

he continued to prospect, hoping to find the mother lode. He was so sure that one of his claims would be a good producer that the Theriault family still maintains the claim to this day.

During the 1920s, a prospector, who didn't have the funds to settle his debt at my dad's tailor shop, gave up seven mining claims located twenty miles south of South Porcupine in MacArthur Township. A small amount of surface showings of high grade gold was found but this disappeared when the drills went below fifty feet. It was, therefore, determined that the claim wasn't worth further expenditure.

While the geologists investigated the area they took shelter in a cabin that had been built especially for them. Later, in the 1930s, when I was about twelve years old, I discovered this cabin while walking the twenty-mile trail from MacArthur Lake to Timmins. The geologists hadn't found enough gold to start a mine, but it was a golden spot to enjoy the best walleye fishing and moose hunting in the area.

It was a two-day hike for a twelve-year-old, from Timmins to MacArthur Lake. Even though there was a trapper's camp midway where we could find shelter for the night, it was still an exhausting trip. At one point along the way, we had to wade through a three-mile swamp which deterred all but the hardiest of youngsters. Most of the guys that made the trip once never did so again. My friends, the Kentys, and a few others, were my regular companions. The treasure of fish and wildlife waiting for us at the end was so rewarding that it pushed us to our physical limits.

During the 1930s and 1940s, this place was a wildlife mecca beyond comparison. One evening while I was cleaning some walleye on the shore, a cow moose and her calf began feeding about a hundred feet from me, just as tame as domes-ticated animals. That night they fed for over an hour and returned to the same place every night for a week or more. A day never went by that we didn't see all kinds of smaller mammals, such as squirrels, chipmunks, mink, porcupine and fox. There were deer on most of the islands on the lake and many beaver lodges on the shores.

One day in the summer of 1934, as my brother Marcel and I were making preparations to leave our camp on MacArthur Lake, an aircraft belonging to the Hollinger Mines, a Custom Waco, landed and tied-up on our dock. The pilot offered us a flight to the airbase in South Porcupine in exchange for a few hours of fishing from our homemade boat. My first flight took only twenty minutes from the camp to town, compared to two full days of walking plus hundreds of fly bites. It was enough to convince me that this was the way to travel in the wilderness.

The very next day, on August 8, 1934, I returned to the seaplane base and began work as a dock boy for Ed Ahr, the pilot in charge. A load of concentrated ore had just arrived from Matachewan and my eagerness in helping unload it got me started in my career as a bush pilot and outfitter.

I worked every day until school resumed in September, then every weekend until freeze-up in late October. The seaplane base was crawling with prospectors, mining engineers, stakers and trappers. When the weather was suitable, the aircraft flew from dawn to dusk. The mechanics were always desperate for someone to help service the aircraft. While one aircraft was on a flight, I had to thoroughly wipe down another in the hangar; back then the engines threw out a lot of oil.

Despite all my duties on the dock and in the hangar, I managed to accompany the pilots on many of their routine flights. While we waited in the bush for a mining engineer to examine a property, I paddled around the lake until I found the best fishing spots. In those days the lakes were so over-populated with pike and walleye that no live bait was necessary, just a good piece of line and a spoon would bring home enough fish to feed everyone at the airbase.

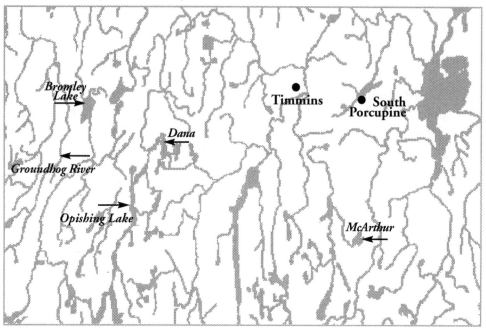

WORKING AT A SEAPLANE BASE

Within two years of working at the seaplane base at South Porcupine, I qualified for my private pilot's license, which I received in June 1936. I continued to work mainly on the dock, loading and unloading the aircraft and helping the mechanics service them in the hangar. The pilots often needed an assistant on longer flights, and since I had both mechanical and piloting skills, I was frequently put in service. It wasn't long before I began to discover all kinds of lakes with spectacular fishing.

One of the highlights of those years was the lake trout fishing on Makobe Lake. While I was stranded there for weather on a weekend in September, I had my first taste of lake trout. A local lumberman, Mr. Harold Wicks, was putting the finishing touches on a log cabin which was located on a small island at the northeast corner, between the small and big lakes. He needed someone to paddle the 16-foot canoe while he tried his luck at catching a few lake trout. I was quite excited about our prospects, as I had never even seen a lake trout except in a magazine.

Mr. Wicks, who often fished at Makobe Lake, knew where to locate the deep holes, since the trout had not yet come to the surface. He used a very short steel rod equipped with a 6-inch reel and about 500 feet of steel monel line. After I had paddled about a mile, he lined up in transit with two high pine trees. At the right spot, he began to let out the steel line slowly to prevent kinks, which would reduce the strength of the line. When about 300 feet of line was let out, he marked the spot with some red paint and I continued to paddle keeping the speed at about 3 mph. Since there was very little wind, I could keep the canoe on a steady course at an even pace. The line was out

for about ten minutes when we had our first strike on the seven-inch Williams wabbler. I watched anxiously as Mr. Wicks played with the trout, tiring it to the point of exhaustion. By the time he brought it alongside the canoe, it had given up the fight. Without using a landing net, Mr. Wicks put his hand into the gills and hoisted the trout into the canoe.

I was mesmerized by the beauty of the fish and wanted to admire it, but by then the lake was dark and the sky overhead merged with the colour of the water—we knew it was the lull before a downpour. Once we arrived back in camp, I had the opportunity to examine this trout closely; it was perfectly proportioned with just a little fat. Obviously the food chain must have been in balance to maintain the maximum growth of the aquatic population.

Mr. Wicks and his hired carpenter, who were from Finland, shared their traditional recipe for baked fish with me. While Mr. Wicks prepared a stuffing of old bread, butter, celery and salt, I cleaned the trout according to his instructions (removed the innards and scales). The carpenter dressed it, placed it in a covered baking dish and put it into the oven of the wood stove for about forty minutes. When it had cooked to the satisfaction of the chefs, the skin was taken off and it was served on a wooden board. The flesh was cooked to such perfection that it fell away from the bones and melted in our mouths. The delicate scent of celery and seasoning from the stuffing made the taste of the fish beyond comparison. To this day, I continue to prepare lake trout and whitefish in much the same way and they are always delicious.

My first experience of lake trout fishing on Makobe Lake left such an impression that I returned there as often as

Harold Wicks at Makobe Lake

new aircraft, delivered on large 5000 EDO floats, with a Pratt and Whitney 450-hp engine. It legally carried 900 pounds and could get off the water in about thirty seconds from full power to lift-off. An Anglican minister, by the name of Harold Smith, who was the chief pilot and engineer, had previously trained in England on large flying boats with Imperial Airways. Since there was very little work in Europe at that time, northern Canada gained one of its best airmen. (Rather sadly, Harold returned to Europe during World War II and was killed when his bomber was sabotaged over Scotland in 1941.) Harold was an ardent fisherman as well. He taught me how to tie flies, make fishing tackle, and repair level winding reels.

The executives of the McIntyre Gold Mines visited the Timmins area regularly from their headquarters in Toronto and expected to be entertained during their stay. We spent a considerable amount of time searching for good fishing lakes to provide them with suitable recreation. On one of our flights with a prospector we landed at Opishing Lake, which is roughly twenty-five miles west of Timmins. While we waited for the prospector to complete his work, the pilot and I appropriated a red canoe which the Department of Lands and Forests had conveniently left in the bush not far from the shore.

We paddled to the foot of the rapids and were totally unprepared for what we found. These are the same rapids which now cross Hwy 101. It was about the first week of July, and even though the flies were still around in full force, the walleye fishing was the best that I had ever experienced. We were using barbless spinners and Heddon Lone Eagle level winding reels with thirty-pound test silk line. No matter what the bait, we had a beautiful walleye on every cast but kept only the

possible over the next three summers and became familiar with most of the good fishing areas, as well as the wildlife that surrounded its shores. Except for a few native people and canoeists from the boys' camps on Lake Temagami, the area remained unknown and unused. When I was released from the RCAF after the war I immediately bought a small floatplane, acquired a cabin on Makobe Lake, and continued to spend my free time exploring, hunting and fishing the entire Maple Mountain area. I discovered that most of the small rivers had excellent speckled trout, especially the Makobe River which empties out at the northeast end of the lake.

During my third summer of working at the seaplane base in South Porcupine, I spent most of my time servicing a Stinson Reliant CF-BGS, which belonged to the McIntyre Gold Mines. This was a brand ones that were over five pounds. During the summers of 1937 and 1938 every executive in the McIntyre Mines hierarchy was treated to a fishing trip at Opishing Lake.

On one of our trips to Opishing Lake we met Mr. Wallingford, a forester from the Timmins branch of the Department of Lands and Forests. He and his colleague had just spent three days paddling up the river system from Timmins. While we chatted about the fishing on Opishing, he revealed his latest discovery to us—lake trout fishing at Dana Lake which was just a few miles away. A few days later, we made a side trip to explore the possibilities at this new lake and met Mr. Wallingford and his colleague there. It had taken them a day to make the trip from Opishing to Dana; whereas, we flew over in a few minutes.

I learned some valuable lessons about fishing for lake trout during the hot summer months at Makobe Lake. For example, when the surface water is warm, the fish tend to feed in the deep water where the temperature is around 41°F. It took me about three hours to find a hundred feet of water, leaving little time for fishing; but the following day, we fished in earnest and the results were well worth our investment. The lake trout fishing on Dana was just as good as Makobe and much closer to the airbase. The company flew in two canoes along with camping equipment, and it became one of our regular fishing spots for the next two summers.

Over the years of working at the seaplane base, I met a countless number of sportsmen, trappers and prospectors. Since many of them came to the airbase regularly to fly into their mining claims or cabins in the bush, I got to know some of them quite well. The owner of a hardware store in Timmins, Mr. Chateauvert, was one of my favourite sportsmen. Every few weeks we flew him and a geologist into Dana Lake for a few hours of surveying. While the geologist scoured the bush for mineral showings, I paddled Mr. Chateauvert around in a canoe in search of lake trout. He always knew the right lure and the right depth to catch lake trout. I don't recall him taking home any fish himself, but he did give me one that weighed about twenty pounds. That was the largest lake trout I saw come out of the area during those summers. We also caught several 25-pound northern pike with either live herring or Williams wabblers in about eighty feet of water.

In the 1930s, all kinds of people who worked in the bush were becoming accustomed to the convenience of using seaplanes as their method of travel. Trappers who usually spent most of the summer months hauling their supplies by canoe into their camps began to hire an aircraft to transport them, and their summer's work was completed in a few hours. One day in the summer of 1937, a local trapper booked a flight to Bromley Lake which is about thirty-five miles west of the base. He paid in advance for the flight and came back a few days later with a canoe, a toboggan and some of his winter supplies. This trapper, Mr. Gagnon, who held the trapping rights to the Ground Hog River, was noted for his expertise at sturgeon fishing. I flew into the bush with him and was impressed by the abundance of wildlife in his area and his knowledge of their activities.

Later in the fall, around the first of October, we dropped in to check on him as we waited for some prospectors who were working at a nearby lake. When we landed the aircraft near his trapper's cabin on the western shore of the lake, we saw several moose feeding in the outgoing river. After a cup of coffee, the three of us paddled to the river to get a closer look at

The view from Ed Ahr's outpost camp on Makobe Lake

the moose. A cow was still feeding there, without a fear in the world about our presence. As we continued paddling down the river there were so many moose I stopped counting and just enjoyed the experience. Mr. Gagnon showed us where the speckled trout had just finished spawning. This area, with its walleye, northerns, speckled trout and moose, was a wildlife paradise. At the time, there were no logging roads to open up the area, and there was only one trapper, Mr. Gagnon, to crop a few muskrats, beaver, mink, lynx and wolves. Even though trappers didn't have quotas then, they knew how to manage their trapping grounds.

Mr. Gagnon was a rare gentleman in the society of trappers; he was well-read, spoke quietly and went about his trade effortlessly. The following summer he also chartered a plane to Bromley Lake, and later I flew in with the J-3 Cub to spend a day sturgeon fishing. He set long lines across the river in about three feet of fast-running rapids and baited large hooks with live crayfish. Within a few hours, he had caught several 50- to 60-pound sturgeon which were towed and kept fresh until they were picked up for shipment to the markets in Toronto.

So many of the people who passed through the seaplane base became important influences in my life. Some of them, like Mr. Gagnon, Mr. Chateauvert and Mr. Wicks, taught me some valuable fishing lessons and gave me a deeper appreciation for the outdoors. Others, like Ed Ahr and Harold Smith, passed on the codes of bush flying and prepared me for the unexpected—which was the cardinal rule in flying. I began my career in good hands and have never forgotten them.

FIRST TRIP TO THE SEAL RIVER

When the McIntyre Mines was awarded a federal government charter to Hudson Bay in the summer of 1938, Harold Smith and I were sent on mail delivery to the villages along the east coast as far as Great Whale River. One of the pilots who had made the trip gave us his charts with distances accurately measured, along with sketches of good landing sites at each village.

Even though the pilot, Harold Smith, was an expert navigator, the prospect of flying over two hundred miles to James Bay made me a little nervous. I had flown more than a hundred miles from the seaplane base on only two occasions, once to Sudbury and once to Chapleau. Nonetheless, Harold put me in the co-pilot seat of the Stinson Reliant so that he could check ground speeds and location while I held the controls. We took off from South Porcupine in the middle of August with a medical doctor and about 300 pounds of mail bags and headed northeast to Moose Factory. Despite my apprehensions, it was a spectacular flight!

Once north of Cochrane, we flew at 5000 feet just below the cumulus clouds, keeping the Abitibi River to our left. Within an hour and a half, we arrived at Moose Factory, which is located on an island with a well-sheltered cove. Harold and I anchored the aircraft at the heavy boat mooring because of the daily five- to seven-foot tide. Even though aircraft landed at Moosonee and Moose Factory on a regular basis during the summer, the native people gathered at the beach to admire the man-made birds. There was still considerable daylight to continue our trip, but the doctor needed to attend to a few patients. The Hudson's Bay Company Store Factor, Rod Duncan, kindly invited us to bunk down in his home.

Early the next morning, two clerks from the HBC Store arrived on the shore to sell us some aviation fuel. As soon as the fog lifted, we departed with about four hours of fuel on board. Our trek took us forty minutes east to Rupert House (Waskaganish) where we delivered and picked up mail. Within an hour we were on our way to Eastmain. By the time we arrived forty minutes later, the wind had picked up, and the river was very choppy; we stayed there less than thirty minutes to provide mail service before heading north to Old Factory. As we approached the village, situated on the edge of James Bay, the rollers were too high to attempt a landing. Since we had a reasonable tail wind, we proceeded further north to Fort George (Chisasibi), arriving there in late afternoon.

The La Grande River was wild with whitecaps near the village where the large boats were anchored. Just south of the village, we found a small section of the river that was quieter. It turned out to be an excellent seaplane shelter. Later, most of the seaplanes made this their regular docking area; however, at the time, there was no road leading to the HBC Store where we could purchase aviation fuel. And because there wasn't a suitable spot to secure the aircraft, I had to stay up all night pushing it up or down the beach as the tide came in and receded.

Because we were the first outsiders to arrive at Fort George that summer, the entire village came to greet us and stayed until it was totally dark. Usually an RCAF survey crew visited the village while they worked in the area, but they were working further north. The next day the doctor was overwhelmed with work and suggested that we spend another day or two in the village. Harold and I weren't elated at the idea of leaving the Stinson in the tidal water for two days, so we opted for a short side trip to pick up an outdoor writer who was fishing forty miles further north on Ominuk Lake along the Seal River. We refueled and headed north for what was to be my most rewarding speckled trout fishing experience.

When we arrived at Ominuk Lake, we met a gentleman by the name of Ben East who was working with *Outdoor Life* magazine. He had chartered a small fishing vessel from Moosonee the first week of July and made his way north to fish the creeks and small rivers along the coast of James Bay. Before leaving Moosonee he had left word with the Anglican minister to hire a seaplane to pick him up if one should happen to fly in, and the minister passed the message on to us.

Mr. East's native guides had set up their tents where the Seal River empties from Ominuk Lake. Fortunately, there was a wide sandy beach for the aircraft. We could hardly wait to catch some trout ourselves, but Mr. East made us join him for a cup of tea and biscuits. It wasn't long before we found ourselves in fishing heaven! It was barely two hundred yards from the campsite to the aircraft, and then another hundred yards to the first set of rapids. I didn't have a pair of waders with me, but my long underwear and running shoes allowed me to wade in the water for about fifteen minutes at a time. The trout were just simply waiting for food. After catching and releasing about a dozen three-pound fish, I was beginning to wonder if there were larger ones that I was missing.

The following morning I was fishing with Mr. East when my question was answered. He let a fly drift very close to shore where there was heavy foliage and

roughly four feet of water. Within a few seconds, a huge, monstrous trout had taken his fly. It swam right across the river. I was sure that the fly rod was going to snap. Mr. East gave me the rod, and I ran downstream about fifty yards before that fish came to a complete stop. Then it turned back towards me. The line went slack, and before I knew it, I was taking off up stream after it. All this time Mr. East was laughing uncontrollably. Needless to say I lost the fish, but we did manage to land a beautiful five-pound speckle later that day.

I had seen sportsmen using fly rods before, but Mr. East was an expert. He had all the latest fly-fishing equipment, and before we left he made sure that I knew how to use it. Harold was so impressed with his knowledge and skill that he and Mr. East chatted about technique and equipment most of the day. By the end of our visit, Mr. East had given us just about every bit of tackle he owned.

We eventually flew Mr. East back to Moosonee after picking up the doctor at Ft. George on the way south. The next year Mr. East sent me a copy of the story that he had written about the speckled trout fishing on the Seal River. My fascination with the Seal River continued to grow, and I made as many trips back as I could manage. By the mid-1950s, I began operating a tourist camp at the same location where I had first fished with Ben East. We continued to correspond while he worked for *Outdoor Life* magazine. Once I established my own camp on the Seal River, he recommended my air service to many trout fishermen.

I have fished the Seal River for some forty years. Each summer I stop there for a couple of days and return to the same holes. I've seen trout up to 8 pounds and loads of them over 24 inches, but my favourite ones are those that weigh about one-and-a-half pounds and come directly from the salt water of James Bay, six miles further west. They fit perfectly into a frying pan and have the most delicate flavour. The Seal River area has changed considerably since a huge hydroelectric power pro-ject was constructed nearby on La Grande. It became too easy for people, especially the construction workers, to abuse the fishing holes. Despite this abuse, the river still has excellent fishing, although it yields fewer large trout.

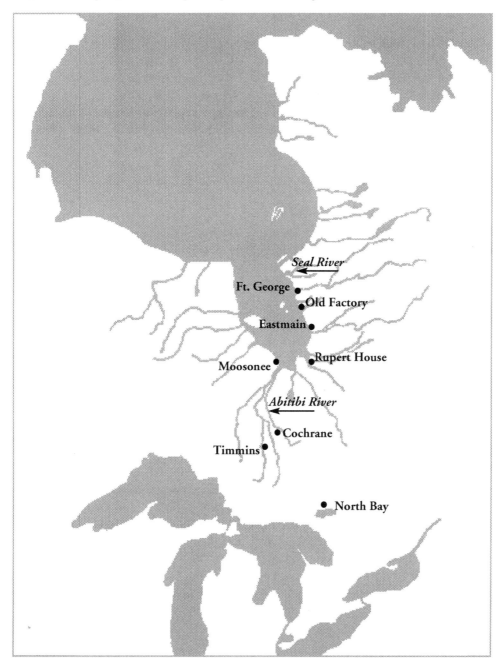

WHEN CALIFORNIA WAS WILD

In the fall of 1938, I was awarded a hockey scholarship to the University of California at Los Angeles. It was a rare opportunity to attend college, so at eighteen years of age, I packed my bags and left Canada for the first time.

My maternal grandmother, Emelie (Leopoldine) Mollot, who was living in Studio City at the time, was happy to have a grandson share her house. I enrolled in the Aerodynamics Program and spent most of my time studying and playing hockey. However, there were always a few weekends over the holidays to explore the surrounding countryside.

On a couple of those weekends I motored up north with some school chums to fish for sea bass south of Carmel. Surf fishing near Point Sur was a novel experience which proved to be quite invigorating. We found a few spots along the rocky coast where we could climb down to the beach and fish off the points with long bamboo poles. We threw our lines out into the heavy surf and let them sit there until a sea bass took the bait. Once the first fish was caught, we cut it up and used the flesh for bait.

It was a glorious experience, as we usually had the beaches to ourselves, and would walk for miles before encountering a stranger. There was no need to be concerned about our safety as we slept in our tents on the beach. Our only companions were the sea otters which came right up to us and ran between our legs. As we caught the fish we filleted them on a table that we had fashioned with some odd pieces of wood. If we had more than one fish on the table, a sea otter was likely to sneak up and grab it before we could clean it.

There were so many fish to be caught that we fished until we were exhausted from holding the long poles. After an hour of fishing, I would change places with a friend who was cleaning the fish. We didn't have coolers, but we managed to find a couple of old metal wash tubs that we filled with ice and covered with canvas. After a weekend of fishing, we all had our fill of fresh fish and took home a few pounds of fillets. These sea bass were the most delicious fish I had ever tasted. My grandmother relished the fillets I brought to her. She cooked them up just as my mother had prepared them—panned steamed with garlic.

When I had just a few hours to go fishing, I found a charter boat in Long Beach which charged two dollars to fish for albacore. Even though that was a lot of money in those days, it was worth the expense. The boat was usually packed with people since it was a very popular outing. The captain of the boat received his directions from a scout who sighted the schools of fish from the air in a blimp. The fish scattered when the captain drove the boat into the middle of the school, but we could still see them by the thousands. We fished from the sides of the boat, and our lines barely hit the water before we had a fish. As soon as we hooked one, we hauled it out of the water and held it over a container in the middle of the vessel while a workman shook it off the barbless hook. We rebaited our hook and threw the line over the side again and again. The whole trip lasted only three hours, but it was packed full of activity. Each of us was allowed to take only one fish home with us. The rest of the catch was sold commercially.

Fishing wasn't my only source of outdoor fun in California; one of my friends from the San Bernardino area took me hunting for mountain quail near his home in the foothills near San Jacinto. The area was mostly desert with a few bushes which often harboured feeding quail. We had the most success using a slingshot to rouse the quail—one of us flung a glass marble into a bush from twenty-five feet away while the other stood by with his gun poised ready to shoot. We also tried jump shooting, but we missed most of the birds as they flew away. These mountain quail had acute hearing and took to the air like bullets once they detected any disturbance. It was quite a contrast to hunting partridge (ruffed grouse) in northern Ontario. Partridge usually wait around for a while to see what's going on before they take off; sometimes you can fire a few shots before they move. But the quail in California were not so dumb. They made us become very quiet hunters because we knew that one little noise would set them off before we were ready to shoot.

There weren't many hunters in the area at the time because most people were afraid of encountering rattlesnakes in the desert. Fortunately my friend's father had taught him how to hunt safely with knee-high boots that were interlaced with steel mesh. This certainly made walking quietly an arduous process. Even though I saw some snake tracks in the sand, I never did come across a live one on any of my hunting trips.

California was a much wilder place in the late 1930s. It was a beautiful paradise for sportsmen; the fishing and hunting opportunities that I had there equaled any that I had experienced in Canada. I left California in 1940 when I was finally accepted into RCAF officer training.

Canada was at war with Germany, and I was ready to serve. When I left California, I never imagined that it would undergo such tremendous growth after the war. I returned in 1981 on my way to New Zealand and found an unrecognizable land of freeways and billboards.

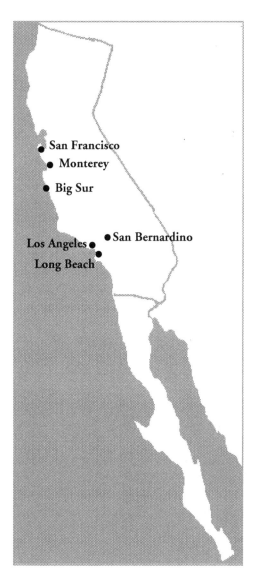

COD FISHING IN PRINCE EDWARD ISLAND

Cap de la Madelane, Quebec, 1941

While I waited for my RCAF pilot training to begin, I worked as a mechanic at the Ottawa Car and Aircraft Company where the Avro Anson was manufactured. Even though there wasn't much time for fishing in those busy days, I always managed to get in a few trips while on military leaves. After graduating in August 1942, with my new pilot's wings, I took the train to Timmins to visit my family. Most of the seaplanes were in hibernation because of gasoline rationing, but I managed to scrounge up a few gallons of aviation fuel for my friend Leo Lamothe's Piper J-3 Cub.

Leo and I did a thorough mechanical inspection of the floatplane and took off on a fishing trip. There were so few people fishing that summer that the fish were happy to see our lures, and I again tasted the fresh walleye that I enjoyed so much. My air force rations paled by comparison. I flew my father into MacArthur township so he could check out his claim. While he was looking at the rocks, I walked along

the trail to a creek which was full of 12-inch trout. That evening we feasted on delicious pan-fried speckles and relished every morsel.

When the annual leave ended in September, I was posted to Prince Edward Island for general reconnaissance. With a last name like Theriault in a French-speaking community, it wasn't long before I met many others with the same name. Since my father's parents had moved to northern Ontario from Acadia, I soon found some first and second cousins, many of whom were farmers and commercial fishermen. My cousins had been in the area for several generations, dating back to about 1780, shortly after the British had defeated the French in Quebec in 1763.

Once the crops were harvested in October, it was cod fishing season, and every able-bodied man was conscripted to help. One of the Theriault families that had a commercial fishing business near the town of Souris on the northeast coast of the island invited me to join them for a day on their boat. It was the most unique fishing experience I ever had because each of us wore a complete rubber outfit with heavy pants, jacket, hat and boots that weighed enough to drag us down fifty feet if we fell overboard. We started out at daybreak in their schooner which was about 40 feet long with a large sail and a 20-horsepower two-cylinder engine, towing three small 14-foot wooden boats equipped with oars.

We sailed about two hours. Then we anchored. While two men remained on board, two men climbed into each of the three small boats and rowed away in a different direction, yet still remaining within sight of the schooner. The rollers were about three feet high, but there was very little wind so the rowing wasn't too strenuous. My cousin Adelard and I rowed one of the boats to our designated area and dropped a line which was as thick as a small rope. Two-inch hooks with a one pound head sinker were tied to the line about four feet apart and were baited with cut fish. We let out the line to a depth of about 100 feet, and within a few minutes Adelard informed me that we had just caught a cod. I held the line and felt the second, third and fourth fish bite. I was excited and started to pull in the line but Adelard signaled me to wait until there were at least twenty cod on the line. About an hour later, we rowed back to the schooner with our line full of cod.

When we were within a few yards of the schooner, we passed the line to one of the cousins on board and he hauled it in. As you can imagine, the line was quite heavy since most of the fish weighed about four pounds each. After one more trip in the small boat, it was my turn to stay on board the ship to clean the cod. It took me some time to get used to the procedure. While my cousin cleaned and salted four cod, I only cleaned one.

By noon our work was done. The schooner was full of fish, and we were on our way back to the dock. Even though it was an exhilarating experience, it was certainly one of the most exhausting fishing trips. I felt relieved that commercial cod fishing was not my profession. There was nothing glamourous about hauling eighty pounds of fish into a boat or cleaning hundreds of fish in a few hours. The endearing part of the experience was the joyful camaraderie of the fishermen. Their labour seemed effortless because they had gone through the motions for years. To them it wasn't drudgery; it was more like a dance in which every movement was brilliantly choreographed. The sea was a delightful addiction to them—they loved the unpredictability of the wind and the waves. After a couple of fishing trips with my cousins, I began to understand their fondness for the experience. I could appreciate its allure, but I still had no desire to be a commercial cod fisherman.

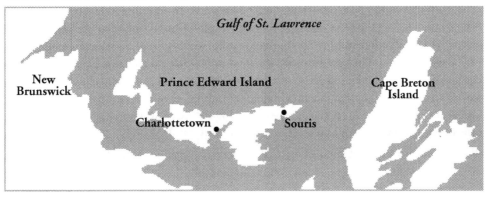

MANITOBA: A SPORTSMAN'S PARADISE

Test flying the Avro Anson in Winnipeg, Manitoba, 1943

Late in the fall of 1942, I was dispatched to the Central Navigation School at Rivers, Manitoba, as a pilot-navigator instructor. This was a very busy training station with about two hundred navigation twin-engine trainers. Students from all over the Commonwealth arrived in Rivers to perfect their piloting and navigation skills before being sent overseas. All of the instructors flew at least a hundred hours a month, but despite our busy flying schedules, I was anxious to find some outdoor activity.

When I arrived in early December, the flatness of the prairies was quite an enigma. There was hardly any snow, just a couple of inches covering the fields, and a cold wind blew at a steady 15 to 20 mph. I only began to realize the potential of this land when I met Vic Caswell at the Bombing and Gunnery School in Paulson, Manitoba. One weekend he took me out rabbit hunting, and to my surprise, we found them in abundance. All the small, wooded barriers between the wheat farms were simply full of small game and the odd deer. The rabbits that I had snared as a boy in northern Ontario were considerably smaller because they survived in cedar swamps and on young spruce during the long winters. On the prairies though, the snowshoes and jacks gorge themselves on left-over wheat and barley.

During one of my rabbit hunting trips near Paulson, I took my quota of snowshoe rabbits and one or two jacks. Then I found some shelter from the cold wind in the lee of an old deserted barn. Even though the building contained remnants of straw and horse manure, it seemed to be abandoned. As I watched a couple of turkeys scrounge for food, one of them took off. I immediately began to wonder if these were domesticated birds.

Two of my mother's first cousins and their families, the Plouffes, had immigrated to Ste.-Rose-du-Lac, Manitoba from France in the 1890s. Their families farmed wheat on the fertile land just south of Lake Dauphin, and they hunted whenever they had the opportunity. When I told my cousins about this experience with the turkeys, they decided to accompany me on my next hunting trip. As we approached the area, it was obvious that these birds had not been disturbed for quite a while. They were not in the least afraid of humans. We determined that the spot where I had first seen them was a roosting area, so we simply waited patiently for their arrival.

Ammunition was scarce during the war, but my friends in the armament sections were kind enough to outfit me with a .22 long rifle which was generally used for target practice. Shotgun shells were unavailable and Imperials were only distributed to the armed forces. Skeet shot loads were just about all that I could get my hands on. That afternoon we managed to shoot two fat, twelve-pound turkeys. I hadn't eaten fresh turkey in many months,

and the feast was especially delicious when they were cooked in the French Canadian style. First, the birds were boiled for about an hour; then they were removed from the water, cut up, and returned to a large pot. They simmered with vegetables for another couple of hours until they made a hearty stew, full of flavour.

During the summer of 1944, while I was stationed in Winnipeg, an RCAF Norseman on floats arrived at the base on the Red River to be used for search and rescue operations in the remote northern regions of Manitoba. Flight Lieutenant Buchanan, a former bush pilot who had flown a Norseman before the war, officially checked me out on the aircraft. Once he was posted overseas, I became the only seaplane pilot in the area, and my hectic work schedule increased exponentially. Between training at the Central Navigation School at Rivers, and working at the McDonald Brothers aircraft plant which was manufacturing the Anson Mk.5, my spare moments were taken up flying doctors and military personnel to isolated areas in the Norseman.

The docking facilities on the Red River were quite adequate for the Norseman, but taking off with a full load was impossible because there wasn't a long enough section of water. We located a much better seaplane base further northeast at Lac du Bonnet. Within a day or two, our staff had the old RCAF base cleaned up and put back into operation.

I made one of my first Norseman trips to Oxford House, an isolated Hudson's Bay Company trading post on Oxford Lake, 300 miles north of Lac du Bonnet. Everyone in the village was on hand to see what we had brought them because the post was visited only once or twice each summer by civilian aircraft which delivered the mail and some supplies. When they saw the doctor and the nurse, plus all the supplies, they were as happy as children at a birthday party. The HBC Factor had a difficult job maintaining some semblance of orderliness.

By evening I had coaxed a couple of the native lads into taking me out fishing. The native people only use gill nets to catch their fish, so the idea of fishing with a hook and line seemed like a waste of time to them. Just after supper, I embarked in one of the canoes with three native lads paddling. Not more than a mile or so from the village, we slipped into a well sheltered bay that had about 10 to 15 feet of water. While they continued to paddle about 30 feet from shore, I let out 100 feet of line from my casting rod.

The native lads must have known that I was due to get a strike; one of them started to chuckle, spoke something in Cree, then all hell broke loose when a big northern pike grabbed the red-and-white plug. This thing was a monster! I'm sure the natives thought that the rod or the line would break as the big fish fought on and on.

After about fifteen minutes, the fish finally weakened and we were able to bring it alongside the canoe. It weighed no less than 25 pounds, but the native lads didn't appear to be interested in bringing it home. Since I had used an inexpensive homemade lure, I slipped the blade of my knife on the line, and we watched it slowly drift downward, back into the darkness. The three native lads were surprised that I could take a fish of that size with a rod and reel because they used a heavy green line that was sharp enough to cut their hands. They didn't set their nets for northerns because they would tear them to bits.

Later that evening in Oxford House, the HBC Factor begged us to arrange for the transportation of fish to Winnipeg. Before the war the native people had a good market for their fish, but once the war started there was no way to transport them to the markets. The lake was full of walleye, the nets were ready, and the men were willing to work, but without transportation it was worthless. We agreed to talk to our superiors about their situation, but we knew that the gasoline rationing would make it very difficult to find a civilian company to transport fish.

The following morning I made an arrangement with my new fishing friends to take home some fresh fish for the staff at the air base in Rivers. They set a few short nets right at the village. Within an hour we had at least fifty large, fat walleye, and in no time at all they were filleted and ready to fly out. Unfortunately, commercial fishing didn't resume until the end of the war. I returned to Oxford House in 1949 with a government survey crew while we were mapping the northern parts of Canada. We saw tons of fresh walleye sitting in a warehouse, waiting for a commercial aircraft to fly them to Winnipeg.

At the end of August 1944, a federal game and fisheries officer, Dr. Harkness, made arrangements for a flight to the Gods Lake area—about 300 miles northeast of Lac du Bonnet and 50 miles east of Oxford House. Since the Norseman had a safe range of only 500 miles, we had to establish a gasoline cache midway. It's easy to drift off course as you fly north over Manitoba because thousands of small lakes begin to melt into each other, and they all look identical. However, at 5000 feet on a clear day, Gods Lake is large enough that it cannot be mistaken. We landed at the native settlement, secured the aircraft and subsequently found that Dr. Harkness and his three assistants could not do all their work that same day. What was there for me to do? Yes, I went fishing.

In 1944 Gods Lake was completely unspoiled country; there wasn't a single outfitter or commercial camp in operation on the lake. During our dinner conversation the native people bragged about the huge lake trout and the enormous speckled trout in the river. They were keen to take me out to prove their boastful assertions and managed to convince me to go out that evening. I went along with their plans because I was anxious to try out my new equipment. That summer I had inherited an almost-new trout rod with a Penn reel that could hold about 400 feet of 50-pound-test silk line. It was my first reel with a star-drag arrangement.

Three of us paddled about a mile from the village before I let out a big red-eye wabbler, a bright silver one. The water is so cold at that latitude that the trout hug the surface all summer long. With this wabbler about 60 yards out and down at a level of 10 to 13 feet, we had our first strike. A gorgeous ten-pound lake trout finally surfaced. I liked the feel of my new rod and wanted to keep on fishing for lake trout, but the native men were anxious to show me the speckled trout in the rapids.

When we arrived, I put on a pair of hip waders and immediately headed downstream with my guides. I switched over to a standard casting rod with 30-pound-test line using a homemade mepp-style spinner. After several casts with no results, I soon realized that I needed to cast a little upstream then allow the lure to drift down a few feet before I slowly

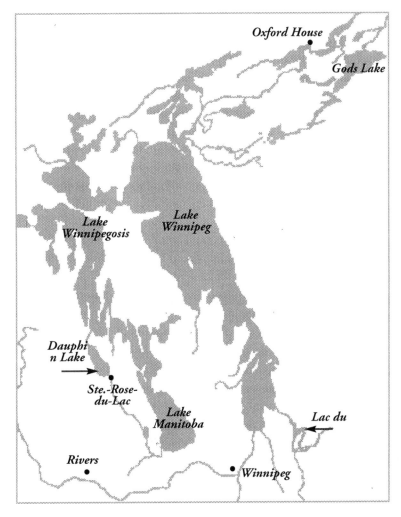

retrieved it. I worked my way downstream for a half a mile using this method and caught a two- or three-pound speckled trout on every cast. When we returned to the canoe, I asked the guides to troll just above the rapids in the deep, calmer water. I figured it would be a good feeding area. On my first strike I caught a large speckled trout, over 27 inches long. My trophy of the season weighed in at just over five pounds!

I never forgot my remarkable fishing experiences at Gods Lake. Fortunately, I had the opportunity to return in September 1949 with a team of surveyors. While they completed their observations, I spent three days fishing in the clear, cool, fall days. The walleye, lake trout and speckled trout were beyond belief. In the same rapids that I had fished in 1944, I could still catch a fish on every cast. The speckled trout were full of spawn, so we fished with barbless hooks and released every one. We found plenty of walleye in the narrows and kept those that weighed five pounds and over. The northern pike and whitefish were also in abundance. In fact, the native people preferred the whitefish to anything else. They caught them in late October, smoked them, and stored them for the winter.

During the fall of 1944 when I returned to Winnipeg from Gods Lake, a Canadian Wildlife survey team organized a flight to an unnamed lake roughly 100 miles north of Dauphin near Lake Winnipegosis. When we arrived at the lake, the water was completely covered with ducks. I had to circle for at least five minutes to clear a place to land. Even while I taxied the Norseman to a small beach, the ducks were taking off by the thousands.

These birds, mostly mallards, a few Canada geese and some redheads, had flown in from the north and were resting and fattening up before they continued their migration south. They would lift off the lake in large flocks, circle and land again. Then another group would do the same. All day long the flocks took off and landed. They seemed to eat all day and quack most of the night. At times the noise was so loud that we had to shout to each other to be heard.

I used an over-and-under 12-gauge shotgun, which I carried as part of our survival equipment, to shoot about fifteen mallards for the wildlife officers. One of them was a taxidermist who preserved birds for various museums and government records offices. By the third day, I couldn't bring myself to shoot another specimen; the ducks had become so tame that they wandered around our camp like pets. In fact, they boldly took the liberty of leaving their mess on the floats of the aircraft.

I never did find out what the lake was later named; however, I am quite certain that today it is accessible by car because roads have penetrated deep into northern Manitoba. The long, narrow lake was a perfect location for growing rice since it was only five feet deep. When we arrived, the wild rice was so ripe that the grains fell into the water at the slightest touch. It wouldn't surprise me if the area is now a prospering wild rice farm.

Once the war ended and my work at the Navigation School was completed, I prepared to return to northern Ontario. Even though I had found plenty of interesting places to fish and hunt during my two-year posting in Manitoba, I was happy to move on. Like all the RCAF flyers, I received a commercial pilot's license when I was discharged. For me, this was my ticket to freedom.

FLYING IN THE LAURENTIANS

By the spring of 1945, hundreds of airmen were discharged from the RCAF and looking for work. I knew exactly what I wanted to do with my new-found freedom—open my own air service in northern Ontario. I was one of a couple of dozen returning airmen searching for information on how to get a license to operate an air service. During the war we had been told our years of dedicated service to our country would be considered in our bid for civilian air charters. However, those promises fell on the deaf ears of bureaucrats at the Air Transport Board. It appeared that no one told the committee members of the ATB that airmen returning to civilian life were a priority. Their allegiances were already made with those who held current licenses.

I was hoping the South Porcupine area would be a good place for me to start because the McIntyre Mines had given me a space in their hangar and a nice little office next door. But it wasn't to be. The fellows who didn't enlist made good connections in Ottawa, and they tied up most of the prime areas. Jack Austin of Austin Airways, who was allowed to keep his aircraft flying throughout the war, was given a series of licenses that completely protected his use of the South Porcupine area—in other words, all returning airmen were shut out in his area. I heard from other airmen that this was the story right across the country.

While visiting friends north of Montreal in early June 1945, I agreed to fill in for one of Wheeler Airline's pilots who was still overseas. The company was resuming operations again after its forced closure during the war years and needed someone to fly their brand new Norseman. My recent experience flying the Norseman

in northern Manitoba proved invaluable, even though flying in the mountains was not at all like the western prairies. The weather in the Laurentians was always turbulent, and the clouds hung over the hills throughout the day.

Tom Wheeler's camps were all within a fifty-mile range of Lac Ouimet in the Laurentian Mountains. The lakes were full of trout because they had been stocked for many years. A caretaker and his family lived at the camps and regularly patrolled the area to ensure that the lakes were protected from trespassing fishermen. These private clubs were well maintained with elegant hotels—indoor plumbing, modern equipment, boats and motors—all in a wilderness setting. The guests were treated to the pleasures of nature, without the discomfort that is often associated with roughing it.

Once we flew guests into the main camp, guides took them fishing by canoe on day trips. The stocked lakes were only a short distance from the main camp, with perhaps one small portage. I learned that there was a ritual involved in guiding the guests to the fishing holes. First, the local guide paddled the canoe to a part of the lake where they would never catch a fish. Then after an hour or so of useless fishing, he took them to another part of the lake where they caught enough fish for a shore lunch. Late in the afternoon, after the guests had sat in the canoe for five hours, the guide took them to the best fishing spots where they caught stocked trout by the bushel. The fish were so tame they would follow the canoe expecting to be fed. Naturally that made the sportsmen very happy, although they had no idea what was really going on.

The guides used this same technique

with the same results throughout the fishing season. It was especially funny to listen to the guests recall the entire day: how they searched for the fish, how they weren't biting, how they caught enough for lunch; then the deluge. To vary the scenario, the guide would take the guests on longer trips, perhaps five or six portages away from the main camp, or on an overnight trip. He would tell the guests, of course speaking with a French Canadian accent, that this lake had big speckled trout, but that it would be a slow process to locate them. After a few hours, the guide would slip over the hole and the guest had a five-pound trout. What an experience! These lakes were so full of freshwater shrimp that the fish grew to four or five pounds in three seasons. It was an old trick but one that brought the tourists back every year.

In my estimation, old Tom Wheeler was the best tourist outfitter in Quebec. His charm and personality attracted all kinds of VIPs, including Prime Minister Louis St. Laurent with whom he became best friends over the years. Sport fishermen came from all over the world to the Lac Ouimet fishing club, just to be with Old Tom because he knew how to make everyone happy.

I flew charter trips to several other fly-in fishing camps that were private clubs for members only and their guests. They were all superior camps with year-round caretakers. The lakes were groomed and well stocked with three or four species of fish. One lake was stocked with walleye, another with small mouth bass, but most of them had either lake trout or speckles. The camp's territory extended over several square miles and often comprised a dozen or so large lakes. Even though I never cared much for catching a fish in such a controlled environment, almost everyone that I flew in that summer raved about the excitement of catching these stocked fish.

By the end of the summer, many pilots, who had returned from the war, were buying small seaplanes and flying into these privately maintained areas. However, they were not treated like guests when they arrived. The private clubs hired patrol planes to protect their fishing lakes. Naturally, the pilots complained to the politicians about the protectionist policies of the private fishing camps.

The lumber companies also voiced their complaints as they wanted road access to cut timber in these area. When the controversy over the private fishing lakes reached the public, they too wanted permission to access the private lakes. The verbal battle for access took place in the taverns as well as the newspaper editorials, and eventually the public won. But it took about twenty years. By then, the fishing in the remote lakes was reduced to a mere trickle compared to the years of glory after the war.

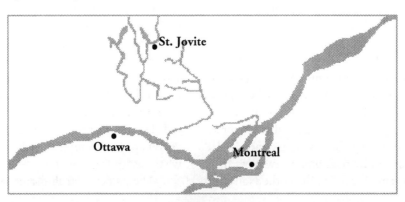

GOOSE HUNTING AT HANNAH BAY

The months following the end of the war were a time of great rejoicing for all of us who had served. We were reunited with our families and friends, and we had time to enjoy our old pastimes. In the fall of 1945, I returned to Timmins and bought myself a new float-and ski-equipped J-3 Cub. Finally I had the freedom I wanted to fish and hunt wherever I could fly. By October, my good friend Alex Hudson and I yearned to hunt geese in James Bay. He had just returned from overseas where he had received a Distinguished Flying Cross while flying bomber command.

We loaded the Cub with provisions for two weeks and flew north to Moosonee. I had made several flights into the area when I worked for Ed Ahr and had become friends with many of the native people whose families hunted geese. The native hunters usually travelled by canoe

along the shore of James Bay to the Harricana River at Hannah Bay where they set up a temporary camp and hunted the geese as they rested and fed on their migration south. Since it was a two-day trip by canoe to Moosonee and only a thirty-minute flight, I made a trip each day taking geese to friends or families and returning with supplies.

The Crees completely depended on the geese for their winter food supply. They would not have the opportunity to hunt again until the birds flew north in the spring. What little money they earned trapping in the winter was spent on clothing and staples such as flour, salt and sugar. Since moose and beaver were becoming more scarce every year, the native people relied on the geese for about fifty percent of their food supply. That fall we were able to supplement the geese with

Hannah Bay hunt, 1956

some harp seals and several hundred pounds of suckers.

The native people ran the hunt like an assembly line in a factory—not a single piece of the goose was wasted. The women and children meticulously plucked every bird, then all the innards were washed thoroughly to be stored and used later for baiting traps for mink, weasel and other small fur-bearing animals. The dogs also received a portion of the hunt, including all the bones.

The Indians always waited for the geese to come within twenty-five yards of their blinds before shooting. By then, they could almost talk to the birds. Usually they would only take one or two younger birds from each family; adults were seldom killed. They used single-shot old Iver Johnson's, but they could reload them so quickly that they could get several shots off in a matter of seconds.

As soon as Alex learned to call geese, he went hunting every day with the native men. He once complained to me that his shoulder was sore after a full day of hunting. He had been using an old Stevens pump and had done away with four boxes of 12 gauge shotgun shells, which meant he had shot at least seventy-five geese. The 24-foot canoes usually arrived in the camp half full of birds. Multiply that by four or five canoes, and we were looking at around a thousand birds a day. Fortunately, it was sufficiently cold to keep the meat from spoiling.

When Alex and I returned to Timmins, we picked up a strong northerly wind—with the Piper Cub flying at 75 mph, we were home in two hours. A week later, Pat Fletcher called me from Moose Factory with news that one of the freighter canoes with two hunters was missing. The canoe had left the camp at Hannah Bay but never arrived in Moose Factory. I refueled the Cub, took on an additional thirty

gallons of gasoline in small cans and flew back to Moosonee, arriving there in the afternoon. Although the territory was held under the license of Austin Airways, they didn't maintain an aircraft in Moosonee. Once a month they sent an aircraft from Timmins which stopped in Moosonee and then proceeded up the coast with mail. If someone was unfortunate enough to get sick in the bush, his only way to the railhead at Moosonee was by canoe in the summer or by dog sled in the winter.

With an observer on board, I immediately set out searching for the lost canoe. We hugged the shoreline of James Bay heading northeast towards the hunting camp. Within ten minutes my observer spotted the canoe, high and dry, near one of the larger creeks. The hunters had paddled upstream for protection from the strong winds, but a high tide had pushed them about a thousand yards from the water. When we found them, they had been waiting for two days for the next high tide to free the canoe. There was a celebration when we arrived back at Moose Factory with the good news. All was well and the anxious moments melted into laughter and cheers.

By then it was October, yet there were still thousands of blues and snows flying in from the northeast and northwest coasts of Hudson Bay. I stayed overnight in Moosonee, listening to the geese on the move. It was difficult to estimate their numbers; however, to this day I have never seen such large numbers of geese. The goose population had risen considerably because there was very little hunting during the war. Old Chief Fletcher told me that this was also the largest goose population he had seen in his lifetime.

In the spring of 1946, Pat Fletcher, Chief Fletcher's son, together with some other native men, decided to open a goose hunting camp for tourists. Jim Bell, owner of Nickel Belt Airways in Sudbury, offered them a Fairchild Husky aircraft to transport tourists to their new goose camp at Hannah Bay. Even though the Fletchers had limited financial resources, the Hudson's Bay Company Store advanced them credit for tents and some supplies to get them started. All went quite well and during the summer of 1946, they were able to book about thirty hunters, mostly from the Timmins, Noranda and Kirkland Lake area.

Once the tourist goose camp became a reality, the chairman of the Ontario Northland Railroad, Colonel Reynolds, saw the potential for increasing traffic on the railroad. In one evening discussion, he made a deal with the Fletchers to ensure the railroad's involvement in future endeavors. Unfortunately for the native people, it meant they took a back seat in the administration and finances of the goose hunting camp. Eventually, they were reduced to working only as guides in the hunting camp they had established. This goose camp at Hannah Bay continues to be run by the railroad to this day.

When goose camps became popular, more tourist outfitters staked their claims along James Bay. Tom Wheeler, of Wheeler Airlines, started a hunting camp at Cabbage Willows, not far from Rupert House. His guests were flown in from St. Jovite, Quebec, a distance of over 350 miles. A little later, Jim Bell and Bill Anderson started a camp at the Albany River. Although the goose population fluctuates somewhat from year to year, James Bay continues to be a hunter's paradise—a place that migratory bird hunters or watchers should see at least once in a lifetime.

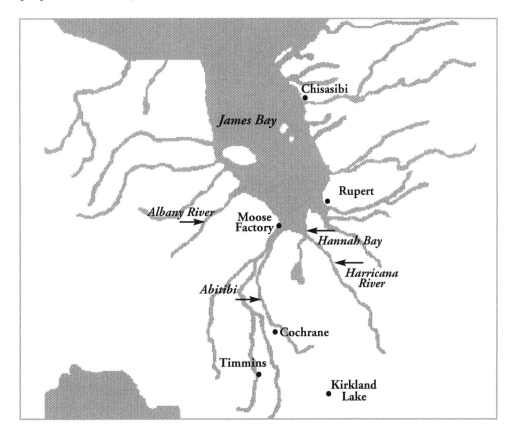

NORTHERN TROUT FISHING

Refueling my J-3 Cub CF-EEU at Temagami

By 1946, a flying school operated by Borden Fawcett in South Porcupine was training new pilots, and the wartime pilots were being checked out on floats. With the end of gasoline rationing, many of my friends took up flying just for sport.

An old friend of mine, Dr. Henry Hudson, received his private license that summer, bought an aircraft, and became quite an avid airman. The flight to his cottage on Lake Temagami took him a little over an hour versus a five- or six-hour road trip followed by a boat trip up the lake. Another friend, Gordon Gauthier, who had flown overseas during the war, became a Piper dealer and sold aircraft to quite a number of people within a one hundred-mile radius. He built a hangar on Porcupine Lake and offered maintenance services to the owners of private aircraft.

During the war the lakes in the Timmins-Porcupine area were virtually abandoned, so the fishing was spectacular when we arrived home. My friends and I pored over maps and planned weekend fishing trips. We hid canoes at our favourite lakes and set up a system of gasoline caches for emergencies. We minimized the danger of unforeseen obstacles by flying in pairs most of the time. Even though we didn't file flight plans, we left notes at our departure points.

I continued to spend much of my time at my cottage on Temagami Lake and helped some of the lodge operators service their outpost camps. When the idea of fly-in fishing trips emerged as a viable means of outfitting, I began to realize that this was a way for me to combine my love of flying with my obsession for fishing and hunting. It took several more years for the plan to become a reality, but in that time, I had the freedom to explore the tremendous fishing opportunities the north had to offer.

On numerous occasions I escorted less experienced pilots to James Bay. Together we established a little tent camp with a gasoline cache on Kesagami Lake where we could refuel when heading north to Fort George and the Seal River. We felt much safer sticking to this inland water route since the Moosonee River at Moosonee has never been kind to light aircraft. Strong winds and high tides can make landing and securing a small seaplane very difficult. Even today when plotting a course anywhere along James and Hudson Bay, I draw a track about ten miles inland, as well as one going directly to my destination. Fog rolls into James or Hudson Bay very rapidly, but further inland the weather is often clearer.

The unpredictable weather can play havoc with even the most cautious plans. There are very few places to safely land a seaplane between Moosonee and Hannah Bay; however, whenever we were in need, we found shelter at a few goose hunting camps along the rivers that flow into the Bay. Further northeast, the area around Rupert House and north of Eastmain has many suitable landing spots in the rivers or lakes. I quickly learned to avoid landing and mooring in the salt water because the tides are often very high and the fog can sit on the coast for days. It's much safer to land a mile or two upstream and then walk back to the coast to fish.

These trips north were periods of great adventure and discovery for myself and my friends. We had the time and the energy to become familiar with many of the lakes and streams along the coast. Each trip was a new and exciting experience because the weather was always changing and we had to make accommodations for it. Often we were forced to land on an unknown river or lake, only to discover that the fishing was exceptional. This country always had something to teach us, and we were its willing students. As we became friends with the native people in the small villages along the coast, they gladly passed on their knowledge of the land and their stories of the wildlife.

Over the years of fishing these trout streams, I discovered that timing the arrival of the trout at one set of rapids is very important. The middle northern portion of James Bay and most of the rivers flowing into Hudson Bay on the east coast are fairly shallow and have one or two sets of rapids from a few hundred feet to one mile upstream. Usually the tide overrides the first set of rapids. From the second set of fast-flowing waters, the rivers are shallow enough for wading, although the pools are roughly eight feet deep. The Seal River, for example, has a large lake about five air miles inland, with interconnecting rivers and rapids for about one hundred miles. Often, within a few days, the entire fish population will move several miles upstream to another set of rapids. When this happens, an aircraft or boat is needed to reach the upper parts of the rivers. Most of the rivers have suitable sections of water where landing a seaplane is quite safe. A short walk to the rapids invariably produces some good trout fishing.

Precaution has always been necessary when fishing the isolated northern streams. Emergency help is not easily accessible. We experimented with various types of apparatus and clothing to determine what was best for the area. I found that a long ski pole, with the lower ring removed, works best for walking on the slippery rocks. Since the weather is generally cool during most of the summer months in this area, I prefer to wear a pair of very light wool underwear and a good set of chest waders with an inflatable life vest. During the months of June and September, the waters are very cold, seldom over 45°F. However, during the middle of July and August, they can be a little warmer and fly hatches will often appear.

I learned the real value of fly fishing on my first trip to the Seal River in 1937. Since then I have always carried two rods in my aircraft: one for fly fishing and one for spin fishing. Once I have located the fish with a spinner, I use the fly rod to keep the fish in the area because spinning baits constantly splash the water and frighten trout away from the shallower pools. Streamer flies seem to work best in the earlier part of the summer, but as the temperature of the water increases, dry flies produce more fish. My largest trout have all been taken on three-inch silver spoons and red-and-white daredevils when the tide comes into the first set of rapids. These silver-coloured trout certainly put up a much better fight. Once the fish have been in the fresh water for a week or two, they seem to lose some of their spunk.

Speckled trout spend most of their adult life in the salt waters of James and Hudson Bay, but during early June, they begin their migration up the rivers to spawn. By July, they have reached sections about five or six miles upstream, and further on up by August. While the trout inhabit the salt water, they are a silver colour. However, about a month after feeding on fresh water shrimp in the streams, they turn darker, and red markings become more prominent. Trout continue to migrate upstream all summer long. Once their spawning period is completed in September, they slowly make their way back to the salt water.

The new spawn hatch in the shallow parts of the river and usually remain together in large schools for up to two years, or until they are about ten inches long. When they leave their birth place, they do not necessarily return to the same rivers. Anglers have caught trout on one side of Hudson Bay that were tagged by biologists on the other side.

My friends and I developed a real fondness for the trout fishing streams along the east coast of James and Hudson Bay. We gained a deep respect for the land and for the people who made it their home. The memories of those countless hours of pleasure and solitude on the trout streams have never left us. Many of my old fishing buddies have continued to fish in these same streams for decades. Our adventurous spirit also led us to constantly search for new streams, for the perfect fishing experience.

For most of my friends, flying and fishing in the north has been a hobby, a way to escape the routine of their daily life. For me, it has been a career that I continue even today, while I am in my seventies. This country has an amazing power over all of us who have come to know it. Year after year, it draws us back; and what draws us has to be more than just the fishing.

Every once in a while, I meet my old friends in the strangest of places up in the north. One day in 1951, while I was flying an RCAF Norseman at Port Harrison, which is half way up the east coast of Hudson Bay, a Super Cub seaplane landed at the base. It was my old friend Gordon Gauthier, all by himself, flying south after having fished at a river just south of Povungnituk. He stayed long enough to buy a drum of gasoline from the HBC Store and then headed south to spend the night at the Seal River, three hundred miles further south, where we had both camped for many years.

A RETURN TO DUTY

G. Theriault, Orville Piper and Cal Hull

While visiting friends in Ottawa in November 1948, I was summoned to re-enlist in the RCAF to participate in a project to survey the Arctic. The RCAF was looking for well-seasoned bush pilots who had experience flying in the barren lands. Since the only maps for guidance in the northern latitudes lacked detail, pilots had to rely solely on their navigational skills. The territory was so immense that even experienced pilots had been known to get lost. I saw the offer as a challenge to my piloting skills and an opportunity to explore and fish new territories in the Canadian north.

SURVEYING THE ARCTIC

In the spring of 1949, the RCAF set up a temporary training base at Golden Lake, a few miles west of Ottawa, where we honed our flying skills on a Norseman. After a month of training, four Norseman float planes headed to the northwestern Arctic, arriving at Yellowknife, NWT about a week later. We flew an average of five hours each day, crossing northern Ontario to Lac du Bonnet, Manitoba, Le Pas, Man., Lake Athabaska, and then to Great Slave Lake. We covered roughly two thousand miles, flew over hundreds of lakes, fought terrible weather on some legs of the journey, but arrived safely in Yellowknife to tackle our first real challenge.

When we arrived we found that most of the lakes to the north still remained ice-bound, so we had to work the areas further south. As the lakes melted, we kept pushing further north. Because the aerial mappers needed to tie in the proper latitude and longitude, we surveyed sites every fifty miles—going east, then west, then north in a checkerboard fashion. We took aerial photographs and compared the site with those that higher flying aircraft had taken.

On a very bright Sunday morning in June, with two surveyors on board, I took off from Yellowknife and headed in a westerly direction for about an hour. Once we found a lake that was large enough to land on, we descended and taxied the aircraft to a sandy beach. We set up a camp in about two hours. Then I had some free time while the surveyors were busy establishing the correct time signals which they obtained from a very powerful radio receiver. When the theodolite was set up, they had to wait until the evening to make the necessary observations.

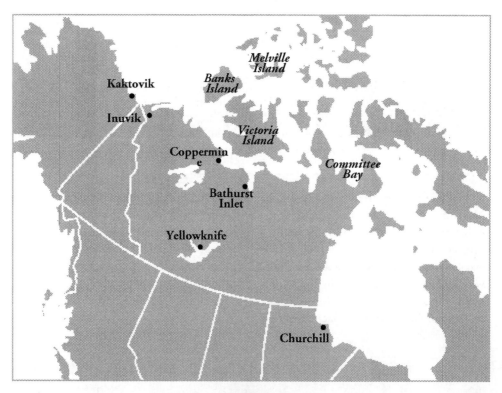

The other airman, Jim Upham, was an ardent fisherman and in no time at all he began to cast from the shore. As I climbed into the aircraft to get my casting rod, I spied a five-pound lake trout right between the floats. The ice had just gone out of this lake and the water was crystal clear. We could see directly to the bottom to a depth of more that thirty feet. I was reluctant to take the time to put my waders on, so I started to cast while standing on the front of the floats. I couldn't believe my eyes—at least half a dozen fish were chasing the lure. They came to within twenty feet, then they must have been frightened by the silver floats because they turned away.

As I searched the water for trout, I caught a glimpse of a fish that must have been the granddaddy of them all. From where I was standing, it looked to weigh about thirty pounds. When I cast a line in its direction, it followed the lure. But like the smaller fish, it seemed to be spooked by the aircraft floats. I yelled to Jim, who was on the shore, and pointed to the fish. He made a long cast with the line passing directly over it and then started to reel in.

Well, the trout went after the lure in a flash, and in a matter of a seconds, the battle was on! This big one fought as vigorously as a small mouth bass, twisting and turning, and generally making a mockery of Jim's fishing skills. Then with a swish of its tail, it headed out towards the middle of the lake. Jim's line ran to the end of the spool and that was the last we saw of the fish. For the rest of the afternoon, we satisfied ourselves catching trout in the four- and five-pound range; however, we often wondered how large that first trout would have been. I never did find out what the lake was named; at the time our charts showed a complete blanked out spot in that area.

As we started to survey points heading east, I had my first encounter with northern pike in the northern latitudes. I had no idea they would be so plentiful and in such a range of sizes. The large ones were big enough to scare you, but we only kept a few smaller ones in the six-pound range since they were even better to eat than the lake trout. Coming out of those cold waters, they were firm and well fed. Whitefish and herring were also plentiful in all those lakes because there was so much food to sustain them. They eagerly devoured the silver-looking baits we offered them; but without a challenge, I lost interest after a day or two.

The RCAF rented seaplane-docking space from Canadian Pacific Airlines in Yellowknife which was also operating a Norseman, running a weekly scheduled flight to Coppermine and Holman Island, 250 miles further north. One evening the pilot, Ernie Boffa, flew in from Plummer's Lodge, which was about a hundred miles further east on Great Slave Lake at the Taltheilei Narrows. A young native girl who cooked at the camp caught the biggest lake trout that I had ever seen. It weighed over 30 pounds and won the Yellowknife trophy-of-the-week award. After it had been registered and admired by all, it was sold to the chap who operated the Wild Cat Cafe up the street.

Since our group was slowly making its way east, we decided to establish a geodetic survey point near Plummer's Lodge. When we arrived there during the first week of July, some workers who were putting up new tents to accommodate the incoming guests lent us their two canoes. Once we tied them together, three of us paddled out a few hundred feet from shore. The waters were so calm and clear that we could see all kinds of big and small fish swimming below. It really was like looking at an aquarium. We dropped anchor and lowered our lures. As soon as the bait was down about fifteen feet, several fish came up to grab the lures. From the surface, it looked to us like the fish were fighting over the bait. While one lake trout struggled to get the lure into its mouth, another would try to take it away. Each of these fish weighed about six or seven pounds. Even though it may seem unbelievable to witness these fish clamoring for the lures, it did get boring after a few hours.

We all decided we needed more challenge, so we went ashore determined to find out where the native girl had caught the 30-pound trout we had seen in Yellowknife. The manager of the lodge pointed out a rocky point within three hundred yards of the camp. After a cup of tea, the three of us got back into the canoes and started out trolling.

Within a few minutes, Jim Upham was all smiles. He had hooked into another big trout and he wasn't going to let this one get away. It put up an enormous fight, dragging us around the lake for twenty minutes or so, but Jim finally exhausted it. I was elated that Jim had landed this big one because I thought it would put an end to the stories about the one that had got away. Even though it weighed over 20 pounds, Jim was sure that it didn't measure up to the previous one. We camped near the lodge for two days and caught an enormous number of fish, but we fished barbless and only took a few back with us to Yellowknife. The cook at the Wild Cat Cafe who served us most of our meals was always grateful for a good catch of lake trout.

By the middle of July 1949, there were only two or three more geodetic survey points to complete near Yellowknife, but we couldn't continue until the ice thawed at Fort Reliance, in the most easterly area of Great Slave Lake. The eastern

end of Great Slave Lake falls within a very severe frost area so temperatures remain much cooler there than in the western sections. When we got the signal that the ice had melted, two Norseman crews quickly moved to Fort Reliance. The signal corps who were based there year round were jubilant when we arrived since they hadn't seen an airplane in six weeks. They were so short on many items that one of the aircraft had to return to Yellowknife the following day for additional supplies.

That first evening, unlike most evenings in the bush, we enjoyed each other's company in comfortable lodgings that the army maintained year round. We chatted for hours and naturally the conversation came round to fishing. A couple of the army boys suggested that we fish the Lockhart River where it empties into Great Slave Lake from Artillery Lake. They described a very round fish with red fins that averaged only a few pounds but fought like the devil and tasted particularly delicious. With our curiosity piqued, eight of us flew to Artillery Lake the next day. We secured the two float planes on a section of beach not more than a quarter of a mile from the upper portion of the Lockhart River.

I tied my aircraft quite a way up the river from the first set of rapids, but the other pilot, Al Marshall, was anxious to get to the fishing. He beached his Norseman about two hundred yards further down river from mine. As my crewman and I passed Al's aircraft, I noted to him that I thought the aircraft would float away if a strong wind came up. But neither one of us was willing to interfere with Al's method of security. He was an excellent Norseman pilot and had been assigned to our detachment as the adjutant, the staff officer who helps the commanding officer with administrative affairs. It was mainly his responsibility to write the reports about the events of the mission.

By the time we arrived at the first set of rapids, the others had just started to fish. Al was the first to catch one. The trout gave him such a fight, that in the excitement of the moment, he went in over his waders. It was not to be the last time Al got wet that day. We spread out on the stream, and each of us began to fish in earnest. About a half hour later, a strong wind picked up, and unfortunately, Al's aircraft came loose and floated about fifty feet from shore. I caught sight of it first and yelled to Al who dropped his rod and began a sprint back down the beach with all of us trailing behind. It was quite a sight to see this big red-headed guy running down the beach tearing off his clothes.

Al was a proficient swimmer who had been on the Canadian national swimming team. He hit the icy water with a crash. Within a minute he caught up to the aircraft and taxied it back to the shore. The water was so cold that there still were ice crystals on the shore from the recent thaw, but Al was too excited to notice that his body was the colour of a cooked lobster. He spent forty-five minutes securing the aircraft and made us all promise that we would not mention the incident to the detachment commander, Art Appleby, who was still in Yellowknife.

This was not a story to be written up in the official memoirs of the survey of 1949. I kept my promise for thirty years. Then one day, when Art and I were remembering old stories, I asked him if he ever heard about the incident with the

Norseman at Artillery Lake. He said he was glad no one ever told him about it because he would have grounded Al for the rest of the mission.

We returned to fishing in earnest as soon as we were all sure that the aircraft would still be there when we came back. Wherever we fished it was the same story; each and every cast produced a trout. None of the trout were over three pounds but they had lots of tenacity. We released most of them and kept just enough for our supper. Since the surveyors were convinced that this lake would be a good location for a survey point, we moved the entire crew from Fort Reliance to Artillery Lake and established a camp about a mile from the Lockhart River.

While the surveyors spent several days completing their work on Artillery Lake, I had some time each day to hike and fish in this outdoor paradise. The landscape surrounding the river, as it dropped five hundred feet over twenty miles, was breathtaking. Each of us had to take our turn hanging on to some of the low trees to admire the magnificent descent at Parry Falls. Those of us who were adventurous spent several hours climbing down the rocky bank to the bottom of the lower falls. We estimated that both falls were at least a hundred feet from top to bottom. The water was so turbulent near the falls that it appeared to boil over, yet we could see trout swimming in it. When the surveyors had finally finished their work, we reluctantly returned to Yellowknife where we packed up all our equipment and headed further north to Great Bear Lake.

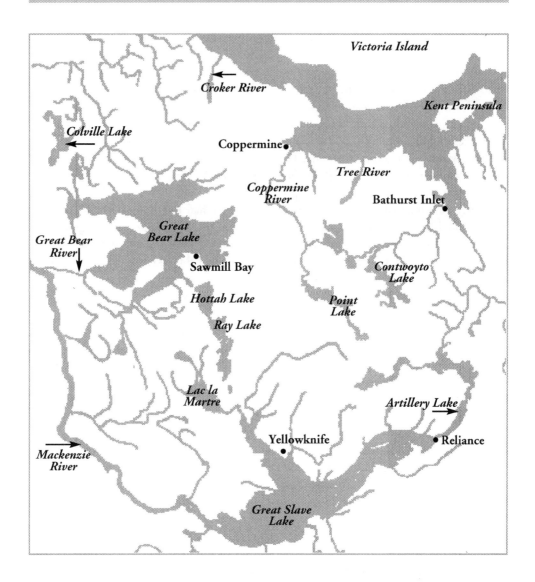

GREAT BEAR LAKE

The hills around Great Bear Lake

When our survey crew arrived at Sawmill Bay on Great Bear Lake on July 20, 1949, there was still ice on the lake. However, we found enough open water near the military station to safely land the Norseman. Sawmill Bay was quite a large military establishment with one of the first Loran Stations in the far north and a 5000-foot gravel strip for wheel aircraft.

The three other Norseman aircraft arrived within two days, and the rest of the maintenance staff and ground personnel arrived on board DC-3s. Our entire team included a detachment of DC-3 photo aircraft plus a crew of thirty men with the four Norseman seaplanes and two Consolidated PBY-5 Canso flying boats. Within a short time, we had our base set up and were ready to start our survey work again. We flew out of Sawmill Bay for several weeks; however, most of my time was spent on remote lakes with the survey crews. Since a Canso aircraft supplied our fuel caches, we could stay in the field and move the surveyors daily, as long as the cloud formations didn't interfere with our observations.

Often we returned to Sawmill Bay late in the evening and had to make the mile-and-a-half trek from the seaplane base to our detachment base in the community. Usually a jeep shuttled us back and forth, but when it was late, we didn't want to wait for the jeep to come for us. It was just a twenty-five minute walk, and we were happy to get some exercise after sitting in the aircraft most of the day.

As I made the walk one evening with my crewman, Laviolette, he pointed out a half a dozen Husky dogs feeding at the garbage dump. We both surmised that a native family had arrived from further north to pay a visit. I mentioned this to one of the local workers at the base. He assured me that no native family had arrived and that those dogs were not of the domestic variety; they were Arctic wolves. He advised Laviolette and I to carry our shotgun with us if we decided to walk in the area, especially in the evenings.

The wolves were not shy and continued to feed at the dump during our stay at Sawmill Bay. They didn't seem to be too interested in humans and ran away if they heard the jeep pass, but they consumed just about every small mammal that came their way. Al Marshall had brought his beautiful little dog with him to the base at Sawmill Bay. One day it just disappeared; only the collar was found.

Al Marshall with his dog

Just as we had done in Yellowknife, we had to survey the area north, east and west every fifty miles. While surveying east of Great Bear Lake near Point Lake, I had the unique pleasure of fishing Red Rock Lake and the head of the Coppermine River. Nature must have created this part of the country with the sportsman in mind—the land was rich with wildlife and scenery. As we caught lake trout on one side of a river, we could admire the barren land caribou standing watching us on the other side. The young calves that had just learned to run were quite a sight as they made ungainly leaps in the air. The caribou were such curious animals. They hung around the camp daily without any fear of us. I could not imagine hunting these tame animals because they didn't make any effort to run away.

From the moment we arrived in

Sawmill Bay, we heard about the tremendous fishing at Gun Barrel Inlet at the southeastern end, where the warmer waters from Hottah Lake empty into Great Bear Lake. The thirty-foot drop from Hottah to Great Bear is followed by a mile long fiord shaped like a gun barrel which makes a perfect habitat for lake trout. Great Bear Lake has become famous for large lake trout in the last forty years, but in 1949, only a few bush pilots and mining exploration companies had ever ventured into the area. During the summer, several thousand trout jam into this small space and when you look down into the water you see hundreds and hundreds of trout piled on top of each other. We also saw hundreds of lake trout in the 25-pound range, just cruising in twenty feet of water. No doubt, it is one of the most incredible wildlife phenomenons.

The sight was so unbelievable that we escorted several groups of honoured guests to witness it. Some took a few fish home to remind them of the encounter, but most simply took pictures. The RCAF had placed a large order for military trainers with the Beechcraft Corporation in Wichita, Kansas. When the president of the company, Mr. Beech, and some of his friends visited the north, I had the pleasure of flying them to Gun Barrel Inlet.

The only boat available was a four-man dinghy with a set of oars. Usually boats weren't necessary for fishing because it was easy to catch trout by just casting a line from the shore, but Mr. Beech had other plans in mind. He was an avid 16mm photographer and had brought along a Bolex camera with a special underwater case which he could hook up to a battery. We rowed out in the dinghy to try our luck at capturing the phenomenon with underwater photography. Mr. Beech lowered the camera about twenty feet into the water. From our vantage point, it appeared that the fish were putting on quite a show. They seemed to think the camera was food, as they swam around it and nudged it.

When the ice completely melted in Great Bear Lake the first week of August, it was recorded as the latest in history. The following year the lake was open the first week of July. We had to establish several survey points on the lake itself so we chose another spot at the mouth of one of the many rivers that flow into the lake. By then the trout population had started to spread out along the shore so the fishing was excellent there as well; however, nothing could compare to the huge numbers of trout in Gun Barrel Inlet before the ice was fully out of Great Bear Lake.

As we continued surveying our points east of Sawmill Bay, I discovered some unbelievable grayling fishing at the Great Bear River which empties into the lake at the southwestern end. We had previously caught some grayling on the Coppermine River and a number of other spots, including some around Great Slave Lake, but the Great Bear River was the highlight of my experience. Fishing grayling is more like fishing speckled trout than lake trout. Even though they can be caught on light spinning tackle, they respond better to fly fishing. Grayling like to follow the fly and will go for it just as you are ready to lift it off the water. Patience and technique are crucial; all too often the impatient fisherman lifts the fly just seconds before the fish is about to strike.

In mid-August Mr. Tom Wheeler and his daughter arrived at the Sawmill Bay base at the invitation of the federal government. Mr. Wheeler was a perennial fisherman, always looking for new territory and a new experience. He accompanied us on a trip to the Great Bear River for a taste of grayling. Old Tom, as I called him, really knew how to handle a fly rod. In no time he had mastered the art of fishing grayling and was catching and releasing three-pound fish faster than any of us.

Mr. Wheeler brought all kinds of fresh food with him for our overnight trip, and he insisted on doing all the cooking. He pan-fried the grayling and served them with fresh salad, fresh cooked vegetables and two kinds of wine. We all felt pampered by this man whose reputation as a top-notch tourist outfitter was respected all over the continent. Mr. Wheeler had perfected the intricacies of the trade at his father's camp at St. Jovite in the Laurentian Mountains, north of Montreal, Quebec. He went on to establish his own successful business, Wheeler Airlines.

His artistry went beyond the level of cooking; he was a master storyteller who kept us enthralled for hours after our feast. We heard about Wheeler's first aircraft, a Waco with a Jacobs engine, which had a notorious reputation for poor performance on floats. When Mr. Wheeler left the airbase a few days later, each of us received a personal thank-you note. Later, he mailed me some photographs of our fishing excursion. He was a great inspiration for me, as I hoped that someday, I too would be a tourist outfitter of his calibre.

ARCTIC CHAR AND THE CARIBOU MIGRATION

Once the surveys to the south, east and west of Great Bear Lake were completed, our crew headed further north. In a month the snow would arrive, and we needed to establish several points on the Arctic Ocean, west of Coppermine. There were ice packs on the Croker River when we arrived, and we could see that the conditions were not going to get any better. I landed at the mouth of the river, selected a sandy beach, dropped off the surveyors, and promptly took off again. With two-way radio communication, I was able to pick them up when they were finished and drop them off fifty miles further west. We eventually reached the Mackenzie River, then turned around, flew back to Coppermine, and began surveying points east.

Leo Manning, HBC Factor in Coppermine, with an Arctic wolf pelt

Today most people have heard about the incredible Arctic char fishing along the Tree River, but in 1949, the area was only known to bush pilots and the Inuit. What an exquisite place to start a survey point! We landed on an inland lake about three miles from the coast and quickly set up our camp. I hiked downstream to the first set of rapids with my crewman, Laviolette. Even though I had heard so much about them, I had never fished Arctic char. With each step towards the rapids, my anticipation was building; it seemed like a very long hike.

When we finally arrived at the rapids, I carefully surveyed the area, looking for the perfect hole. I tried to keep my excitement under control as I dropped a red-and-white daredevil into a hole which was about 20-feet deep. I paused for just a few seconds to allow the bait to settle before reeling in. Then I got a jar that almost pulled the rod out of my hand. I was still using the level winding reel, a Heddon-type, that Ben East had given to me in 1937.

This fish never surfaced, it just pulled and pulled for what seemed like an eternity. I didn't know who was going to tire first, but I was too pumped up with excitement to feel fatigue. Only when my hands were red and sore did the fish finally surface and show its red colour. Although it weighed about ten pounds, it had fought like a twenty-pound northern pike. Even when I had the char on shore, I was cautious since it was such a powerful one. As I watched the char in the shallower parts of the rapids, I could see that many of them were over 15 pounds and a few were even bigger. That day, Laviolette and I caught char until our hands were too sore to continue. Each one was a new challenge to our waning strength. We released most of them and kept a few to savour with our evening meal.

The following morning we had an unexpected visit from a couple of Inuit men who had set up their camp further downstream. They had seen our aircraft and walked up the river just to have some conversation and a cup of tea. They too were catching char, but they were smoking them for their winter food supply. Their methods differed from ours, as they were catching them with gill nets in the shallow parts of the river just after they had spawned.

While we were stationed at Coppermine, I was sent on a trip with an RCMP detachment in search of a cairn that had been erected by some of Franklin's men as they made their way south. Inspector Larson had been informed by some native travellers that they had seen a cairn near Turnagain Point on the Kent Peninsula. We landed at the mouth of a small river that flowed into Dease Strait and proceeded along the coast by foot until we found a six-foot heap of flat boulders that marked the location of some remains. An official photographer from Ottawa recorded as the officers removed several stones from the base of the cairn and pulled out the written notes and utensils that had been left there for future travellers. The notes verified that the men were on a southward journey after their vessel had been frozen in the ice. There was no mention of Franklin himself; however the records stated that they had left the bodies of two men at an Eskimo village on Victoria Island. Here was another piece in the puzzle of Franklin's last expedition A few years later another cairn was discovered two hundred miles further south of Bathurst Inlet.

As we worked our way eastward, we set up a base at the small community of Bathurst Inlet and two young Catholic missionaries offered us space in their comfortable lodgings. Without their willing assistance it would have been a very time-consuming process to fuel the aircraft. The 45-gallon drums of gasoline were several hundred yards from the shore at low tide.

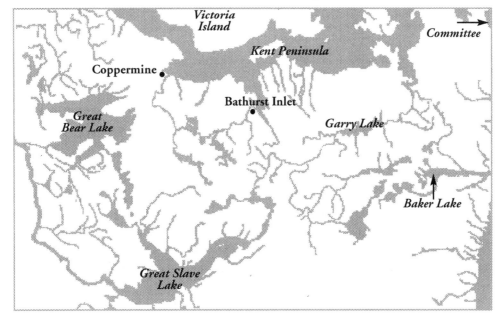

Every morning the missionaries helped us roll the heavy barrels to the aircraft, then hand-pumped two barrels for our daily flight.

As we flew around the Kent Peninsula, we saw a large caribou herd begin their migration south. During the last week in August, we witnessed the herd cross the river at a spot just south of Bathurst Inlet, about two miles from our camp. By then the new calves were running with confidence. The herd was so large that it took three days to complete the crossing; however, once they had crossed the river there wasn't a single caribou left to be seen. We followed them by air as they headed south; then we turned eastward in the direction of the other survey crew. Their detachment had moved to Garry Lake where they completed the checkerboard of survey points as far east as Chesterfield Inlet.

Before we made our final departure from Bathurst Inlet, the entire Inuit village and the two missionaries took us on an excursion up the river to a place where the Arctic char had gathered by the thousands. At one point the water in the rapids was so low that the natives used only a short pole with a handmade spike to spear the fish as they rolled over the rocks. Every year the Inuit camped at this part of the river where they caught and smoked their winter supply of char. Their winter food store also contained caribou meat which they dried or stored on the permafrost, a foot below the surface.

As we flew two hundred miles southeast towards Garry Lake, we saw the caribou herd, with a pack of wolves following them. We also spotted a herd of musk ox, and photographed them as proof that they migrated from the islands. Musk ox had never been seen before on the mainland.

By September the cool weather was upon us, and the snowstorms triggered the geese to start their southward trek. The head surveyor needed only two more geodetic points in the area before the end of the season. My detachment volunteered to establish one about three hundred miles north near Committee Bay. The Canso put in a cache of fuel on Brown Lake, and we started north on a bright sunny day at the beginning of September. We arrived at our destination and discovered that the ground was already frozen. We worked quickly, stayed only one night, and started back south to Garry Lake, flying in snowstorms all the way. While refueling at Brown Lake, one storm was so intense that we ceased pumping fuel into the aircraft and wondered if we were ever going to get out of there. Eventually the storm abated, and we took off for Garry Lake, arriving just moments before the darkness settled.

When the cool September air and snow flurries settled into our Garry Lake camp, we could certainly feel the chill from the north winds that were blowing constantly. Fortunately, our work was completed for the season so we packed up our equipment and flew south to Baker Lake. When we arrived, the HBC Factor, Sandy Loonan, invited us to stay with him in his modern home. After living in tents or in the aircraft for two months, we all enjoyed the comfort of a bed and a solid roof over our heads. The following morning we departed for Churchill, roughly 350 air miles further south. In 1949 there were no worthwhile charts to navigate by, so we used the old-fashioned type of dead reckoning and a sun compass, although we did have an air direction finder (ADF) that could be tuned into the Churchill radio range once we were within a hundred miles.

While flying south we constantly searched for the caribou migration. It was hard to believe that we had not seen a

On the barren lands with a caribou

single caribou since leaving Baker Lake, even though the herd had passed through Garry Lake only a week before. We wondered if they had changed direction. About an hour after departing from Churchill, we saw the first of the stragglers 2000 feet below us—about three thousand head, comprised of mostly females with young ones, loosely spread out. A few minutes later we spotted the main stream. Three aircraft, flying in loose formation roughly a half a mile apart, flew over the herd for a hundred miles. The never-ending herd stretched as far to the right and left as we could see.

We attempted to record this incredible journey using the only camera available to us—an RCAF issue Fairchild-type which took 4x4 inch black and whites. Needless to say our photographs didn't do justice to the natural wonder that we had witnessed. However, the event has left a deep impression in my memory. A biologist based in Winnipeg later told me that the 1949 migration of caribou exceeded

two million head. This large herd began to dwindle a few years later and declined to less than five hundred thousand.

Since I witnessed that great trek in 1949, I have flown thousands of hours crisscrossing the north country—Ontario, Manitoba, Quebec, Labrador and the Northwest Territories—with float planes during the open water season and on skis in the winter months. To this date, I have not seen a herd of such great magnitude.

With the number of large dams being constructed to produce electric power, it may well be another century before it is ever seen again. The dams create extensive lakes which cover large areas of the caribou food supply. These new lakes force the herds to alter their migration routes. Often the caribou have to cross new rivers and suffer the consequences. In one instance in northern Quebec, ten thousand head of caribou were swept into the rapids as they attempted to cross a newly created river.

ANOTHER ARCTIC SUMMER

In June 1950 I flew an RCAF Norseman from the Rockcliffe airbase near Ottawa to Yellowknife, NWT where I was joined by Bud Richmond, the pilot of a Canso flying boat. The two of us were to finish the survey work that we had begun in 1949, and install shoran sites in conjunction with the high level photographic airplanes. The loran sites, which we had established in 1949, were long range navigation sites, whereas the shoran sites were a short range navigation system. Both functioned on the same principle of determining position by measuring the time interval of a pulsed radio signal between two or more fixed ground stations.

Survey crew at Lac la Martre, 1950

We immediately set to work installing three different sites within eighty miles of Yellowknife. Bud flew in the heavy equipment which was used to construct the forty-to-sixty foot towers and I flew in the personnel and lighter stuff. Between the two of us, we managed to move things fairly quickly because the weather was unbelievably perfect for flying—sunny and clear.

Once the new sites were established, I returned to inspect some of the geodedic survey points that we had put in the year before. And, of course, I fished the same rivers to renew my memories of the incredible trout fishing. I spent about two weeks in Yellowknife, flying into Ft. Reliance, Artillery Lake, Lac la Martre, Rae Lake, Point Lake and Contwoyto Lake. By the first week in July we moved further north to Great Bear Lake and began to work northwest on Colville Lake,

Five Lakes and Ft. Franklin. Once we set up three triangulation sites in the area, I had time to return to Gun Barrel Inlet and was amazed that it was still the same—the fishing exceeded even my memories.

We continued to move further northwest, along the coast as far as Tuktoyaktuk, where we installed a station in the Inuvik/Aklavik area. At the beginning of August, we received a telegram from Ottawa authorizing us to fly beyond the Canadian borders to continue our survey work towards Point Barrow, Alaska. Another team had started from Nome, Alaska with a Norseman and a Canso and were to meet us there. The Korean War had just begun and there was an immediate call to finish the Distant Early Warning Line sites as soon as possible. The DEW Line project had been fairly secretive up until then; however, with the threat of the Korean War so close to our borders, the project became top priority.

We flew approximately fifty miles west of Tuktuk along the coast and established a site on a little lake just three miles inland. There were no detailed maps at the time, so we didn't know how close to the Alaska/Canada border we actually ended up. We pushed further west another fifty miles and put in a site along the Hulahula River, two miles from the mouth on the Arctic Ocean.

The ocean was completely frozen at the time. Only the mouth of the river was open for landing. Since we couldn't land at the Inuit village, Kaktovik, on Barter Island, because of the ice, the native people came over to visit us with their dog teams. They kept a boat on the river and delighted us with a trip up the river.

We camped along the river for about a week while the surveyors completed the triangulation between the site on the Hulahula River and the one we had just established fifty miles further east. The area was one of the most spectacular I had ever encountered in the Arctic. The mountains were only about fifty miles inland. The two large peaks of Mt. Chamberlin and Mt. Michelson stood out like pyramids on a desert. When the sun shone on these snowbound mountains, as

late as 10:00 P.M., they glistened with an orange-yellow colour as if they were torches in the sky. In fact, each peak is no higher than 2800 feet above sea level, yet they seem like megaliths in the vast expanse of ice and snow along the Arctic Ocean.

The Brooks Range extends for about six hundred miles—from the Canadian border on the west, to the Chukchi Sea on the east. While spruce and alders grow on the southern slopes of the range, the steeper northern slopes are barren and remain snow covered year round. As we walked along the banks of the Hulahula River, we encountered two feet of snow within three miles.

This area along the Hulahula River is one of the most prolific calving grounds for the Porcupine herd of caribou that winter on the other side of the Brooks Range along the Porcupine River and the Yukon Flats. Every year the herd travels north through the mountain passes which have been carved by three rivers: the East Fork Chandler, the Sheenjek and the Coleen, that flow south into the Yukon River. Even though we placed our camp site away from the grazing herd, we soon found them in our camp at all hours of the day and night. They make an

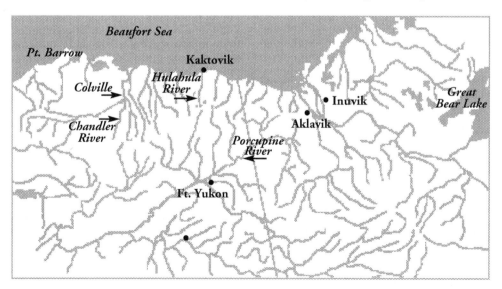

unmistakable noise—their ankles are loosely jointed so the cartilage clicks as they walk. Once the snow melts from the tundra, the caribou find plenty of food and few predators to disturb them as they rear the new calves. The wolves that preyed on them throughout the mountain passes usually remain further south where they can find more shelter. The only aggravation in the tundra is the ever-present mosquito which seeks out every living creature, whether caribou or human.

The caribou are one of the tamest creatures that I encountered in the Arctic. Whenever I ventured from the camp at least one of these curious creatures would follow me. And when I stopped to fish along the bank of a creek, they would stand about fifty feet from me and watch my activities.

Within a few days of camping along the Hulahula River my whole body became sensitive to the slightest movement of the caribou, the birds and the wind. Such a deep silence penetrated the area that the sound of a ptarmigan flushing as I crossed the tundra echoed like thunder.

The weather was optimum for our work. A high pressure system moved into the area and remained during our entire stay in Alaska. The sky was so blue and cloudless that we wore our dark glasses all day and well into the night because of the intense glare from the snow-covered mountains and the frozen ocean. With twenty-four hours of daylight and perfect weather conditions, we worked around the clock until we finished the surveys.

Once the surveyors were satisfied with their work, we moved further west to establish three more sites. The first one was situated between Kaktovik and Prudhoe Bay, about three miles inland on a small river that flowed into the Beaufort Sea. We put in the second on the Colville River, a couple of miles inland, before the estuaries begin. The third was located about sixty miles inland, near the junction of the Colville and the Chandler Rivers.

We set up our camp at the third site and between flights I had a few opportunities to fish the creeks that emptied into the Colville River. It didn't seem to make any difference what kind of lure I threw in. There was always a trout or a salmon clamoring to take it. Very few people had ever visited these waters, let alone fished in them. The thrill lasted about an hour or two, and then I was lulled into observing the activity of the wildlife that surrounded me. There were countless birds feeding and nesting in the area, including Arctic terns, snow geese, blue geese and white-fronted geese.

By mid-August, our installation sites were established and the other survey team from Nome had arrived to finish the points further west. When we returned to Coppermine and Bathurst Inlet to verify the previous survey points, we were just in time to witness the caribou migrating off the Kent Peninsula. Even though I had also seen the migration in 1949, the movement of so many animals was still an awesome sight.

We continued northward to Victoria Island where we installed fifteen new sites; then we moved on to Banks Island and Melville Island. There was very little time for exploring the fishing opportunities because of our tight schedule; however, I did manage to discover some incredible Arctic char fishing in a few rivers that flow into the Queen Maud Gulf and McClintock Channel in the southeast section of Victoria Island. The fast-flowing rivers are so shallow in this area that landing on them was virtually impossible. We had to land on the ocean and walk up them. I encountered char on these rivers that were as thick as on the Tree River the year before. The fishing is a tourist outfitter's dream; however, it would be a nightmare to worry about transporting the fishermen into the area. The only sensible way to accomplish this feat would be to fly guests by helicopter from Cambridge Bay and that would be quite an expensive proposition.

When our work was finally completed, it was the first week in September, and most of the wildlife was on the move. Everything seemed to be heading south as we made our way to Bathurst Inlet and subsequently to Yellowknife where we spent a few days resting and reorganizing for the flight back to Ottawa.

My second summer in the Arctic had given me an opportunity to feel at home in the environment because I was accustomed to the barrenness and the wildlife that inhabited it. My first experience in 1949 was exciting, but my second experience was more settled. I could appreciate the subtler details. I felt that I hadn't just visited the northwestern Arctic, I had actually lived there and breathed in the landscape. It had become a part of me.

July 1950, about 75 miles north of Yellowknife

RELAXING WITH THE PRIME MINISTERS

As an officer in the RCAF I had many opportunities to fly dignitaries to a variety of destinations. Often high-ranking government officials needed to be flown from Ottawa to Washington, D.C., or other cities for official meetings. However, there were other destinations where the dress was informal and the purpose was relaxation. On numerous occasions, I was called upon to escort dignitaries such as the Prime Minister or his cabinet ministers to a secluded lake for a few hours or a few days of fishing, hunting or just plain relaxing.

The year before Prime Minister Mackenzie King retired in 1948, I had several opportunities to socialize with him at his summer home at Kingmere, a small lake in the Gatineau Park, where he loved to spend the weekends. He enjoyed the simple pleasure of sitting on his verandah and chatting about all the unimportant details of life.

One day while we were talking on his dock, he asked me, in his very shy way, if I would do him a favour. He had some young children visiting him from Ottawa, and he wanted them to see the country from the air in my J-3 Cub which I usually flew to the lake on the weekends. He even offered to pay for the gasoline for the trips in my Piper Cub. Naturally, I agreed to the flights but wouldn't accept payment for the gasoline.

All that afternoon, I packed the children, two at a time, into the rear seat of the Cub. After each fifteen-minute sightseeing flight, the Prime Minister and my friend, Bud Richmond, helped me unload and refuel the plane. I tried to convince the Prime Minister himself to come up for a spin, but he politely declined saying that he only flew when he was on business. He preferred to have his feet on the ground when he was relaxing.

Later, while we were sitting on his verandah sipping some cool drinks, he asked me what the average air force pilot earned as a yearly salary. I told him that I was making about $4800 a year; however, this could increase with a higher rank. He then asked what a similar pilot flying for T.C.A. (Trans-Canada Air Lines) would make, and I told him that they would make about $10,000 a year. He expressed concern that our salaries were too low considering the high level of responsibility we had. Then one of the other air force officers asked him what the Prime Minister of Canada earned. He was silent for a while and then responded that he made under $10,000; this was in the summer of 1948!

When Louis St. Laurent became the Prime Minister in November 1948, we found a boss who really liked to relax in a boat or canoe. I had flown Mr. St. Laurent to Wheeler's camp on Lac Ouimet on numerous occasions while he was Minister of Justice. Tom Wheeler had an open door policy with Mr. St. Laurent and his associates who loved to fish for trout. It was good advertising for Wheeler Airlines when the Prime Minister regularly visited his establishment.

If Mr. St. Laurent only had a few hours to relax and fish, I flew him in the Norseman to a private camp north of Ottawa which was owned by a lumber company; we could leave Ottawa after 5:00 P.M. and return by 10:00 P.M.

I always enjoyed fishing with him because we would just paddle a 16-foot canoe out onto a lake and sit for hours. There was no competition, no hurry to catch a fish. It seemed to be a way of meditation for him. After a few hours of fly fishing his whole countenance brightened and the weight of his office seemed to grow lighter on his shoulders.

Catching a fish seemed less important to him than the experience of just sitting in the canoe moving his fishing line in and out of the water. In the privacy of nature he seemed to allow the pressure of governmental business to dissolve. The hours spent with him in a canoe were beyond the realm of time. The transforming power of nature worked its magic on us both.

When the leader of a nation takes some of his valuable time to spend a few hours fishing, this is newsworthy. Occasionally the press found us and took pictures of the Prime Minister with his catch of the day, if there was one. The photographs that appeared in the local papers were undoubtedly the best advertisement the sport of fishing could have had. I'm sure it helped the young people realize the value of the sport.

AN ICE SKATING FISHING TRIP

When I returned from the northwestern Arctic in September 1950, I received a short vacation. Then my wife, Joan, and I were posted to Goose Bay, Labrador, a large military base serving both the Canadian and American armed forces. Between September and the end of October, I flew a DC-3 on scheduled flights from Goose Bay to Montreal, Frobisher Bay, and other points north. In a period of thirty-five days I had flown about a hundred and forty hours, so around the first week in November, I was granted three days off.

I met a couple of native men by the name of Beauvais who worked at the base. They lived in a community about five miles further northeast called La Vallee Heureuse, which means Happy Valley in English. This was apparently the name of the Montagnais village long before the Canadian military arrived in the area at the beginning of World War II. The Beauvaises told me about a river that was full of sea-run speckled trout. When the river froze, the trout would run up it to spawn near the open rapids. The only way to reach this river was to cross Lake Melville by boat then walk down the Traverspine River.

Once the ice was about three inches thick, the native men attached their tie-on skates, and skated down the river looking for the migrating trout. The timing was critical because the trout were only visible through the ice when the river had just frozen. Once it snowed, the fish were hidden.

Those of us at the base who were good ice skaters were excited about a skating-fishing party. Gus Delaire, the chief cook at the airbase, and I, organized an outing for the first week in November.

The parents of the Beauvais family had a cabin up the river where we could spend the night after a day of skating and fishing on the Traverspine.

When the day of our trip arrived, the weather was quite clear, but the temperature hovered around 20°F. Four of us from the base, plus two of the Beauvais brothers, crossed the Melville River in a 20-foot boat while the ice was forming around us. Once we arrived at the landing on the Traverspine River, our bodies felt like frozen logs. Our anticipation of the fishing ahead of us kept us going as we walked a mile or so down the shore until the ice was thick enough to carry our weight.

We hurriedly put on our cold ice skates and began skating on three inches of glassy ice. As soon as our bodies got into the rhythm of skating, we started to thaw out and enjoy the bright sunny day. A half hour later, when we had covered about four miles on the ice, we arrived at the Beauvais family home where we ate a hearty breakfast in their two-story log cabin.

By noon, we were well fed and ready to begin fishing. Each of us carried two short poles about 24 inches long with a line about the same length. We used a barbless hook with lead on it (similar to a jig) and a piece of red thread wound tightly on as bait. As we skated up the river, we were followed by two men, each pushing a komotik—a wooden barrel on a homemade sleigh used to transport the fish back to the camp.

About a mile further down the river one of the Beauvaises spotted the shadow of a school of trout under the ice, so we quickened our pace to get ahead of them. We skated up to the next sand bank and dug little holes in the ice with our axes and waited for the school to swim by. The sand banks which extended twenty feet around each bend in the river were covered by just eighteen inches of water. The trout always cut the corners at the bends and swam over the shallow sand banks.

Even though we each had two lines, one in the right hand and one in the left, we could put only one line in the hole at a time. As the fish went around the bend, our lures were ready to tempt them to stop and eat. When a trout went for the lure, we quickly jerked the line out of the water, and the fish flew off the barbless hook. While we pulled one line out of the water, we dropped the other line into the hole to keep the fish around the hole. If you were fast enough, you could keep your arms moving constantly. We pulled out as many as we could; sometimes about 150 trout came flying out of these holes in just a few minutes.

Eventually one school of migrating trout would be joined by four or five hundred more trout in another school, and in no time, there were about fifteen hundred trout moving up the river. Since they were easy to spot under the ice, we simply skated up to the next bend, dug our holes across the sand bank, and waited for them. As they passed by underneath, we'd catch another hundred or so.

Meanwhile, the men with the komotiks were following behind us and picking up the fish. We continued skating up the river until the barrels were nearly full of fish—all between half a pound and a pound and a half. By then, it was about 4:30 P.M. and the temperature started to drop rapidly, so we skated back to the cabin.

We spent the night with the Beauvais family in their beautiful log cabin where we ate trout, drank homemade wine, talked and played music late into the night. Gus had brought a packsack full of delicacies with him from the base, and he and Mrs. Beauvais cooked up a banquet for us. I played my harmonica and one of the native men played the violin while the others danced until the early hours of the morning. It was a day and a night to remember.

When I returned to visit the Beauvais family a few weeks later, the ice was too thick and dull to see the schools of fish swimming underneath. We skated all the way up to the rapids where the fish were spawning. There were so many fish we could have walked across the river on their backs. Since they were all full of spawn we didn't take any fish, but we admired them.

During my visit old Mr. Beauvais told me about spending the winters at the Minipi River with his father on his trap line. He said that it was common to catch northern pike that weighed between 25 and 30 pounds. He also described one section of the river that was full of speckled trout ranging in size from a few pounds to ten or twelve pounds. Even though the section of river where the speckles could be found was just about a mile long, he couldn't remember the exact location. The Minipi River, which is west of Goose Bay, flows one hundred miles north/south into the Churchill River.

The following summer, in 1951, I began my search for this one section of river that had the legendary speckles. Whenever we had a day off or an excuse to fly the Norseman into the area, we searched for this speckled trout haven. We thought it would be a great fishing camp for the military, if we could find it. We found pickerel (walleye), lots of pike and whitefish, but no speckles. Despite the disappointments, I continued to believe Mr. Beauvais' story, although many of my companions thought it was an old man's fantasy.

Finally, around the beginning of September, our search ended. On that eventful day, I had a plane load of military personnel who were all avid fishermen. After landing and securing the aircraft, we set up a small camp, and then two of us hiked about a mile and a half on an old trappers' trail to the foot of the falls. On our first cast we caught a speckled trout, the first one we had caught on the Minipi.

We were so elated with this trout, we hurried back up the trail to show the others our good fortune. To our surprise, they too were catching them fast and furious. In fact, most of the trout were above the rapids, not far from where we had secured the Norseman. Down the river, in only four or five feet of water, there were thousands of fish. That day, one of the men, Sergeant Clark, caught a trout that weighed in the eleven pound range. Four

of the men decided to camp at the spot to fish for a few days. My crewman and I headed back to Goose Bay with the trophy fish which later ended up on the wall of the President of the Canadian Pacific Railway.

When I returned to pick up the fishermen, they had caught countless numbers of fish, but with no way to preserve them, they had kept only a few of the big ones. I stayed overnight with them and landed the biggest speckle that I had ever caught—it weighed about nine-and-a-half pounds. As soon as I returned to Goose Bay, I put my trout in the freezer to preserve it until I could have it mounted.

A short time later, my wife and I permanently left Goose Bay when I was posted to Edmonton, and I forgot the fish in the freezer. As luck would have it, someone ate it.

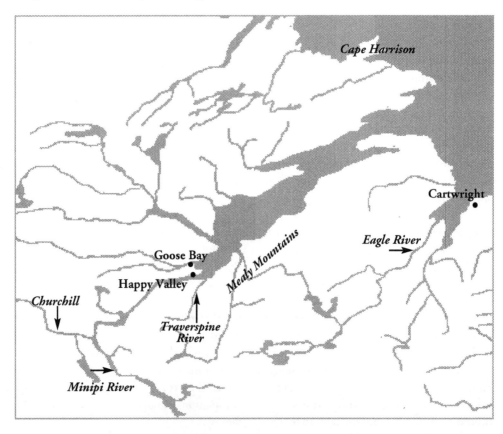

SALMON FISHING

Salmon fishing was often on my mind while I was stationed at Goose Bay. In October 1950, I flew into the Department of Transport weather observation facility at Indianhouse Lake (Lac de la Hutte Sauvage) in northern Quebec with their winter oil supply. By the time I arrived, the salmon had finished spawning. These fish had migrated about four hundred miles up the George River from Ungava Bay to spawn in the fresh, clear water.

This was not the time or place for sport fishing. There was such a multitude of fish, the native people were catching them with pond nets, similar to large minnow traps. Without refrigeration, they had to leave the fish in the nets until an aircraft arrived to transport them to the southern markets.

The following summer, starting in mid-July, I fished the George River at just about every set of rapids. It was a fabulous area to bring in dignitaries and high-ranking military personnel to experience the best fishing the north had to offer. We would land just above or below a set of rapids, secure the aircraft at a beach, and walk to the rapids where the fish were waiting for us. The cold waters produced four different species of fish: speckled trout, Arctic char, lake trout and, of course, salmon. The salmon would only hit flies, but the char would hit spoons, plugs, or whatever you threw at them.

The variety and plenitude of fishing along the George River has earned a reputation as one of the finest spots for sport fishing in the world. The spectacular fishing is complemented by breathtaking scenery and an abundance of wildlife along the shores of the river. While fishing along the river, it is not uncommon to see a caribou herd en route to the feeding grounds further north. Even today this herd is estimated to be around 600,000 head.

Many outfitters have capitalized on the tremendous fishing and hunting in the area over the past forty years. The numerous commercial camps along the George River now offer a full range of accommodations for fishing from July until the end of September, and for hunting from August until the end of September. Each hunter can easily attain his quota of two caribou, if he so desires.

In the late spring of 1951, I began preparations to take advantage of the fabulous salmon fishing on the Eagle River which flows into the Labrador Sea near the community of Cartwright. I managed to convince one of my frequent passengers, Mr. Joey Smallwood, the Premier of Newfoundland, to construct a small chalet on the Eagle River. Once Mr. Smallwood agreed to the plan, we put a crew together, procured some materials, and constructed a comfortable cabin for dignitaries to sample the province's finest salmon fishing.

By the time the salmon started running at the beginning of August, the camp was set up and ready for guests. Premier Smallwood had lined up a few parties of VIPs to break in the new fishing camp. On one of those excursions, I flew His Royal Highness, Prince Philip of Great Britain, into the camp along with his entourage of bodyguards and friends. When catering to royalty, you need a chef who can cook for the occasion, so we flew in Gus Delaire who had cooked for Louis St. Laurent, the Prime Minister of Canada.

On the first day of this fishing expedition, I guided Prince Philip up the trail to the biggest pool. We could catch grilts, the smaller, tasty salmon, along the river near the cabin, but the big salmon would only feed in a large pool which was about two miles up the river. As we were fishing in the pool with double-hook silver doctors, we could see a fifteen-pound salmon cruising in ten or twelve feet of water. It surfaced then rolled over without touching one of our flies. Prince Philip was an excellent sport fisherman who had fished the best streams all over the world, but that big salmon was eluding him. He was using a twelve-foot bamboo rod, split canes as we called them, standing about four or five feet above the pool. To get close to the salmon, he had to wheel the line out about a hundred feet. Then if a big one hit, he had to use a back-up spool with another couple of hundred feet of line because the fish would take as much line as it could for his run. Did they put up a good fight!

Once Prince Philip and his group felt comfortable with the fishing, I had other chores to do, so I returned to the camp. Before leaving, I told them that the chef was planning on serving their supper at 6:00 P.M. Gus was such a perfectionist when it came to his cooking that he insisted on serving the meal the moment it was ready. When Prince Philip's group didn't arrive by the appointed time, I set out on the trail in search of them. I located them a half hour later, but by the time we got back to camp and they had washed up, it was 7:00 P.M.

They had been so absorbed with the fishing, and in particular with that big salmon, that they had lost track of the time. Gus had to reheat their meal that he had meticulously prepared for 6:00 P.M. After the meal Gus approached Prince Philip, and in his thick French Canadian accent, introduced himself, then chided him for his tardiness. From then on Prince Philip and his group enjoyed every meal when Gus had it ready to eat. The following day

A member of Prince Philip's group fishing the Eagle River

Prince Philip lived up to his reputation as a fisherman and caught the big salmon that had eluded him the first day.

The camp on the Eagle River was such a success that over the past forty years the military has made continual improvements to it and still uses it exclusively for special guests of the federal government. One of the native men from Cartwright has established a small fishing camp about a half a mile away; however, he limits the number of fisherman to around ten at a time as the government only allows a specified number of lines in a pool. Since the salmon fishing season on the Eagle River only lasts about four weeks, from the beginning until the end of August, only a select few people can enjoy the experience of incredible salmon fishing there each year.

One day as I was flying between the base at Goose Bay and the fishing camp on the Eagle River, crossing the jagged peaks of the Meely Mountain range, I spotted the crash site of a World War II bomber that didn't have a white X painted on it. (All the downed aircraft that had been located were marked with a white X on the fuselage.) We circled the site and landed on a nearby lake that was about 150 yards wide. Once we found a beach and secured the aircraft, we walked about a quarter of a mile before we found the wreckage of an American B-24 and the remains of seven crewmen. The plane had been missing since 1943. Quite by accident, I discovered that the long narrow lakes which run northeast/southwest between the spikes were fishing treasures.

A Canso flying boat arrived from Ottawa plus all kinds of U.S. military personnel to conduct the investigation. Since we had to set up a camp for those working on the site, we flew in tents and camping equipment, plus a 17-foot square stern canoe. One evening I had a few moments to relax, so I paddled out on the lake to try the fishing. To my great delight, I landed several five-pound speckled trout.

Once I located the trout on this particular lake, I figured that the numerous lakes in these mountains would also have them. Sure enough, every lake we tried was full of trout in the three- to five-pound range. Later, others took advantage of the great fishing, and today most of the lakes in the Meely Mountains have commercial outfitters who fly in sportsmen from Goose Bay.

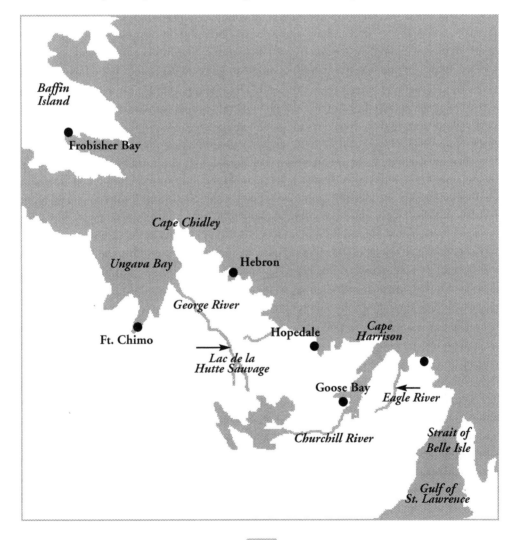

A SEAL HUNT IN HOPEDALE

In 1950 the military base at Goose Bay serviced all the native villages further north. We flew DC-3s on wheel/skis to Frobisher Bay, Pond Inlet, Arctic Bay, Clyde River and Fort Chimo (Kuujjuaq) on scheduled flights, and Norsemen on floats or wheel/skis to the smaller villages that didn't have landing strips.

As I flew north of Goose Bay along the Labrador Sea on search and rescue missions or medical evacuations to villages like Hebron, we found spectacular salmon fishing along with Arctic char and speckled trout in all the rivers that empty into the ocean north of Hopedale. But unfortunately, it is extremely difficult to safely land at the fishing spots because the winds can blow haphazardly in this area from 50 to 100 mph. The unpredictable weather makes flying so dangerous that even today there are no commercial sport fishing camps in the area.

Around the first week in December the ice was usually frozen to a depth of about two feet in the villages along the Labrador coast so we could safely land the DC-3 on wheel/skis. As we flew northwards along the coast on supply trips and medical evacuations, we could see herds of harp seals migrating south to their winter feeding grounds through the Strait of Belle Isle to the Gulf of St. Lawrence or off the Grand Banks where there was plenty of cod. They had spent the summer feeding on fish further north, but once the ice started to form they headed south.

Whenever the seals migrated, whether it was north or south, they traveled in groups of five to ten thousand, about two or three miles apart. On one flight we could easily count 150,000 to 200,000 harp seals. From 2000 feet up, their black and white bodies bobbing along the shoreline looked like penguins gliding over the waves. It was a sight to see them all swimming in such harmony!

As soon as the ice started to melt, usually around the beginning of June, the seals would begin their trek north. Along the way, the seals stopped at the rivers that empty into the ocean to feed on the fish. The coast is full of narrow fiords, about 8 to 15 miles long with 4000 foot high mountains on either side. Whenever we flew by during the migration, it was not uncommon to see ten thousand seals feeding in the well-protected fiords. They usually remained in the salt water, feeding on the fish that were entering and leaving the rivers to spawn.

One fall day we received an emergency radio call from the Grenfeld Mission in Hopedale. All the northern villages along the coast—Cartwright, Cape Harrison, Hopedale, Nain, Hebron, Cape Chidley—had a Grenfeld Mission. These missions were founded at the turn of the century by Sir Wilfred Grenfeld, a member of the British Parliament. All were maintained by the Anglican Church.

Volunteers at the mission educated and cared for the native people, both spiritually and physically. Well trained graduate nurses supplied medical and ambulatory care and operated radios to communicate with points south. Most of our medical evacuation flights took place because we received radio calls for help from workers at a Grenfeld mission.

We flew into Hopedale with a Norseman and waited for several hours while the doctor took care of the emergency. Just after we arrived, some native men returned to the village with a load of harp seals and were heading back out again. I didn't hesitate to accept when they

A nurse from the Grenfeld Mission helps load a patient
into an RCAF Norseman on skis

invited me to join them. It was such a calm day that we could navigate along the shoreline quite easily in their 24-foot freighter canoe with an 18-hp motor. The seals swam along the coast as close to the shore as possible. When a herd passed us, there were so many of them swimming together it was easy to navigate the canoe along side one of them.

The native hunting technique was so perfect it can only be considered an art. One of the men harpooned a seal with a spear with a 50-foot line. An empty 5- or 10-gallon barrel was attached to the line. Once a hunter had harpooned a seal, another hunter would drop the barrel overboard. Then they would go after another seal. This way they could kill a half dozen seals, then return to pick them up, because the barrels would prevent the dead seals from sinking.

When the native people killed a seal, no part of it was wasted. They used the skins for their clothing and their kayaks and sold a few pelts to the HBC Store in exchange for cloth or metal tools. They ate the meat near the ribs and melted down the fat for oil. Their homes were heated with seal oil, and they cooked their food over it.

In 1950, the native people in the remote areas still lived in tents in the summer and ice houses (igloos) in the winter. Even though they had other sources of food, such as fish and caribou, their way of life revolved around and depended on the harp seal. Their tents were made of caribou hide, and they used the caribou bones for tools, but caribou were not as prevalent as the seals. In a good year a caribou herd would pass close to their village. But, more often, the hunters had to travel inland to find a herd, whereas the seal herds always passed by their village every spring and fall.

DR. HENRY HUDSON

I was just a teenager when Dr. Henry Hudson moved to Timmins as a practicing dentist. He built a house on the shore of the Mattagami River across the river from my family's boat house. We eventually became good friends because he liked to fish with us at Sandy Falls.

Over the years, Henry became fascinated with airplanes. When I returned to Timmins after World War II and bought a J-3 Cub, Henry decided it was time to learn to fly. He took flying lessons from Borden Fawcett in South Porcupine and received his private license shortly afterwards. In 1946 he bought his own Piper J-3 Cub and began to fly regularly to his cottage on Temagami Lake.

Once Henry had his own aircraft we flew together on several fishing trips, each with our own airplanes. In 1946 we flew up to the Seal River. The following year we made our first trip to Sutton Lake. A few of us who regularly flew up to the eastern coast of James Bay to fish for speckles established a fuel cache midway on the trip at Kesagami Lake so that we didn't have to land at Moosonee.

After I re-enlisted in the RCAF in 1948, Henry and I continued to correspond and planned to meet again in Timmins while I was on leave in September 1951. He intended to fly north to the Seal River with a well-known hockey player, Bill Barilko, but expected to be back in Timmins by the time I arrived there.

I had been posted to Edmonton, Alberta from Goose Bay, Labrador and was driving across the country from Montreal with my wife and son. On our way north from Montreal to Timmins, we spent a night with our friends, Norm and Agnes Wickens, in Temagami. As we were preparing to leave the following morning, we

heard the news on the radio that Henry's plane was missing en route to Timmins.

By the time we arrived in Timmins a few hours later, the RCMP had already arranged for search and rescue flights from Kapuskasing and Timmins. I knew Henry's flight plan because we had made the same flight to the Seal River together: he would stop in Kesagami Lake on his way south to refuel; then proceed directly to Timmins.

I accompanied Art Appleby of the 413 Squadron in a RCAF Norseman to check out the location of the secret fuel cache on Kesagami Lake. When I discovered that the gas cans and the fuel were both gone, I realized that Henry must have passed through Kesagami Lake, otherwise they would still be there. We had made a pact to take the cans whenever we used the fuel and to replace both on the next trip north.

The area between Kesagami Lake and Lillibelle Lake, near Cochrane was searched thoroughly for five weeks with DC-3s, Beech 18s and every other available aircraft. There was a lot of public pressure to continue the search because Bill Barilko was a famous hockey player for the Toronto Maple Leafs. Finally, after thousands of hours of searching without finding any trace of the aircraft, the rescue mission was called off.

For many years, people speculated about the disappearance of Henry's aircraft. I always had a feeling that Henry had been forced down somewhere because of bad weather.

One day, ten years later, while Holly Parsons was flying in a helicopter sketching timber north of Cochrane for the Abitibi Pulp and Paper Company, he spotted something yellow in the forest. When the helicopter hovered lower, he determined that it was an aircraft, but he couldn't identify it. He reported the sighting to the Ontario Provincial Police. A team was dispatched to investigate the crash. The OPP officers discovered Henry's aircraft and the remains of two bodies.

Since Henry could have landed on several lakes between Kesagami and Cochrane, we can only speculate that the weather must have deteriorated very suddenly. When the plane was first reported missing in 1951, there were all kinds of rumours about its disappearance. Some people believed that the plane had crashed because it was overloaded—with the floats full of speckled trout. I never believed those stories because I knew that Henry wasn't the type of fisherman to bring fish home with him. He enjoyed eating fish on the trip, but he rarely took more than one big trout home with him.

When the airplane was found in 1961, there was no sign of fish in the floats or any other kind of overload. I visited the crash sight to determine if there was any part of the aircraft worth salvaging and to pay my last respects to an old, dear friend.

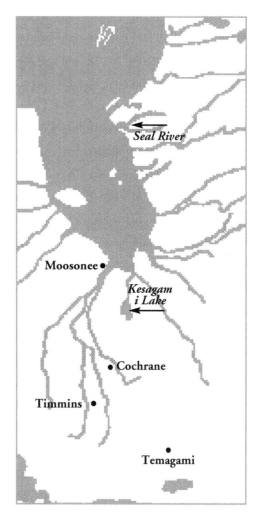

NORTHERN ADVENTURES FROM EDMONTON

In the fall of 1951, I was transferred to the RCAF base, Northwestern Air Command, at Edmonton, Alberta. We flew DC-3s on scheduled trips to Whitehorse, Winnipeg, Churchill, and Coral Harbour on South Hampton Island and medical evacuations to Cambridge Bay, Yellowknife, Fairbanks and other northern points. On occasion we flew for an army detachment out of Churchill, Manitoba, and made parachute training flights for the Princess Patricia detachment in Calgary.

The RCAF eventually assigned us some Fairchild C-119s (Boxcars) when our transport duties increased. Since Canadian troops were active in the Korean War at the time, we also picked up injured men at the McChord Airbase in Tacoma, Washington, and transported them east.

By the time I arrived in Edmonton in November, the winter deep freeze had already begun. After settling into work at the base and a new home on the outskirts of the city, I finally found some time around mid-December to hunt prairie chickens and Hungarian grouse not far from our home. The large grain farms were separated by a couple of hundred yards of bush which was prime country for grouse, rabbits and deer. The season for upland game hunting extended well into

the winter. I went out at least once a week with a few other airmen and we easily shot as many birds as we needed. There were only about 75,000 inhabitants in Edmonton in 1951; the oil industry, which later brought prosperity to the city, had only just begun development.

Once the rivers started to open in the Whitehorse area in the middle of June 1952, our fishing trips began in earnest. We usually arrived at the base on a scheduled flight around 4:00 P.M. Since it was daylight well into the evening we had time to enjoy the scenery and the fishing. We found Arctic grayling in all the little rivers that were just ten or fifteen miles from the airbase. Once we became familiar with them, we set our sights further.

The pilot of a search and rescue Otter, based in Whitehorse, flew us into some of the rivers that flow into the Gulf of Alaska. In mid-July he flew Squadron Leader Ken Dobbin and me past Lake Labarge into the Kluane Lake area. About an hour out of Whitehorse, we landed on a picturesque, long, narrow lake in the mountains, with an interconnecting river that flowed about twenty-five miles to the ocean. Once we landed and tied up the aircraft on a beach, we hiked about a quarter of a mile along the shore, donned our Air Force-issue waders, and waded thirty or forty feet into the cold waters.

In just a few hours, we caught several different types of salmon: coho, steel heads, king salmon, and silvers. The steel heads ran up to nine pounds. The silvers ran three or four pounds. Their size wasn't as impressive as their numbers. The fish were biting on spinning tackle using mepps, daredevils, and jigs in fast water. While we were fishing on one side of the river, there was a grizzly bear mother with two cubs on the other side. We didn't seem to bother them, and they didn't seem particularly interested in us; there was

enough fish for all. When we departed, we left a few fish on our side. We expected the bears would take up our fishing spots once we were gone.

Whenever we had time on these short trips, we hiked up the slopes that surrounded the lakes to look for game. We easily saw the potential for big game hunting in the Kluane Lake area because we frequently sighted mountain goats, mountain sheep, mule deer, and moose at five or six thousand feet above sea level.

The black moose were feeding on mountain ash and alders along the high plateaus where there were relatively few flies to bother them. These were some of the largest moose I have ever seen. On one trip we saw a black moose that easily weighed 2000 pounds carrying a 70 inch rack. Today the Kluane National Park Reserve covers approximately 8500 square miles and preserves the wildlife for all to enjoy.

By early September the geese began their migration south. The Canada geese fly southwest hugging the coastline of Hudson Bay from Churchill to Fort Severn, and then head due south. The blues and snows ("wavies" as the Cree call them) fly further down the coast to Winisk. Our scheduled flight from Edmonton to Winnipeg to Churchill, Manitoba, often gave us a day layover at the base in Churchill. When the geese began to fly south, Ken Dobbin and I took advantage of the situation and arranged a hunting trip.

Squadron Leader "Bounce" Weir maintained a Norseman on wheels for Search and Rescue missions. (His nickname "Bounce" was attributed to the highest bounce that any airman had made while landing a Norseman on wheels.) He flew us into prime Canada goose hunting territory, fifty miles south of Churchill, early in the morning, landed on a gravel esker, and picked us up late in the afternoon. The timing was perfect. The geese were so plentiful that we didn't have to build blinds. We were fortunate enough to make two of these trips in the fall of 1952; one about two weeks after the first.

Before I was posted to Edmonton, an old friend, Matt Berry, the owner of Yellowknife Airways, told me about several farms around Edmonton that allowed hunters onto their private land to hunt the ducks that fed on their grain. During my flights on the DC-3, going in and out of the airbase, I located several lakes and ponds within a forty-mile radius where several hundred flocks of mallards and teals were nesting.

By hunting season, I had rounded up a few hunters at the airbase. Eight of us headed out at daybreak to one of the ponds that I had located from the air. There were thousands of ducks resting on the long swamp when we arrived, but within a few minutes the majority of them took off to feed in the nearby fields. We managed to shoot about a half-dozen birds and then sat waiting in our makeshift blinds for the rest of the morning.

Every once in a while a lone duck would take off, but it was usually too far away for us to get a good shot. The only one of us that bothered with these strays was Bill Shearer, a check pilot for the 435 Squadron. Bill wasn't much of a hunter, although he enjoyed the company of hunters and the outdoors. He was shooting downwind at the fast-flying teals and missing them all until one small teal fell. The wind was pushing this duck straight down an alley at 65 mph when Bill popped out of the blind and his bullet managed to find it.

Once Bill retrieved his bird, he carefully examined it and then declared that this was the only Protestant duck in the area; all the others that had eluded him must have been Catholics. Bill himself was a staunch Catholic and quick to make fun of hunting on Sundays.

When I figured out the feeding patterns of these local ducks, I decided that morning hunting wasn't worth the wait. Most of the flocks were leaving the ponds in the early morning to feed, returning in the afternoon to rest, then feeding again until almost dusk. I located a small lake that was covered with ducks, about ten miles south of the airbase. Squadron Leader Dobbin and I drove to the area, wearing our uniforms, of course, and talked to the farmer about hunting on his private property. He happily gave us the key to his gate, and we hunted there for the remainder of the season. There were probably several thousand ducks—mostly mallards and teals—on the lake at any given time.

We arrived in the early evening as the ducks were returning to the lake to roost for the night and hunted from several small one-man blinds fashioned from chicken wire and covered with grain. If the wind was blowing from the north, we used the blinds at the south end of the lake so the ducks would fly over us. When the winds shifted, we moved to our other blinds.

We only had about twenty minutes to shoot when the ducks arrived, but there were so many of them that we usually filled our quota. They came in low enough over our blinds that we could pick out the young ones since each pair of ducks usually had between six and eight following close behind. Aside from the fact that they were the easiest to shoot and the tastiest to eat, we also figured it was less disruptive to the family and the flock to shoot the young ones rather than the adults.

IN THE BUSINESS OF FLYING

Loading and refueling the Norseman at the Chapleau airbase

When World War II ended in 1945, I resigned from active service duty. I remained on reserve for three years before I rejoined the RCAF in 1948 to fly a Norseman with the survey teams in the western Arctic. By the time the majority of the surveys were completed in 1953, my obligation to the air force was fulfilled. Since I had flown many high-ranking government officials around the country, including the Prime Minister and several cabinet ministers, I had contacts in the government when I decided to apply for a charter to open my own air service.

I was looking for a place to set up an airbase, run a flying service, and establish outpost camps for fishing and hunting. There were numerous places in northern Canada that were perfect for hunting and fishing. However, most of them were in such remote areas that they didn't offer any

services or easy access by road. In the fall of 1952, my wife, Joan, and I had two young children. We were eager to locate our airbase in a community with schools and hospitals.

I would have liked to return to my hometown of Timmins, Ontario to establish my airbase since I was familiar with the surrounding lakes and rivers, but the existing air services had sole rights to fly commercially in the area. As I looked further afield, the town of Chapleau, 120 miles west of Timmins, became a possibility. While I worked at the seaplane base in South Porcupine I had flown into Chapleau twice; once in 1937 on mining charters and again in 1948 to fight the forest fires. On both occasions the local people told me about the excellent walleye and northern pike fishing in the nearby lakes.

CHAPLEAU: MY FIRST AIRBASE

Ed Ahr and I arrived in the town of Chapleau in April 1937 flying a Custom Waco that belonged to the Hollinger Mines. We registered at the Queens Hotel, and then Ed made two trips into Brett Lake with supplies for one of the many mining camps in the area. As crewman, I loaded and unloaded the aircraft and kept it serviced between flights.

We weren't the only aircraft in the area at the time; during our three-day stay in Chapleau, I counted eighteen different ski-equipped planes flying charters. All the mines needed supplies flown into their camps to carry them through the three- to six-week spring break-up period. Aircraft were freighting supplies into Swayze Lake, Brett Lake, Lee Lake and another small lake near the Kenty Mines.

The mines at Lee Lake were also serviced by dog teams or horse-drawn sleighs on a winter road that had been cut directly east from Chapleau, but these trips took about two days. Several old timers from Chapleau, including Mr. Vezina and Leona McCrea's father, Mr. Burns, told me stories about running a team of horses from Chapleau to Swayze Township in the 1930s. Eventually, the expense of the horses

and the drivers cost more than an air charter. As aircraft became readily available, gradually all the mines in the area were serviced by air.

In 1937 the community of Chapleau was like a western town with a frontier attitude; even the stores had fashionable false fronts. The highlights of the main street were the Chapples department store and the Queens Hotel. The hotel had little balconies on the front where the airmen sat and socialized after they finished flying for the day. All the famous bush pilots of the time—including Matt Berry, Phil Sauve and Punch Dickins—came to Chapleau at some point because aircraft supplied the mines in Swayze Township for at least five years.

At first Swayze was a very good gold producer, but as the shafts went below a certain depth, the ore bodies disappeared. Once the war came along in 1939, many of the men were recruited so there was a shortage of labor. The mining companies must have felt they had cleaned out the ore bodies by then because they closed down and left everything there. When I returned in 1948 to fight the fires, I flew over Swayze and could still see all the original

The town of Chapleau during the winter of 1955

buildings. In 1954 when I arrived back in Chapleau, most of the old buildings at Swayze were still standing even though many of the roofs had caved in. A few years ago I flew over the site and could hardly find a building; a few logs were all that remained of the bustling mining community. Nature had been at work over the past fifty years, reclaiming its territory.

By 1953 Chapleau was prospering as a major railroad centre for the Canadian Pacific Railroad. A road south to Thessalon and Sault Ste. Marie had been constructed in 1948 to haul out the burnt timber after the fires, so the town was easily accessible for American sportsmen in Michigan and states further south. In addition, it offered services such as schools and a hospital.

In 1953 I notified the RCAF that I intended to resign at the end of my five-year commitment, instead of taking a permanent commission. Shortly afterwards, I was posted to an all-weather squadron in North Bay, Ontario because that was the closest base to the area where I planned to establish my own air service. We were flying T33s and I was in charge of checking out the pilots in the Link trainer. On a couple of occasions I flew north to Chapleau with the

Norseman pilot from Trenton to assess the situation before my charter was approved.

By January 1954, I was officially given an honourable discharge from the RCAF and my charter was approved. I left Joan and the children at her parents' home in Belleville and headed to Chapleau to set up operations. With my meager pension from the air force, I could only afford a Stinson Stationwagon on skis and a set of floats to change over in the spring.

When I arrived in Chapleau, I bunked down at the YMCA, bought an old boat house on the Chapleau River, and hired two carpenters to winterize it. I immediately started flying several crews of prospectors who were looking for uranium—the Cold War was well underway and uranium was a hot item.

In the early spring, I flew out an entire crew of surveyors that was stranded on the bottom of Windermere Lake. The ice had started to melt earlier than was expected. The Department of Lands and Forests had flown them in with a deHavilland Beaver, but they couldn't fly them out because the Beaver was too heavy for the thin ice. It took me ten days to transport eighty men in the Stinson Stationwagon. I was busy flying charters

1955 with the Stinson Stationwagon in Chapleau

right up until the ice started to melt on the lakes. Then I took the train to Belleville to pick up my wife and two children.

I arrived back in Chapleau with my family in a snowstorm on May 5th, and my son, George Jr., was born three days later. My wife had her hands full with children and setting up a new home, while I was busy changing the Stinson over to floats with the help of an engineer who had worked with the Department of Lands and Forests.

I had trained as a mechanic in South Porcupine and written my license in 1938. It had expired while I was in the RCAF and I was too busy flying to renew it. Fortunately, a very talented engineer/bush pilot by the name of Fletcher, who had a small repair service in Missinabie, helped me in the early years. I did most of the work on the airplane, then he inspected it and signed it out. Fletcher was originally from New Brunswick and had learned to fly with the Eddie Rickenbacker school back in the 1930s, before he worked as an engineer for the Ontario government.

Over the years, Fletcher and I became good friends, swapping stories about our experiences flying in the north.

Setting up the airbase was an all consuming process that occupied my waking hours and much of my sleep. When I wasn't flying the aircraft, I was servicing it or wading through the ocean of paper work that went along with reports to the Department of Transport. At times, flying seemed to be the easiest part of the business.

The town of Chapleau proved to be a perfect location for an air service. There was plenty of charter work as well as many excellent fishing and hunting opportunities. The walleye and northern fishing was highly rated, and the speckled trout fishing was better than I expected. As I entered my first year of operation, I was certain that I had made the right choice. Despite the long hours of work, it was a fulfilling experience to create something of my own. I was doing everything I enjoyed—flying, exploring, and fishing. Every moment was worth the years it had taken me to get there.

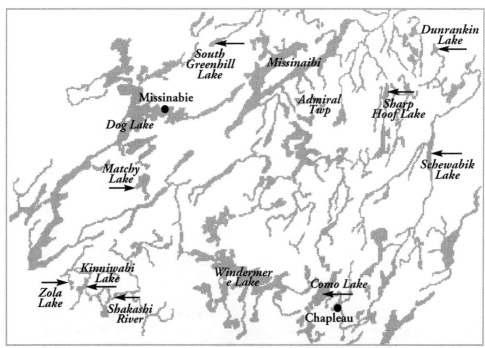

A BIOLOGIST SOLVES A FISHING PROBLEM

In the summer of 1954, I flew charter trips for three lodges on Dog Lake, near the small community of Missinabie. One of the lodge operators wanted to offer his guests speckled trout fishing on day trips, since Dog Lake only had walleye and northern pike fishing. We flew together to a lake further south that he had heard was full of speckled trout. This lake, Zola Lake, was too small and rocky to land the Stinson safely so I landed just a few miles away on Kinniwabi Lake. We hiked to Zola Lake on a trail that a mining company crew had blazed.

The speckled trout fishing exceeded our expectations. There was an abundance of fish in the one- to two-pound range—the perfect size for pan frying. And they were delicious! We set up a temporary camp on the west side of Kinniwabi Lake and carried two canoes over the one-mile trail to Zola Lake. Later that summer, when the lake's popularity grew, I flew in two 12-foot boats as well.

During my first summer operating the air service in Chapleau, an old friend of mine, Whitey Canon, a biologist from the Arlington Heights/Chicago area, visited my family. Whitey's talents as a biologist and woodsman were well known when I became acquainted with him during the 1940s on Lake Temagami. While he was the director of a boy's camp, he set up a restocking program for the Ontario government to reintroduce walleye and northern pike into the lake. I wanted to spend my first summer in Chapleau exploring the lakes and testing out the fishing before I established my own outpost camps, and Whitey was the perfect companion. He was an ardent fisherman who knew more about fish and their habitat than anyone I had ever known.

One afternoon we flew into Kinniwabi Lake to pick up two fishermen, and were confronted with a perplexing situation. Zola Lake had produced plenty of speckled trout all summer long, but the two fishermen, Al Snyder, a writer for the *Sudbury Star*, and his friend, hadn't caught a trout in two days of fishing. Al described how the fish were jumping all around them but wouldn't bite on anything. They had tried every lure in their tackle boxes. This was very unusual—the speckles usually bit on just about anything in Zola Lake.

Since I didn't have any other pressing trips that day, I suggested that we all hike back to Zola Lake to try our luck. Maybe Whitey or I had something in our tackle boxes that the trout would find interesting. As we arrived at the boat landing we could see the trout surfacing. They were swimming around huge lily pads that were swarmed by dragonflies.

Whitey quickly grasped the situation. He informed us that the fish were feeding on eggs which the dragonflies were attaching to the underside of the lily pads. When a dragonfly landed on a lily pad, its tail would sneak under the pad and deposit its eggs. This explained why the fish weren't biting the lures, but then we had to figure out how to get some bait that simulated the dragonfly eggs.

Whitey suggested that we walk back along the trail to find something that harboured insect eggs and also resembled the dragonfly eggs. After walking a few hundred yards he spied an old, rotting log. When we broke it open with an axe, we found thousands of white eggs laid in a nest by some red ants. We scooped up about a hundred eggs, put them in a bucket, and returned to Zola to see if they would attract the trout.

Whitey stripped all the feathers off a few flies, then he put a little white grub at the end of each one. Once we each had one of these altered flies on our line, we paddled out into the lily pads. We dropped our flies down about two inches below the surface of the water. Within minutes each of us had a trout on our line. A couple of hours later, we had caught our limit of trout and released about fifty more.

Al Snyder wrote up the story for his paper, extolling praise for the American biologist who solved the mystery of the trout that wouldn't bite. I asked Whitey how he had known what the dragonflies were doing on the lily pads. He related an experience he had fishing for bluegills in one of the chain of lakes north of Chicago. One year in the fall, he made a trip to a lake which was famous for its great bluegill fishing. That day, no one had caught a fish. He knew that the fish had to be feeding on something, because he could see them in the water around the beds of cattails. He stripped one of the cattails and

figured out that the fish were feeding on eggs that were deposited on the cattails, just below the surface of the water. Whitey was able to use this experience to help us solve the puzzle of Zola Lake.

We willingly passed on this secret to our guests who fished Zola Lake. Even though the dragonflies only lay their eggs for about five days in the summer, a fisherman would be very disappointed if he didn't know how to fish for them at this time.

The cold water of Zola Lake and a regular diet of freshwater shrimp produced firm tasty trout with flesh that was almost red. They were the favourite of so many fisherman that we flew the same guests in year after year.

We set up a tent camp on Kinniwabi Lake in 1955. A year later we received permission from Algoma Ore to use their small cabin at the north end of Zola Lake, if the guests were reluctant to camp out in tents. Once the lakes in the area became accessible by road, when Hwy 101 opened between Chapleau and Wawa, the fishing declined rapidly.

Unloading the Beaver at the dock on Kinniwabi Lake

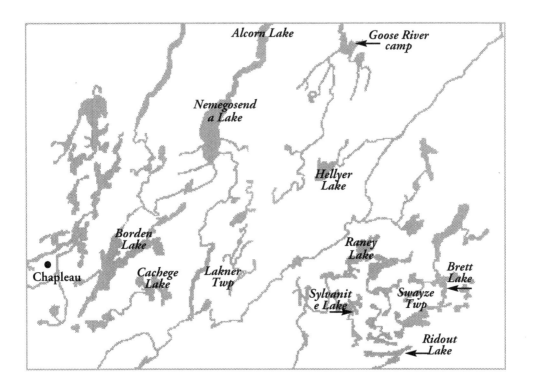

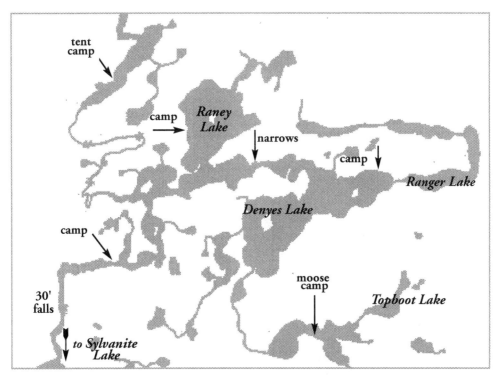

RANEY AND DENYES LAKES

Dick Ryan at Raney Lake falls

Chapleau was a bustling little town in the summer months. Mining companies, road crews, fire fighters and fishermen all wanted air charters. There was never a dull moment nor a spare one. I kept my aircraft flying from morning till night. While I was flying a charter trip, I was busy looking for good fishing lakes. During my first year of operating the air service in Chapleau I didn't have my own outpost camps nor the clientele to fill them, so I relied on the charter work to fill my time.

Several lodge operators in the area needed their camps serviced regularly and were anxious to hire someone who took an interest in locating additional fishing "hot spots." Chapleau Lodge on Borden Lake had good lake trout fishing in the spring and fall and northern pike throughout the fishing season. However, most of the sport fishermen also wanted the tasty walleye. One of the local trappers had told me that Raney Lake produced exceptional walleye fishing, so Dick Ryan, the owner/manager

of Chapleau Lodge, and I flew there one afternoon to test it. Since we didn't have a canoe with us, we secured the aircraft on a beach below the falls and fished from the shore.

Well, I hadn't seen such a concentration of walleye since my early years fishing in the Timmins area. Within an hour Dick had landed a ten-pound walleye and a fifteen-pound northern pike, plus there were so many smaller fish that we caught one on every cast. It was a walleye fisherman's paradise! The lake became such a hit with the fishermen that we flew in guests from his lodge on a daily basis. We built a small dock near the falls where the fishing was excellent in the spring. Then once the spawning was over, we had to fly in a couple of canoes because the fish spread out into Raney Lake.

The walleye generally spawn from about the 10th of May until the 20th. The northern pike spawn from the beginning of May to the 15th. During that time, the fish feed on minnows and crayfish which come down from other lakes into the fast waters near a set of falls or rapids. The fish concentrate in the warmer waters at the foot of the falls when the ice melts. Towards the end of June the lakes warm up, and the fish begin to spread out. As the minnows and crayfish fan out into the lakes, they are followed by the walleye and pike.

When fishermen are looking for fish, they have to find the minnows first. As the minnows move out in the early morning and the late evening, the walleye come out to feed on them. During the summer these are the best times to fish. June is an excellent month for fishing, despite the annoyance of the black fly hatch. The fish feed just as aggressively in July and August, but because they are dispersed throughout the lakes, the fishermen have to locate them on the shoals and rocky points.

Raney Lake, which is thirty air miles east of Chapleau, has about a hundred miles of shore line and numerous islands, offering many places to fish. In 1955 I received a Land Use Permit to build an outpost on an island in the north end. I flew Axel Romanon in to begin constructing a tent site there. He built one 14 by 17-foot tent base with walls, three smaller 10 by 12- foot bases and a floating dock. Axel had a fondness for sauna baths, so he also constructed a small log house near the water for bathing and a dock in front of it for a cool dip after a hot bath.

We didn't use the site in 1955 because of the fires, but while Axel was building the camp, he located some of the best fishing spots nearby. He continued to guide the guests for three seasons while he built a cabin and cleared the land.

The whole area around Raney Lake was full of game and plenty of fish. Denyes Lake, which is connected to Raney Lake through the narrows at the east end,

produced walleye fishing that equaled what we had found at Raney, so we established an outpost camp there as well. During the winter months a herd of about 150 moose yarded near the south end of Denyes Lake. Even though they scattered during the summer, there were always several that remained nearby to feed in the outgoing rivers. Both camp sites on Raney and Denyes were prime moose hunting sites, yielding several moose from 1957 until 1970.

The Raney/Denyes Lake area also contained one the largest population of beaver in the Chapleau area. Gilbert Clement's family had trapped in the area since the 1920s, when his father had started his trapline at Ridout Lake. The Clements were very conservative trappers who knew exactly how many beaver they could take from each lodge and still maintain a steady population. There were about thirty beaver lodges near our camps on Raney and Denyes Lakes. The activities around each lodge provided hours of entertainment for the guests. They could watch the beavers traversing and felling the trees along the shore to build their lodges and dams.

Many guests returned to Raney Lake or Denyes Lake year after year. Some returned every year for fourteen years because the area provided hours of wildlife adventures. There were numerous families of muskrats, particularly in the long reeds at the east end of Denyes Lake and the north end of Raney Lake. A large colony of loons nested on both lakes during the summer and were often seen with young ones riding on their backs. A family of osprey nested at the north end of Denyes Lake and another family nested at the narrows between Raney and Denyes.

Every year a group of bald eagles was found nesting in a dead jack pine on the south shore of Denyes. Guests came yearly with their binoculars to observe them. The rivers were full of blue bills and the hiking trails were full of ruffed grouse.

Every year from 1959 on, Leo Vesco, an ardent walleye and northern fisherman from the Detroit area, booked a trip to Raney Lake for six men. Leo always wore one of our name tags that read "I have flown with Theriault Air Service." One year I counted twelve of these badges on his hat. Over the years he witnessed many changes to the camp. On his first few trips, he and his friends used square-stern canoes and small 3-hp motors to travel around the lake. Later they used twelve-foot aluminum boats. When Leo began his trips to Raney Lake, he stayed in the cabin that Axel built. Then he stayed in the new cabin that we had to build after the original was burned down by Harvey Clough and his group.

Harvey was another regular at our Raney Lake camp. He brought up a group from Stoney Creek, Ontario for numerous years. In 1960, on one of these trips, he accidentally put some smoldering cigarette butts in the trash after a late night card game. The men woke up a few hours later to a cabin full of smoke. They escaped unharmed through the windows, but they didn't have time to retrieve any of their belongings.

Their fortune improved later in the morning when I arrived unexpectedly with Pitt Thomas in the Norseman. Their mid-week trip wasn't scheduled until the next day, but I wanted to check out Pitt on the Norseman, so we decided to deliver some gas and supplies a day earlier. As we secured the aircraft, the charred remains of the cabin were still smoking. Harvey's group was huddled together in the sauna bath since it had started to drizzle in the early morning hours.

Pitt and I flew the men back to Chapleau; however, the men wouldn't disembark from the aircraft until they were properly attired. We scrounged enough clothing for one of the men, and he drove to the local department store to purchase six sets of clothing, one for himself and one for each of his buddies. When the men were re-outfitted with gear and food, we flew them to Sylvanite Lake where we had just acquired a second cabin from another outfitter.

Within a month we had the cabin at Raney Lake rebuilt; it didn't have the charm of the original log cabin that Axel built, but it was roomier with more windows. Harvey Clough continued to make his annual fishing trip and probably made about twenty-five trips in all. He and his wife tried fishing in other areas and one year we flew them north to Kesagami Lake, but they always came back to their favourite spot—Raney Lake.

The area was so popular with our guests that we asked the Department of Lands and Forests for a permit to build a lodge to accommodate a few more guests. They denied our application because they wanted to ensure the continuation of the excellent fishing. We acquiesced and discontinued flying day trips into the area from the lodges.

A few years later an individual was allowed to buy a five-acre parcel of land on Denyes Lake for private use. Then someone else was given permission to build a lodge there which accommodated twenty-five people. Once the lodge was operational, we felt obliged to sell our camps. With the increased traffic on the lakes, we couldn't offer our guests wilderness fishing experiences since they were constantly meeting ten other boats on the lake.

NEMEGOSENDA LAKE

When I first arrived in Chapleau, a local business man, Arthur Grout, owned an outpost camp about twenty miles northeast on Nemegosenda Lake. The walleye and northern pike fishing was very good, and the lake trout fishing was excellent in the spring and fall. During my first summer in business I regularly flew guests into his camp from spring until the end of the moose hunt in the fall. The log camp had been built in the 1940s and was very popular with the tourists; however, by 1954 it was quite run down. A few years later Mr. Grout sold his camp and the new owners subsequently updated the camp and the facilities. The camp is now called the Chapleau Outpost and is still in operation, even after several changes of ownership.

Just before the ice melted in the spring of 1956, we built a tent camp at the north end of Nemegosenda Lake on a sandy beach. It was just a short walk to the mouth of the river where the guests could fish from an old dam that had been built by a lumber company in the early 1900s. There was so much food flowing into the river that the fish concentrated in that area. For years that was the favourite fishing spot for all our guests. Most parties caught at least one or two large walleye in the ten-pound range, right at the dam.

Since the lake was often rough, we left our boats along the shore at the mouth of the river where they were protected in a cove. The guests usually motored down the Nemegosenda River, past Alcorn Lake, to fish for the biggest walleye and northerns. Along the way they counted the wildlife. The river was full of game, especially moose, beaver, muskrats and bear from early spring until late fall. Except for a few trappers, and a brief period of lum-

bering at the turn of the century, the area was untouched and very primitive. To this day, it remains much the same, except that there are fewer moose because of the pressure from hunting. The government of Ontario has recently declared the area a waterway park. I think that in the next few years all hunting and trapping will be prohibited as well.

In the spring of 1957 we constructed two small cabins on a four-acre plot of land along the west shore of the lake. The location became one of the most popular with the tourists. The fishing even surpassed our expectations. Our cabins were booked continuously from the middle of May until the end of the moose hunt in October.

During the summer of 1958 we hired a couple of dock boys from Chapleau, Freddie Schroder and Vince Creighton Jr., to help us load the aircraft on our busy days. In the middle of July, I flew them into Nemegosenda Lake for a vacation. When I returned to pick them up, they had their limit of fish to take out. They claimed that they had caught a fish every time they cast at the mouth of the river.

Vince's father, Vince Creighton Sr., was the Chief Conservation Officer in Chapleau at the time. He paid me a visit shortly afterwards to discuss the fish that his son had brought home. When he and his colleagues had examined the scales on the fish, they determined that the two-pound walleye were about fourteen years old, even though a fourteen-year-old walleye should weigh at least four pounds. This suggested that the lake had an overpopulation of walleye.

Vince Sr. recommended that we remove some of the fish and use them to restock other areas. Freddie and Vince Jr.

returned to Nemegosenda with barbless hooks and pond nets to round up a couple of hundred walleye in a pen. A Department of Lands and Forests aircraft transported the fish to other lakes in the area. They continued to remove fish that summer and the following summer. Today there is an excellent population of walleye in Nemegosenda Lake, although it suffered a severe blow in the early 1960s when high waters wiped out their spawning areas.

Nemegosenda Lake camp, 1962

During our first year in business in Chapleau, I met Mr. Ralph Stedman from Flint, Michigan. We had the pleasure of taking care of him and his son Larry for many years. He was such a naturally amicable man that within a year or two our business relationship turned into a long-standing friendship between our families. In the fall of 1956 my five-year-old son, John, and I accompanied Mr. Stedman and his son, Larry, to our little tent camp on the north end of Nemegosenda Lake. I didn't have any boats at the site, so for safety we tied two canoes together—a 17-foot square-stern with a 9-hp motor and a smaller 16-foot canoe, loaded with our gear. We motored down the river to

Alcorn Lake and spent the better part of the day still fishing for walleye.

Once we had our fill of catching walleye in the holes along the shore, we decided to troll down the center of the lake. I was using a red-and-white daredevil in hopes of tempting a northern pike to hit my line. Most northern pike are found in shallow water near weed beds, but the big ones like the deeper water where they feed on smaller fish. Ralph and Larry were using casting reels, whereas I was using an Alcock spinning reel with about 300 yards of 6-pound-test line. It wasn't monofilm line; it was actually made of silk, like the thread used on parachutes.

All of a sudden I felt my line tighten, as if I had hooked onto a huge log. Ralph immediately saw my line go down and told his son Larry, who was running the motor, to turn around because he thought my line was snagged. There was no reverse on motors back then, so Larry turned the boat around and I held the rod up. We motored back up the river a hundred yards. The line was still out another two-hundred feet. At this point, I began to entertain doubts about this snag. Larry pushed the motor a little faster until we were about a hundred feet from where the line was hugging the bottom. Only then did I confirm my suspicions that this had to be a fish. Whatever was on the line took it on a run for another couple of hundred feet.

We had to wait ten minutes to get a glimpse of the fish. As soon as it surfaced, I knew it was a northern. It barely stayed on the surface for a few seconds before it dove to the bottom, pulling at least fifty yards of line. Then it sulked and pulled and held the six pounds of drag. We sat in this suspended state for several minutes. I knew that if I expected to land this fish, I had to make the next move.

I asked Larry to paddle the canoes so

that I could put side drag on the line. The northern made a dash, and we followed, running the motor slowly enough to keep the pressure on. After a few minutes of this chasing game, the fish stopped, turned ninety degrees and took off a little faster. By now we were in the middle of Alcorn Lake, at a depth of thirty feet with the fish still close to the bottom. The pressure was so intense that I could only imagine that I had foul hooked a fifteen-pound northern by the side or the tail.

It seemed like we had been trailing this fish for an hour, but when I looked at my watch, it had only been about twenty minutes. My hands were sore and tired, but I wasn't about to give up until I had gotten a good look at my opponent. Finally, the fish eased up and I could reel in some of the line. This time I got it within thirty feet of the boat. From our vantage point, we could see a huge northern. It looked like it was about five feet long. I knew my line couldn't handle much more pressure and I figured that if this fish decided to take another dive for the bottom, it was going to take all my line with it. I began to feel satisfied just to have seen this monster.

Just about the time I was giving up all hopes of landing it, the line slackened. I quickly used the opportunity to reel in. My last ditch effort to get the fish close enough to the boat paid off. Fortunately, the fish seemed to have given up all its will power. By the time I got it within a foot of the boat, there was no fight left in this brute. Larry leaned over the boat and got his hands on the gills. With a little help from Ralph, he managed to hoist the fish into the small canoe.

My young son took one very nervous look at the fish and said, "Is that an alligator, Mr. Stedman?" His fear of the fish soon subsided and curiosity took over. He climbed over to the other canoe, examined it and decided it was the biggest fish or alligator he had ever seen. It was a huge one! The fish turned out to be a 35-pound northern—the biggest one I ever caught. We had the fish officially weighed and measured and the Stedmans took it home to have it mounted.

I continue to use a red-and-white daredevil to lure northerns to my line, but so far, I haven't had a strike that is bigger than the one I landed at Alcorn Lake. In 1958 I saw another northern caught at the Seal River that weighed 35 pounds. A couple of other big northerns in the 20- to 25-pound range came out of Alcorn Lake during the first few years we were in business. Later Brunswick Lake also produced a few in that category.

Nowadays huge northerns are quite rare in northern Ontario. There are several lakes, like Rice Lake, where it is common to catch 10- to 15-pound northern pike. It takes between fifteen and twenty-five years for a northern to grow to 35 pounds in the cold waters of northern Canada. Very few ever reach that weight because there are so many fishermen who are willing to keep them at ten pounds. Today the really big ones are confined to the areas north of the Albany River that are not accessible by road.

1955: FIRES AND TROUT

When the spring of 1955 arrived, we were prepared for a tremendous fishing season. We had established outpost camps on Zola/Kinniwabi, South Greenhill and Missinaibi Lakes. I had also applied for three more Land Use Permits on Raney, Denyes and Nemegosenda. Once I had six spots where I could fly fishermen, I began to buy new boats and equipment for the outposts. The lodge operators were pleased to have someone supply boats in these lakes for their day trips. During my first few years of business, their guests continued to be my main source of income.

Spring arrived exceptionally early in 1955. Since there hadn't been much snow during the winter, the ice melted from the Chapleau River in the middle of April. I had left several crews in the bush cutting the right-of-way for the highway between Chapleau and Wawa because they had permits to burn until the beginning of May. From the time the ice melted until May 5th, I flew out the entire crew of sixty men. Then I started to fly supplies to Raney Lake to build a tent camp. While Axel Romanon was building the tent camp at Raney Lake, I flew in another crew to quickly assemble two tent bases at Kinniwabi/Zola Lake. By the second week of May we were ready for the first guests that arrived.

It was so warm in early May that you could see heat waves over the Chapleau River. It hadn't rained yet and the snow had melted early; the fire hazard was exceptionally high. In the middle of May, the water in the lakes had dipped to the normal level for the beginning of August. On May 19th, I was on my way to Kinniwabi Lake, crossing at the south end of Como Lake, when I noticed smoke in Admiral Township. Even though I had two passengers on board, I turned around and returned to Chapleau to report the fire. When I advised the Chief Forest Ranger, Ernie Morin, about the fire, he immediately tried to contact his Beaver aircraft, but the pilot was doing a "fish survey" in Bisco.

While others at the Department of Lands and Forests continued to radio the pilot of the Beaver, I took Ernie up to assess the fire. By the time we arrived, about a hundred acres was on fire, and the lookout tower on Sharp Hoof Lake was directly in the fire's path. When we returned to Chapleau, the Beaver had arrived back at the base and the pilot was ready for his directions.

The pilot, Lou Poulin, loaded the Beaver with a fire crew, dropped them at one end of Sharp Hoof Lake, and taxied to the north end to pick up the family that had already walked down from the tower. By then the fire was all around them and Lou did a tremendous job of flying those people out. Half an hour later the tower burned to the ground.

Six hours later, the fire that began in Admiral Township had travelled twelve miles and was about a mile wide. It was completely out of control. All travel was immediately halted. I flew into Kinniwabi Lake and transported the guests back to Chapleau. Axel Romanon, the carpenter, was the only one in Raney Lake at the time. He decided to remain since he was on an island.

Even though I had tent camps ready for fishermen, I didn't fly a single tourist into the bush until September 17th, when the fires were under control. Every available aircraft was put to use fighting the fires. The Admiral Township fire burnt thousands of acres. And there were many more fires that year. At one point, there were so many fires burning that the smoke could be seen as far as Chicago.

At the turn of the century, the Ontario government had a policy of handing out huge timber limits to companies such as Abitibi. The companies had so much land that they didn't have the resources to cut it all. The ideal method of forestry, like gardening, is to cut the forest while it is in its prime because when a forest becomes over mature, it is like dynamite.

In 1955 the forests burned incredibly quickly because they were full of over mature trees and dry underbrush. The forests might have been cut sooner if the government had granted parcels of land to smaller jobbers. As it happened, the government spent an enormous amount of money; first to fight the fires, and then to hire logging companies to haul out the burnt timber once the fires were extinguished. It wasn't until 1957, two years later, that the land was cleared and replanted.

While I was based at a Department of Lands and Forests camp on Dunrankin Lake for one month, I flew from Alsace to Dunrankin at least ten to fifteen times per day to resupply the fire crews. I was full of smoke, and the aircraft had so much soot on it, the crews had to wash it down every couple of days. The water in the lakes was the temperature of a warm bath all summer long. As part of their daily ritual, the fire fighters would jump into the lake with their clothes on. They took off their clothes, washed them in the lake, then hung up them up, and within an hour they were dry.

Usually the mosquitoes and black flies can drive a sane person around the bend during the spring and early summer in northern Ontario, but we didn't have a problem with them that season. They died off quickly with the heat and lack of humidity.

Fires were burning in every direction around us, but we felt somewhat safe at the camp on Dunrankin because the area was one of the first to burn when the fires started. Even though all the trees on Dunrankin had burned, an insect, which we called a buzzer, would come out at night and burrow into the charred wood. There were so many of them buzzing that it sounded like a thousand chain saws going all night long. When daybreak dawned, the buzzing stopped and we didn't hear it again until sunset.

On a rare day, when it rained and we had some reprieve, we could rest and think about something other than fire. Dunrankin Lake was full of speckled trout, and Dunrankin Creek, which was a forty-five minute walk from the lake, also had tremendous trout fishing. Bob Landgeran and Lucien Morin, who both worked for the Forestry Department in Foleyet, had fished the Dunrankin Creek on several occasions in previous years. On a few evenings, when the firefighters had everything under control and there was no flying, we walked down the trail.

No tourists fished that summer because the bush was closed to the public, but that didn't stop the Forest Rangers. The speckled trout fishing was so incredible that the three of us returned with enough fresh trout to feed our entire camp of thirty men. That was about the only fish I tasted all summer long. The following year, I returned to Dunrankin Lake and stashed a canoe along the shore so we could fly in fishermen on day trips. The lake continued to be a great spot for speckled trout—until a lumber road made it accessible in 1962.

THE PERILS OF WINTER FLYING

Winter flying with wheel/skis is a far more delicate operation than summer flying with floats. The severe and unpredictable weather conditions can make survival a challenge to the most seasoned bush pilot. The only way to fly safely in northern Ontario winters is to be prepared for all possibilities in the air and on the ground. Spending the night in the bush, when the temperature drops to -40°F, is not something I look forward to, especially if I am unprepared for the event.

When I first established the air service in Chapleau, there was a demand for winter flying because of the extensive mining activity and highway construction in the area. In the fall of 1955 I made an agreement with a local businessman, Arthur Grout, and his partner, to fly their crews into the bush throughout the winter. The crews were cutting the right-of-way for the road to Wawa. They couldn't begin cutting until the middle of October because the government had been late awarding the contract. By then the weather was turning cold and the lakes were freezing.

When it started to freeze, ice accumulated on the floats. The crews had to help me break the ice off between flights. To save time, the owner of a garage in Chapleau lent me a steam jenny which produced enough steam to thaw the floats in a few minutes. I managed to fly about sixty men into the bush before we were forced to stop until the ice had frozen solid on the lakes. At the end of December, I resumed flying with wheel/skis and transported 120 men into the bush in teams of six to eight.

As the weather turned colder in January and February, I was busy flying the crews in and out of the bush. They could only work a week or two at a time. In early January, twelve inches of blue ice covered the lakes, with a half a foot of snow on top. When a snowstorm dumped an additional two feet of snow, the ice cracked under the heavy load. Then the water seeped up and flooded parts of the ice producing slush.

It's very difficult to determine if there is slush on a lake until you actually begin landing the aircraft. By maintaining the air speed at 30 mph and letting the plane down gradually, you can test the solidity of the ice before you come to a stop. If the aircraft starts swinging from side to side or one ski drops before the other, there is water underneath the snow, and a new landing site must be located.

The area around Chapleau, in the boreal forest, is particularly prone to slush in the winter. Further north, around Moosonee, the problem is not landing in slush but landing on lakes which are covered with three-foot snow waves.

When slush conditions on the lakes made landing the aircraft precarious, the work crews had to tramp the lake with their snowshoes to pack the snow and prepare a runway. This was time away from cutting and burning—an expensive procedure for the contractors. In fact, the expenses ran so high that they were $250,000 over budget when the right-of-way was finally cut. Obviously Mr. Grout and his partner had not anticipated the inclement winter weather conditions and the roughness of the terrain when they had submitted their bid to the government.

One afternoon in February 1956, I flew a supervisor to one of the camps to deliver supplies and to check on the progress of the crew. The men had prepared a runway for our arrival, but when I turned the aircraft around and moved off the runway a few yards, the slush consumed us. From that moment on, it was a race against time to raise the Stinson before the watery mush hardened and trapped it.

The men cut long poles with their chain saws while I retrieved two hydraulic jacks that I routinely carried in the aircraft for emergencies. It took all our manpower and ingenuity to lift the plane onto the poles, and then onto the packed ice. The seven cutters and I laboured until late in the evening to raise the aircraft. If the crew hadn't been there to help with the operation, I would have spent many days in the bush and may not have been able to save the aircraft.

My night in the bush with the cutting crew was relatively enjoyable because they had a good tent camp with heaters and comfortable cots. Unfortunately, I've also had to endure less comfortable nights in the bush. On another occasion, I spent three nights in late March at our tent camp on South Greenhill Lake with Jim Cachege and Bill Terrien. We planned to spend the afternoon setting up the tent camp. When the top layer of ice gave way near the shore, the aircraft sank half a foot to the second layer of ice—leaving us immobilized. Even though we made a runway with our snowshoes, it didn't freeze for three days. By then our emergency food supply was very low.

March is one of the most unpredictable times for winter flying. The snowstorms appear out of nowhere and surround the aircraft in all directions. It is relatively easy to fly in a snowstorm in January or February because the fine, dry snow allows about two miles of visibility. However, in March the heavy wet snow cuts the visibility to about a hundred yards. There is nowhere to go but down. I've spent a few nights in trappers' cabins while a March snowstorm dumped about nine inches of snow.

Snowstorms, slush and thin ice are just a few of the hazards of winter flying. With experience, you begin to sense when a situation can develop into a problem. When a trapper, Larry Bean, arrived at my office requesting a charter flight to the Dominion Gulf camp on Nemegosenda Lake, I sensed a bad situation. I was concerned that the lake had not yet frozen sufficiently to safely land the Cessna. Larry assured me that the ice was six inches thick at the east end where the camp was located. He had just walked out of the camp and was anxious to return with food and Christmas gifts for his wife and children. Despite my misgivings, I sent our pilot, Hugh Kutner, on the flight.

When Hugh landed near the camp, the ice near the shore cracked and the aircraft sank to the wings. Fortunately they were able to push open the doors to escape from the water-filled plane. The children threw them some boards and some rope, and they scrambled onto the ice and then into a warm cabin to thaw out. All the supplies that were still inside the aircraft stayed under water for days.

We maintained radio contact with this camp because Dominion Gulf had entrusted us with the property while the mine was inactive over the winter. The trapper and his family lived in one of the cabins and acted as caretakers to prevent unwanted visitors from snooping around the core shacks and pilfering the samples.

Hugh radioed me at the airbase with news of the mishap. I flew into Nemegosenda Lake the next day with a light aircraft, a Cessna 120, that belonged to one of the lumber companies. Since all the supplies were still underwater, we needed to fly in more food for the family. The canned goods were fine once we were able to get them out of the water, but everything else was ruined.

There wasn't much we could do about the aircraft because the ice surrounding it was too thin to erect a tripod to lift it out. Eventually, after the new year, the ice thickened to about ten inches. Art Thibault and Marcel Paquette accompanied me back to the site, and we cut the ice around the aircraft with a chain saw and hoisted it up. After two weeks in the ice, the wings were frozen and there was no way we could thaw them out quickly. I tried unsuccessfully for three days to thaw them with a Herman Nelson heater. The weather was so cold that I could only thaw out one part at a time.

I wasn't able to completely thaw the wings until the weather warmed up in early April. Then I had to remove all the instruments, and the engine had to undergo a complete overhaul before it was air worthy again. It was a rather expensive and time-consuming process to rescue the airplane. But, I learned to trust my intuition and refuse to fly when I had doubts about the conditions.

Cessna 180 that went through the ice on Nemegosenda Lake in December 1961

WHITEFISH AT SYLVANITE LAKE

The tremendous walleye and northern fishing on Raney Lake led us to discover similar fishing opportunities on other lakes in the area. We established outpost camps on Denyes Lake and Sylvanite Lake. Both had excellent fishing and plenty of game. Raney and Denyes were large lakes with many miles of shoreline. Sylvanite Lake was a smaller body of water which offered more protection from the winds. We constructed the floor for a cabin at Sylvanite Lake in the fall of 1957. Then in January 1958 Jim Cachege and I hauled the rest of the building materials to the site, and Jim spent a month building a 16 by 14-foot cabin.

The fishing at Sylvanite Lake was steady for several years, then I noticed that the walleye population was declining abnormally. Since we had been careful not to over-fish the lake, I knew there had to be some other factor that was adversely affecting the fishing. Something must have been eating the walleye spawn before it had the opportunity to hatch.

I discussed the situation with a naturalist at the Department of Lands and Forests. We both agreed that the proportion of coarse fish and game fish in the lake was out of balance. Lakes in northern Ontario usually have a mixture of game fish, like walleye and northern pike, and coarse fish, like suckers and whitefish. When the coarse fish overpopulate a lake, the game fishing deteriorates steadily. Eventually it is difficult to find a single walleye. The only way to correct the balance is to remove some of the coarse fish, so we started netting the whitefish in the fall when they were running up the river to spawn.

Since the whitefish usually only spawn for two weeks at the end of October, the timing has to be perfect. Once we knew they were beginning their run, we flew in for a couple of days of fishing. But it wasn't exactly fishing in the way we usually think of fishing. Unlike game fish, whitefish don't respond very well to bait fishing. When you do manage to catch one, any jerk in the line is enough to rip the hook out of its soft mouth. If you are an expert fly fisherman who likes to fish in the very early hours just before daylight or in the late evening during a mayfly hatch, you might catch a few. However, they are usually caught with nets. Commercial fisherman on the bigger lakes in the Northwest Territories use gill nets. We could only legally use dip nets.

As soon as it got dark, the whitefish started their run and we took our flashlights down to the river. We waited for them just off shore or in a boat. All we had to do was dip the net into the water and haul them out. It wasn't uncommon to take fifty to one hundred fish in an evening. Since my family could only eat about twenty whitefish over a winter, we invited many of our friends to come and fish with us.

Whitefish are recognized worldwide as one of the finest tasting freshwater fishes. At the time, during the mid-1960s, Canada was the leading commercial exporter of whitefish. Because the soft flesh spoils very quickly, whitefish are often smoked before they are shipped. When we caught them in the late fall, it was cold enough in the bush to keep them frozen until we stored them in the freezer. Some of our more enterprising friends smoked them in their homemade smokers.

Not too many fishermen who are accustomed to the thrill of catching game fish relish the less challenging chore of scooping fish up with a dip net. Yet Walt Stevens, from Xenia, Ohio, came up to Chapleau in late October for several years just to enjoy a few days of whitefish fishing. He loved eating whitefish, and he loved spending a few days on Sylvanite Lake with our gang of friends.

Because the whitefish run only at night, we had the whole day to socialize and hunt the ruffed grouse that abounded in the area. Aside from the usual social activities of eating and drinking, we tried out our new card tricks or jokes and played some music to wile away the daylight hours. By the end of October, I was usually quite exhausted from a long season of flying fishermen and hunters. The moose hunters had left, and the chore of closing all the camps had finally come to an end. Now was my time to just relax and enjoy life, without a full schedule.

We didn't have a lot of cash when we started the air service. We were buying airplanes, boats and motors, and building outpost camps. Fortunately, I became friends with some people in Chapleau who were exceptionally kind to us. Gilbert and Conrad Tremblay helped us on their days off from the CPR. They loaded and unloaded the aircraft, refueled them and pumped the floats. They also enjoyed the opportunity to fly into the bush with me for a little fishing or hunting. Fishing for the whitefish at Sylvanite Lake was one of their favourite ways to relax before the winter freeze.

When Bill Terrien retired as a conductor on the CPR, he was another regular at our airbase. He came with us to Sylvanite Lake for the annual whitefish holiday. One year he had it in his mind to shoot a moose. He had shot deer in his younger years in southern Ontario, but at sixty-eight years of age, he had never shot a moose.

Once we finished our chores in the late afternoon, Bill asked me where I thought he would find his moose. I knew there were plenty of moose around because the previous moose hunters at Sylvanite Lake had seen about seven of them in the area. I told Bill to head east in the boat. Past the point and around the corner in a bay, he would see a moose. Jigs Tremblay knew I was giving Bill a line but he went along with it just to see if Bill was really taken in by my apparent ability to predetermine where a moose would be.

The two of them set out in the boat; Bill was in front and Jigs was running the motor. Just as they rounded the point, to their surprise, they saw a young bull standing at the bottom end of the bay. They got close enough for three shots, but all three missed the moose. The water was quite choppy and Bill didn't have much practice shooting from a boat, especially on a windy day. I was quite surprised myself to hear the three shots.

The hunters returned to the cabin without their moose, but they were full of excitement about getting three shots at one. We stayed up quite late that night netting the whitefish and talking about the moose they almost shot. Late the next morning Bill asked me again where I thought he would find a moose. Again I told him to go past the point and he would find a moose in the bay.

Jigs laughed because he was certain that their three shots had scared away all the moose in that part of the lake. But Bill was a trusting soul, and he managed to convince Jigs to run the boat for him. When they passed the point, they saw the same moose—not ten feet from the spot where they had seen it the previous evening! This time they managed to get close enough and Bill knocked it down with two shots.

I must admit that this time I was really surprised to hear the gunshots. Bill was so thrilled by the experience that he couldn't contain himself. He was still shaking when he arrived back at the camp. He could only watch as Jigs and I cleaned his moose. For years Bill talked about shooting that moose. Everyone in the town of Chapleau who knew him must have heard the story at least twice.

One day in July, I made a check trip into the second cabin at Sylvanite Lake. The four guests were happy with the fishing but distressed by the number of mice in the cabin. They had set the traps we had given them and were catching about a half-dozen mice each day. However, they were still bothered by more of them each night. I only knew one other way to get rid of so many mice—I flew our family cat into the camp.

Within a few weeks, the camp was clean of all the mice inside and outside of the cabin, as well as all the other small mammals, such as the squirrels and chipmunks. Cats have this nasty habit of going after anything that moves.

After the last of the fishermen left in the middle of September, I returned to the camp to prepare it for the moose hunters. I expected to pick up the cat at the same time, but there was no cat to be seen. The weather was beautiful and the cat had no reason to come near the camp. I didn't worry because I knew I would return again soon with the moose hunters. My only problem was dealing with the constant questions of my children who were wondering what had happened to our family pet.

As the moose hunt progressed, I asked all the hunters at Sylvanite Lake if they had seen a cat. One group admitted to having seen it but said that it wouldn't come near the cabin. They had tried to entice it with some food but it wasn't interested in what they had to offer. My final hope was that we would find it

while we were catching the whitefish in the fall.

At the end of October, I flew Raymond Burnett and some other friends from Chapleau into the camp to catch whitefish. I neglected to tell them about the cat. Late one night, as they were playing cards after their fishing expedition, they heard an animal noise outside. One of the guys was sure it was a bobcat. A couple of others were sure it was a house cat. When they went outside with their flashlights they couldn't confirm their suspicions.

The next morning, while they were cleaning their whitefish at the foot of the rapids, they heard the characteristic meow again and there was our pussycat on the other side of the creek. One of the men rowed over and the cat jumped into the boat. After several months in the bush, the cat was very thin and quite skittish, but it readjusted to life in our house and soon looked healthy again. We kept the cat until our family moved to Montreal in 1966. Then it became the chief mouser in the Martel Lumber Company kitchen.

The morning after a night of catching whitefish

SECRETS AND MINING COMPANIES

One sunny afternoon in the summer of 1954, I was sitting on the dock at my airbase in Chapleau chatting with a friend, Art Thibault. A stranger approached us and introduced himself as Mr. Parsons. He had just walked out of the Lackner Hill area because the aircraft he had chartered to fly him and his crew of five men out of the bush never showed up.

I agreed to transport the rest of his crew out of Ten Mile Lake, even though the lake is only about a half-mile long. There was just enough room to fly out one passenger and a couple of hundred pounds of gear. When I finished transporting all his crew, he presented me with a purchase order made out to the Dominion Gulf Corporation. That afternoon was the beginning of a long association with "Red" Parsons and Dominion Gulf. Several other mining companies chartered our air service because of the service I had provided to Dominion Gulf.

Red and his crew travelled to their offices in Kirkland Lake by train. He returned to Chapleau a week later with another mining engineer and crew of six men. They chartered the Stinson to transport them back into Ten Mile Lake where they set up a camp at a trapper's cabin on the north end. Some of the crew hiked into a small lake north of Lackner Hill and set up a tent camp to be closer to the staking activity.

Once they had completed an electromagnetic survey at the base of the north end of Lackner Hill, Red chartered the Stinson to fly him to another outcrop near Lougheed Lake, about fifty miles north of the Lackner Hill area. These two outcrops, which are about four hundred feet high, are the only hills in the Chapleau area—the obvious places to do geological surveys.

Red set up an airborne centilometer in the back of the Stinson, and we headed towards the second outcrop, flying at 1000 feet. As we flew over the east side of Nemegosenda Lake, the machine signaled the presence of something below. We circled the lake several times while Red tried to make sense of the reading from the machine. Instead of continuing on to the second outcrop, we returned to Chapleau and took on more fuel. Again we returned to Nemegosenda Lake, took more readings, then flew on to his camp at Ten Mile Lake.

The following morning we flew along the east shore of Nemegosenda from north to south with two centilometers. Both machines rattled off the same signals. Red returned to Chapleau with me and made a few phone calls to his office. I knew Red was on to something big. We didn't discuss the nature of his findings and I was just as happy to remain somewhat ignorant.

Within a week, another geologist, an executive of the Dominion Gulf Corporation, arrived in Chapleau and Red brought him by my office. Once we started talking, I began to sense the purpose of the conversation. They were trying to determine if I had any prospecting interests which would compromise their operations in the Nemegosenda area. I assured them that my interests were strictly in the air service. Their mining activities would be kept confidential. They both seemed relieved by my disclosure and indicated that they would return with more business.

A few days later I flew Red and four licensed stakers—the men who set the corner posts for the mining claims—into the east side of Nemegosenda Lake. There they staked about seventy claims. Red was not satisfied that they had staked enough claims to cover the anomaly. He planned to return in January with another group of stakers to finish the area. However, he was concerned that in the interim, someone else would sneak in and stake a few claims in the middle of theirs. I again assured him that we would maintain strict confidentiality about their business in the area.

Red and a crew of sixteen stakers arrived in Chapleau in January. I flew them into Nemegosenda Lake where they staked over two hundred claims. Dominion Gulf had never maintained such secrecy in all the years that it had staked in the Timmins/Kirkland Lake area. Somehow the news of their interests always leaked out and other prospectors rushed in to grab claims.

Once they were finished staking as much of the area as they wanted at Nemegosenda Lake, they made their intentions public. A few local prospectors did arrive to stake claims on either side. Even though the Dominion Gulf crew was looking for uranium, they had found columbium at Nemegosenda Lake. Columbium is a very rare earth used in alloying steel to control the temperature in jet tail pipes.

Once the stakers had delineated the area, construction workers arrived to build accommodations for the drill crews. Dominion Gulf contracted the drilling to Heath and Sherwood of Kirkland Lake. They maintained about twenty men at the site year round.

Over the next three years, we flew about two hundred tons of ore to Chapleau where it was transported by train to Denver, Colorado for processing. Unfortunately, the site at Nemegosenda Lake never went into full production because a richer deposit was found near Oka, Quebec. By 1964 the mine at Nemegosenda was abandoned. Since then the silvery metallic element called columbium has been renamed niobium. It is now used in superconductivity research as well

as steel alloys and arc welding. It is entirely possible that at some time in the future the demand for it will escalate, and the Dominion Gulf claims at Nemegosenda will become a financially viable asset.

Once we had established a reputation as a reliable air service with discretion, we had several firms charter our aircraft for surveying and staking. One winter a couple of mining engineers chartered our Beaver aircraft, but they wouldn't give me their destination until we were in the air. They installed their equipment in the aircraft and then attached a long trailing antenna out the back. I filled the belly tanks and the two wing tanks with enough fuel to keep us flying for about five hours.

They asked me to fly over the Dominion Gulf site at Nemegosenda Lake. They took a few readings on their instruments, and then they requested that I fly over to the Timmins area. As we approached Timmins, they directed me to an area north of the Timmins airport. We remained airborne over a designated area for a couple of hours before returning to Chapleau.

Every Sunday that winter and the following winter, I flew similar charters for these same engineers. They told me that they had heard from Red Parsons that I could be trusted to keep the nature of my flights confidential. I had no idea what they were looking for, or what they had found. Some time later, I read in the newspaper that this area became known as the Kidd Creek Mine.

The mining charters were an important part of our flying service because they provided us with the financial basis to build our outpost camps. Recently I met an old friend, Dr. Joubin, who found the largest uranium deposit in the world in the Elliot Lake area. He still remembers how our ability to maintain secrecy allowed him to stake without interference.

FLYING TRAPPERS

Most people are happy to spend a day or a week in the bush and then return to their comfortable home in the city. They would never consider spending a cold winter in the bush without the convenience of stores or neighbours. In actuality, very few people could survive isolated from civilization, yet most of the trappers I have known function best in that situation.

When I worked on the docks at the seaplane base in South Porcupine, I had many opportunities to meet the trappers who chartered aircraft to fly their supplies into their camps. I soon developed a deep respect for them because they had cultured a relationship with nature which went beyond the norm.

In the fall of 1954 I began flying a few trappers from Chapleau into their trap lines. As the years passed, I routinely flew them into the bush in October, flew them out for Christmas, returned them to their camps in early January, and then flew them out with their furs in the spring. For those who remained in the bush all winter long without a break, I flew in more supplies in January. During the summer, when the trapping season was over, many of them worked as guides for me or other outfitters.

The first time I flew Emile Bouchard to his trapping grounds on Round Lake, which is part of the Shakashi River, we saw seven moose feeding in the river as I landed the Stinson. When we began to offer moose hunting package trips in 1955, we used this location as one of our prime hunting outposts and Emile became one of my guides. He worked with me for about fifteen years as caretaker at our Brunswick Lake camp and our northern camps on the Belchers and Long Island.

Another trapper, Jim Cachege, who had a camp about fifteen miles east of Chapleau on Cachege Lake, worked for our air service in the summer months as a carpenter, building my new outpost camps. I flew him into his camp for the trapping season. Then he came to work for me in the summer. We operated together this way for ten years or more. I liked to hire trappers as guides because they were all excellent woodsmen who knew where to find the fish and game.

During the war years no one trapped. After the war there was a lot of outside work, so trapping wasn't a serious business again until the 1950s. Fortunately by then the Ontario government was better organized to handle trapping licenses. When we started flying trappers into the bush in 1954, there was such an abundance of game—beaver, muskrats, and marten—that it was not uncommon for trappers to bring out their full quota of pelts after a season on the trapline.

Trapping was often a family affair; I flew Doc Potts and his family into their camp on Siwash Lake, John Bain and his family into Swayze Lake, and Gilbert Clement and his family into Ridout Lake. Many of the trappers were a mixture of native American Indian and French Canadian. Cree and Ojibwa were the predominant native tribes in the Chapleau area. There were some Algonquin who came from the North Bay area to trap.

The Clement family had been trapping in the Chapleau/Bisco area for several generations when I met Gilbert Clement's father at Brett Lake in 1937. After I set up my outpost camps on Raney and Denyes Lakes, I made an arrangement with Gilbert to use his trapper's camp on Ridout Lake in the summer and fall while he used my cabin on Denyes Lake in the

*My son John with a winter moose hunter at the Clement's
trap line in 1963*

winter. My cabin was in the middle of his trapping grounds.

My son, John, spent two weeks with the Clement family one winter when he was about twelve years old. He had the time of his life learning to snare rabbits and prepare the hides for tanning. Today Gilbert's son, Peter, still traps in the Raney River area and operates a lodge on Ivanhoe River North.

The area around Chapleau was so rich with game in 1964 that the Department of Lands and Forests arranged for two native families from Moosonee to trap the area twenty miles south of Biscotasing on Marionette Lake. The families arrived in Chapleau by rail, purchased their supplies at the local grocery store, and then we flew them into the chosen location.

One of the mothers had a seven-month-old baby with her and the other mother had three small boys. When the local trappers flew into their camps, they had a well-built cabin to protect them from the elements. These native people flew into Marionette Lake in December with just a couple of canvas tents and the knowledge of how to survive off the land.

Our Chapleau airbase was located on the river near the public school. During one morning recess, some of the children at the school observed the native family as we loaded them into the aircraft. Their curiousity was piqued when they saw such small children preparing for a trip into the bush in the middle of the winter. They tried to imagine what life would be like without all the conveniences and decided that they would like to send the native family some Christmas presents. They collected fifty dollars to buy some supplies and gifts for the children. We offered the use of our Cessna 180 to fly their purchases to the two native families.

The pilot, Dave McConnell, and his wife, Jackie, who was a teacher at the public school, flew the Christmas goodies into Marionette Lake on December 23rd. When they arrived in the camp, the men were out on their trap lines. The women and children disappeared into their tent as soon as they began unloading the aircraft. They carried the gifts up to the tent and with some hesitation, the two mothers, who didn't speak English, accepted them. The two men arrived in the camp shortly afterwards. Since one of them spoke

English, Dave and Jackie explained the nature of the gifts to them.

Both families appeared to live in one long tent, about twelve feet by twenty-five feet, which was erected in a sheltered area on a point. An additional windbreak of evergreen boughs protected the tent from the harsh north wind. The floor was lined with more evergreen boughs and a pole held down the tent flap at one end. One small airtight heater kept the tent warm enough for the families, but the women cooked outdoors on a camp fire. The men had constructed another small shelter of trees and foliage to store the furs that they had collected. To those of us who were accustomed to central heating and the conveniences of indoor plumbing, their life seemed harsh. To them, it was their way of life and they seemed to flourish in it.

Austin Airways had been freighting native families into the interior of northern Quebec and northern Ontario to trap since 1945. They flew a family of four along with their winter supplies, a canoe, a sleigh and their dogs, from Great Whale River, Fort George or Paint Hills, into one of the inland rivers in September. The following spring the family canoed back to the village with their furs. From 1966 until 1972, we continued this inland freighting from Fort George with a Beech 18 on floats in the fall and made a service trip with a Beaver on skis to each family in January.

Since the 1960s, trappers have faced two major changes: first the snowmobile arrived to make their life easier, then the decline in the demand for fur sent many of them looking for new careers. Our business declined with the local trappers as soon as they could afford to buy a snowmobile. The federal government now pays many of the native people along the coast of James and Hudson Bay to forgo trapping because of the limited demand for furs. The flamboyant activities of animal rights groups has been the largest cause of the decline in trapping.

Wherever I travel now, I see such an abundance of beaver in the lakes and ponds that I worry about their overpopulation; it has become common to see four beaver lodges on a pond instead of one or two families. When a species overpopulates, inbreeding is a very serious concern for the future evolution of that species. Even before the Europeans settled on this continent, the beaver population was controlled by the native people who hunted them for food and clothing. I think we have yet to learn that when we discipline ourselves to use nature's resources intelligently, with strict controls and quotas, we are rewarded with a bountiful harvest every year.

Native family trapping on Marionette Lake in December 1964

HURRICANE & MOOSEHUNTING MISADVENTURES

No one forecasted that Hurricane Hazel would pass through northern Ontario with such tremendous winds in September 1955. I was certainly not prepared for it when it arrived. The morning the hurricane hit, I was on a flight to Camp 88 on Esnagi Lake. Suddenly the air sheer became so unstable over Como Lake that I couldn't keep the aircraft horizontal. With some good luck, I managed to turn around and the Stinson made it back to Chapleau.

Earlier that fall I had secured a contract to fly charters for a firm that was building the railroad from Hemlo to Manitowadge. I bought a Fleet Canuck aircraft from Pineland Timber and hired another pilot. When the pilot realized the ferocity of the sheer as he took off from Hemlo, he tried to turn around but the airplane got sucked into some telegraph wires and flipped over. Fortunately the pilot was not seriously injured, however, the Fleet Canuck had to be sold as salvage.

So far 1955 had been a most memorable season—first there were the fires that played havoc with the fishing season—then the hurricane arrived to give us another setback. After flying steadily on the fires for about four months, the government owed me approximately $14,000, but with the bureaucratic procedures in the government offices, I wasn't paid right away. In fact, I didn't get paid for six months. With all that happened during the fall of 1955, our cash flow was very limited and our luck didn't improve much after the hurricane.

When the moose hunting season began the first week in October, we were able to fly a few moose hunters into our new outpost camps on Raney Lake and Nemegosenda Lake. We also took two moose hunters and Emile Bouchard from

Dalton into his trapper's cabin on Round Lake. In order to prevent people with aircraft from landing on just any lake and shooting the moose, the Ontario government only permitted air services to fly hunters to recognized, licensed outpost camps. Since Emile had a Land Use Permit for his camp on Round Lake, we could fly hunters there.

It was a perfect season for moose hunting. The moose population in the Chapleau area had expanded to an incredible size because hunting had been closed for a number of years to allow the herds to grow. It was common, and not at all unusual, to count ten to twenty moose on a fifteen-minute flight from the airbase. However, our bad luck continued and the fall moose hunt cost us an additional $500 when we were fined for a moose that was killed at Schewabik Lake.

The lake is situated on the edge of a game preserve. When the moose finally collapsed after it was shot, it had strayed about 250 yards into the preserve. A game warden arrived, saw us in the preserve with the moose, and I was fined for taking a hunter into a restricted area. Nowadays similar situations are quite common, but the authorities are a little more lenient. They realize that if you hunt on the edge of a preserve, sometimes a wounded animal will, of its own accord, make its way into a non-hunting area. Moose aren't expected to abide by the limits of man-made boundaries. We probably could have paid a smaller fine if we hadn't been advised to take the case to court. These are things you learn with experience.

Back in 1955, dealing with the government officials in the Department of Lands and Forests was quite a delicate affair, especially if you happened to be the first French Canadian in the area to hold an air charter. The province was run by a Masonic group that was very protective of their own kind. French Canadians were definitely not their kind.

Today it's a totally different atmosphere. The bureaucrats come from a more varied background, but in 1955 we needed someone to champion our cause. Fortunately my wife, Joan, was the daughter of a Mason. Otherwise our life in Chapleau would have been very uncomfortable.

When my father-in-law, Capt. John Watson of Belleville, Ontario, who was a pre-eminent Mason, heard that our company was not being treated fairly by bureaucrats in the Department of Lands and Forests, he spoke to his Member of Parliament, who was also a Mason. A short time later we were given what we needed to get our outpost camps underway.

Moose running into the game preserve on Schewabik Lake

PLANES, BUGS & MECHANICS

In the spring of 1956, when I finally received the money the Ontario government owed us for fighting the fires the previous summer, I took the train to Toronto and purchased a new Cessna 180 from an old friend of mine, Jack Sanderson. Jack and I began a long friendship when he delivered a Stinson Reliant to the McIntyre Mines while I was working there as an apprentice. After the war, he began his own company, Sanderson Aircraft in Toronto and held a dealership for Cessna aircraft.

The new Cessna 180 (CF-HJJ) could carry 600 pounds, and with an additional 30 mph, it got off the water faster than the Stinson Stationwagon. I kept the Stationwagon for the summer. Then in the fall I traded it in for a Stinson Reliant, that could carry 1000 pounds.

We hired a young pilot, Henry Korpala, from Island Lake, to fly the Cessna. When he arrived at our airbase in June, with his brand new commercial pilot's license, he was wearing a beautiful grey linen suit with white shoes and a straw hat. We were so busy flying on a forest fire that Henry started work the day he arrived. He flew the Cessna for twelve days straight, fighting the fire. By then his suit was black, his blond hair was black, and the airplane was black with soot. Henry gained a tremendous amount of flying experience his first summer, flying about four hundred hours in four months.

When the Cessna was ready for its first 100-hour inspection, Fletcher and I went over the procedures with a representative of Sanderson Aircraft who was in the area selling an aircraft to another carrier. I was sure that the Continental 225-hp engine, called the O470-A, still had a few bugs in it that needed attention. The representative from Sanderson gave us some good advice about cleaning the filters on the hydraulic lifters. These were notorious for accumulating dirt. When we pulled the filters during the inspection, they were so dirty that they collapsed. From then on we changed the oil every fifty hours and pulled the filters every twenty-five hours. When the filters were heavy with dirt, the hydraulic lifters made the engine run roughly, and in a few cases, this had led to engine failure.

We flew the Cessna on floats for five hundred hours in the summer, and then installed a pair of skis on it in November. Fletcher and I had received installation diagrams for the Federal skis, but when we went over the diagrams with an engineer from the Department of Lands and Forests, Hank Warner, we were perplexed by the suggested procedure. The bungee cords were set from the front of the skis directly to the leg at a 45° angle. The rear bungee cord was fastened in the same way.

We modified the design slightly by outfitting the skis with an additional cable that fitted directly up and down vertically from the ski to the airframe. Even though this modification was not approved by the Department of Transport, we all felt that the safety of the aircraft would be jeopardized if we followed the suggested installation procedure. Over the winter, several aircraft encountered problems with the same skis that had been installed according to the suggested procedure. My friend, Leo Lamothe, was flying his Cessna out of Blind River when one of the skis flipped over in the air. He was forced to land with one ski upside down.

The Cessna 180 was a remarkable little aircraft. The first models, however, had a few little glitches that were potentially fatal. One snowy winter day I was returning from a charter flight with a crew that was surveying the right-of-way for the highway from Chapleau to Foleyet. The engine suddenly quit over Mulligan's Bay. Fortunately I still had good height and I was able to land the aircraft in front of the Department of Lands and Forests' airbase.

Hank Warner briefly inspected the aircraft and determined that the vent on top had clogged during the snowstorm. This blockage was preventing air from getting into the tanks. We took the cap off one side of the top of the wing, and I was able to start the engine and taxi the aircraft over to my airbase. Later that day Hank and I drilled very small holes in the tops of the caps and on top of the wings where there was a little bit of a flap that covered part of the tank.

I never had another engine failure while flying the Cessna in a snowstorm. However, a lumber company aircraft had a complete engine failure under similar flying conditions on a survey flight north of Cochrane. When they made a forced landing along a power line, one of the men was severely injured and the aircraft was completely destroyed.

Winter flying makes excessive demands on light aircraft, especially when the temperature falls below 0°F. On one very cold day the passenger door opened during the flight and gave both myself and the passenger a scare. We installed heavier door springs on the two doors to prevent future accidental openings. Whenever I made alterations to the original design, I informed Jack Sanderson so that he could notify the makers of the Cessna. He also included the information in a newsletter which he sent to all his customers. Unfortunately the news about the weak hinges on the doors didn't reach one owner of a Cessna 180. His aircraft crashed in the New York City area that same winter when the doors flew open on a very cold day.

Each aircraft has its own personality. After a while you get to know when it is performing at its best and when it needs a little attention. When I sold the Stinson Stationwagon in the fall of 1956 and purchased a Stinson Reliant from Parsons Airways in Kenora, I quickly realized that this aircraft, which I had flown in 1938 when I was an apprentice with the McIntyre Mines, was not performing up to

Loading the Stinson Reliant CF-BGS on the dock in Chapleau

its potential. The first thing I did was measure the length of the propeller. It measured 8 feet 5 inches; at least an inch shorter than it should have been. And the blades had been worn to a very narrow status. After Hank Warner and I installed a new propeller, the change in performance was amazing. I was airborne in 30 seconds with an 800-pound payload versus 40 seconds with the old propeller.

Hank also suggested that I could enhance the performance by inserting wooden plugs in the flaps to set them at a 30° angle rather than the standard 60° angle for these vacuum-operated flaps. The standard had been set for aircraft flying on wheels, not on water, and this modification suggested by Hank adjusted for this change. The procedure hadn't yet been approved, but the engineers at the Department of Lands and Forests were using this same modification on their aircraft. With the adjustments to the flaps and the new propeller, the Stinson Reliant began to operate almost as efficiently as the new deHavilland Beaver aircraft.

The following spring I acquired a couple of Norseman canoe carriers. They had been in storage in a hangar in North Bay ever since the federal government had sold their fleet of Norsemen aircraft to the Norwegian government. A talented young welder at one of the local garages in Chapleau made some alterations to the canoe carriers to fit the Stinson. This new design allowed the carriers to slide up or down so that we could carry a 12-foot or a 14-foot boat. A few years later the DOT approved this novel type of modification and it became standard in the industry.

Before we built our own maintenance hangar in Chapleau in 1960, I had a nose hangar in front of the office on the river. This allowed us to do inspections and minor repairs during the summer. In the winter months, I had to fly the aircraft to Harry Sturck's operation in Orillia for the 100-hour inspections. When we built our hangar, we hired our own engineers who were licensed to do all of the required inspections and maintenance. Unfortunately, the town of Chapleau didn't offer much for a young engineer, so our staff changed yearly.

Our fortunes changed though in 1964 when we hired Mike Papalinski and he settled in Chapleau with his family for seven years. Mike was by far the best mechanical engineer that had come to Chapleau. We had no trouble finding apprentices who wanted to work with him. Once he left, we again had difficulty finding engineers who were willing to move to such a remote section of northern Ontario. When my son, George Jr., obtained his aircraft mechanics license in 1976, he became our chief engineer. Now, since both John and George Jr. are outfitters, they have all their inspections done by engineers in Sault Ste. Marie.

Mike Papalinski (on the right) with apprentice Gerry Henderson working on a DC-3

TROUT FIT FOR A QUEEN

When people think of eating freshwater fish they immediately think about trout. Trout are such sought-after fish that fishermen have been known to forgo the worst kinds of weather and travelling conditions just to catch a few of them. In 1939 the Queen of England was travelling across Canada by train. The people of Chapleau wanted to give her a special gift that she would always remember. They decided that they would provide her with some fresh fish for her dinner.

The Chapleau area was renowned for its walleye fishing, but the mayor didn't think that this fish was appropriate for royalty. A few of the local fishermen were trout enthusiasts and had located a few streams to catch their favourite fish. The only difficulty was that these streams were not very close to town.

The local authorities concurred that it was worthwhile to send a couple of fishermen on a canoe trip to bring back some trout in time for the Queen's arrival. Basil Collings and Tommy Godfrey set out in their canoes and travelled for a day and a half until they reached the Goose River. They succeeded in catching several speckled trout. They arrived back in Chapleau in time for the mayor to present the fish to the Queen, who was very pleased with the gift. The newspaper reporters who travelled with the Queen had a field day with the story, and several outdoor magazines published articles on how the Goose River had provided royal trout fit for a Queen.

When I arrived in Chapleau in 1954, the Goose River was still one of the prime spots for speckled trout fishing, but very few fishermen were willing to travel a day and a half by canoe to reach the streams. Even the local fishermen were happy to charter an aircraft to fly in for a day of fishing, rather than spend days in their canoes. The lodge operators were also willing to charter flights for their guests to give them the opportunity to fish trout. Once I began establishing my own outpost camps, I applied to the Department of Lands and Forests for a Land Use Permit to build a camp on the Goose River.

In the spring of 1956 Gilbert Tremblay and his brothers built a tent camp at the Goose River on Renee Lake for speckled trout fishing. The trout in these waters ran up to three or four pounds, but they couldn't be taken in large numbers like at Zola Lake. The largest trout that I ever saw come out of the Goose River was six-and-a-half pounds. The location had a lot of fast water flowing into the lake. The outgoing river provided spectacular scenery, with a fast-running stream and good portages to take the guests to the fishing holes.

Quite a number of canoeists flew into the camp at the Goose River. They paddled to Lemoine Lake where we picked them up and returned them to Chapleau. Others just canoed down the river five miles or so, spent the night camping along the river, and then canoed back to the camp at Renee Lake the next day. There is a set of rapids about every mile along the stream and the fish were usually caught just below the rapids. Once a couple of trout were taken at a pool, the rest were spooked, so the fishermen had to canoe to the next set of rapids to continue fishing. Most of the fishermen travelled to three or four sets of rapids in one day of fishing to catch their limit.

If the fishermen wanted to catch northern pike as well as trout, there were a few lakes within a comfortable portage. One small lake was such a popular spot for pike that we stashed a canoe on it. The fishermen only had to walk two hundred yards along a trail that we cut through the bush to get to the lake.

The river system, which extends all the way from Lemoine Lake to Renee Lake to Hellyer Lake, is a thirty-five mile stretch of water with forty-one portages. Canoeists could run some of these portages when the water was high in the spring. The area was full of game, particularly moose, so the fishermen who were photographers had many opportunities to take pictures of moose of all sizes. We also ran a moose hunt in the area in the fall. It never failed to satisfy our expectations.

Many of our guests found that this river system fulfilled all their fishing and outdoor desires, and they returned year after year. Bill Maki, a Finnish lad from Iron Mountain, Michigan brought several groups of guests into the area for eight years.

When Hwy 101 was completed to the Shawmere River, lumber companies moved in to cut timber and built roads deep into the area. In a very short time the fishing was reduced to a trickle, so we abandoned our outpost camp on Renee Lake. Today a good trout fisherman might catch the odd trout there, but it requires a lot of luck and plenty of patience.

Tommy Godfrey and friend with speckled trout

RECORD TROUT AT FOOT LAKE

During the summer of 1956, some local trout fishermen, Tommy Godfrey, Basil Collings, and Tee Chambers, hired me to fly them into a lake for a couple of days of speckled trout fishing. I dropped them off on a little island along with an old, red canoe that belonged to Tommy. The water in the lake was as clear as any stream in the Arctic. I could easily see down about thirty feet.

The following day I dropped in to check on them, and, to my surprise, they had a stringer of trout that could have won all the prizes at a fish derby: every fish was over six pounds and one of them weighed ten pounds! Finding this lake was like hitting a jackpot.

Five years earlier the Ontario Department of Lands and Forests had secretly stocked the lake with speckled trout. Somehow this knowledge leaked out and Tommy got wind of it. The lake was full of fresh water shrimp, so within two years a trout grew to four-and-a-half pounds. It was a prime location for trophy trout. In fact the lake, known as Foot Lake, produced the largest speckled trout by weight for North America in 1956.

Before I got too excited about Foot Lake, I made a trip to the Department of Lands and Forests and inquired about using it as a regular fishing spot. Since they were anxious to keep the knowledge of the lake quiet, they advised me to use the lake sparingly, and to make sure the fishermen didn't bring in minnows as bait. We were allowed to leave a canoe on the island. For the remainder of the summer, I made just three more trips into this little "gold mine" of a trout lake. Every party landed speckles between six and eight pounds. Most only took out one big fish because the limit was ten pounds plus one trophy.

By the spring of 1957 most speckled trout enthusiasts had heard about Foot Lake because of the record trout. I received many inquiries from fishermen looking for the ultimate experience. Bo Randall and his fishing buddies, Al Cameron and Hank Beehler, made a trip into the lake and caught several in the seven and eight-pound range. But they didn't find the trophy they were looking for. Several other groups caught a few fish that were suitable for mounting. We were very selective and flew in just a few "lucky" parties each year to Foot Lake. The Department of Lands and Forests continued to monitor the growth of the trout in the lake as part of their ongoing research. We were careful not to over-fish it and deplete the stock before they had collected all their data.

Eventually the experiment was forced to end when the Ontario government opened the trout season during the winter months. At the time the snowmobile companies had powerful lobbies working in the Ontario and Quebec governments. Together with the help of some fish and game clubs, they were able to persuade the governments of both provinces to open the season after the trout had spawned. Up until 1960, the trout season was only open from May 1st until September 15th. Once fishermen with snowmobiles could travel into the trout streams and lakes, it wasn't long before the trout population suffered a quick demise.

When the lake trout season was closed all winter in the Sudbury area, the fish population remained fairly constant for decades. Within four years of winter fishing, it was difficult to find a single trout. Then the snowmobile fishermen advanced further north to the Chapleau area and the decline of the trout population continued. Most outfitters were totally unprepared for the winter traffic in their areas and had no way to protect their interests. The snowmobilers arrived at Rollo Lake near Chapleau and forced their way into the camps, cut down the trees for firewood, and then left their garbage. Wherever they went, the snowmobile fishermen left a trail of garbage and destroyed property. The Department of Lands and Forests were overwhelmed by the onslaught of snowmobile fishermen and didn't have the equipment to police all the lakes.

When the speckled trout season opened in the winter, Foot Lake suffered a tremendous blow that destroyed the fish population. One winter day I flew over the lake and counted at least fifty snowmobiles. I returned in the spring to find about five tons of garbage sitting on the ice. Whatever the fishermen didn't want, they just left behind. All the garbage ended up in the lake and the crystal clear water was history.

The snowmobile itself isn't the evil creature that is to blame for the blow to trout fishing in Ontario and Quebec—they are wonderful machines that have opened up tremendous opportunities for winter travel. However, some people use them without a conscience. They don't think of the implications for the future when they take out more fish than their legal limit or leave garbage behind. They behave like looters in an inner-city riot. If there are no policemen, they just take whatever they can get their hands on. It's a sad comment on human behaviour that so many people take advantage of nature when there is no one to police their actions.

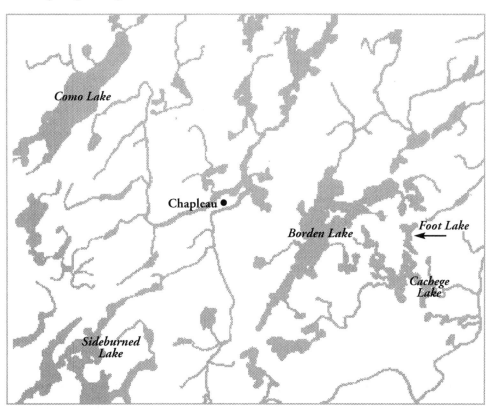

WAITING TO HUNT MOOSE

In the fall of 1958, Howard Shelley of "Michigan Outdoors" recommended our air service to Fred Bear of Bear Archery in Grayling, Michigan. Mr. Bear arrived a couple of days before the moose hunting season opened. We flew him into a lake south of the Nemegosenda River where his guide, Jim Cachege, was already at the camp getting things in order for the hunt. The day before the season opened, Jim and Mr. Bear went out fishing on the lake and surveyed the area for moose. They saw several small-antlered moose, but Fred was looking for a big bull.

When they returned to the camp late in the afternoon, they prepared their meal and planned to go to bed early so they could get up and start hunting as soon as the season opened. As they were washing their dishes, a big bull moose with about a 60-inch rack appeared on the shore of the lake not more than a hundred yards from their camp. Jim looked at Fred and said, "There's your moose, if you want it."

Fred looked at his watch and said, "Hunting season doesn't start for another twelve hours." Even though Jim tried his best to convince Fred that he might never see this moose again, Fred wouldn't shoot it. The moose hung around near the camp for about three minutes before it headed back into the bush. Fred and Jim spent the following week looking for that big bull. They never found it. The next year Fred returned to the Chapleau area and shot a bull with about a 58-inch rack at Moore Lake with Doug Saunders as guide.

When I told Howard Shelley the story about Fred's refusal to shoot out of season, he laughed but concurred that people like Fred Bear give hunters a good name and keep the sport of hunting clean. I had a somewhat similar experience with

goose hunters in James Bay. On several occasions I had guests who wouldn't shoot on Sunday. In fact, most of the native guides wouldn't shoot on Sunday either.

I have certainly had many opportunities to learn the art of waiting as it applies to moose hunting. My old hunting buddy, Bill Clarke, and I made a trip to Keifer Lake, about twenty miles west of Timmins. We waited and waited and finally, when we had given up waiting, our moose appeared.

As we were paddling a canoe across the lake, we saw a cow moose swim to a point, then climb up on the shore and head into the bush. We quickly paddled to the shore. I dropped off Bill at the tip of the point, and then paddled to the other end. I started walking down the point towards Bill and we presumed that one of us would meet the moose. But neither of us did. Eventually we met each other and pondered the situation over our lunch of cold sandwiches.

How could we have missed that moose? We passed an hour or so discussing whether we should make another attempt to locate this moose or move on to another area of the lake. Then we heard something moving behind us. We turned around and there was the cow, trotting down the path about seventy-five feet from us. Within seconds we had collected ourselves and Bill tried to shoot it while it was on the run. He couldn't get a clean enough shot to kill it.

We chased after the moose and caught up to it as it neared the water again. This time Bill had the opportunity to get a clear shot. The moose must have lain down somewhere in the bush while we were walking the point, and then got up to move while we were discussing our

Fritz Slifcak with bull moose

plans. Our wait was certainly worthwhile on that occasion.

A few years later Bill and I flew to Nemegosenda Lake with Gilbert Tremblay to clean the camp before we closed it for the winter. We already had our share of moose hunting for the season and didn't plan to hunt anymore. Then Art Thibault came over from the mining camp to borrow the canoe to make his final trip down to Alcorn Lake.

Art had been waiting patiently throughout the season to hunt this one big bull that he had seen during the summer. It was already noon and we were reluctant to begin the trip at such a late hour. Art was persistent and we finally consented to accompany him. His description of this huge bull made us all wonder about the reality of his story. We set out in the square stern canoe with a smaller one in tow, just in case we found the moose that Art had

been waiting for.

As we entered the Alcorn Lake from the river, on the left-hand side around the first bay, we saw the biggest bull moose that I had ever seen in northern Ontario. We turned our canoes around but the bull didn't move. It just stared at us with its black eyes. Gilbert, Art and I drove the canoe right at the bull. When we were within a hundred yards of it, Bill fired and hit it in the neck. The moose crashed into the water and we continued moving towards it. As we got closer, it got up on its four legs, hesitated while it eyed us again, then sank down on its hind legs. Before any of us had time to think about reloading the gun and shooting again, Art jumped out of the canoe. He waded over to the moose, and slit its throat with the hunting knife he always carried on his hip. It was quite a fitting end to a long wait.

THE WINTER MOOSE HUNT

When the Department of Lands and Forests announced in January 1958 that there was to be a winter moose hunt the following winter, I began to locate the moose yards. Moose, which are quite solitary in the summer, group together during the winter. They feed in mixed forest areas that have an abundance of aspen (poplars) and alders to eat as well as spruce or jack pine to protect them from the winds. Once the food is used up in an area, they move as a group to another. Generally moose find an abundance of food in a forest about five years after it has burned. This is where I began searching for them.

From my aerial surveys, I discovered that there were no moose yards near any of my outpost cabins. There was a large yard close to our cabin at Denyes Lake, but we had promised this cabin to the Clements for the winter trapping season. We set up a tent camp near the cabin, and the Clements guided our guests during the six-week hunt. We also set up tent camps at Johanson Lake, Little Service Lake and King Lake, which were near large moose yards. The fires of 1948 had passed through the Johanson and King Lake areas, so there was still a lot of feed for the moose. Each yard that we located contained over a hundred moose.

By December 5th the ice was thick enough to fly the first hunters into the bush. Every group of hunters had a local guide to assist them in winter camping and locating the moose. Many of these guides, such as Marcel Paquette, Ross Sawyer and Doug Saunders, remained in the bush for six weeks, guiding one party after another. All the camps were equipped with air tight heaters that kept the tents warm night and day. Early in the fall we split six cords of wood for each camp to keep their heaters constantly full. In addition to moose hunting, many of the guests spent time ice fishing, hunting for partridge (ruffed grouse) and snaring rabbits. It was a great winter camping experience and we never had a single complaint about the weather, even when it was -40°F.

When the weather is calm with no perceptible wind, the moose are very difficult to hunt because they have extremely good hearing. Moose don't see well; however, they can hear a hunter a half mile away on a calm day. If it's a windy day, a hunter can position himself downwind from the moose and move up to it without being heard. The winter weather in the Chapleau area is usually cold and clear with no wind and only a few inches to a foot of snow until mid-January. Then the snow starts to fall more frequently. This weather pattern can make it quite a challenge to hunt moose, since it requires a lot of patience and quiet hunting.

Despite the challenges, the winter hunt was such a novelty that we had a television crew come in from Michigan for a TV show called "Michigan Outdoors." The first year of the hunt, I flew Howard Shelley into Denyes Lake where he interviewed three hunters from West Branch that had bagged a couple of moose. His film of the camp was a big hit with the viewers. Howard returned the following year to take more film. By then I had so many hunters who wanted the experience of a winter moose hunt, because they had seen the TV shows, that I had more hunters call than I could handle.

It wasn't until the last year of the winter moose hunt that Howard decided to hunt for his own moose. By the 12th of December 1961 our hunt was off to an excellent start, with several moose killed and many more sighted. I called Howard in Pontiac, Michigan and suggested that he come up as soon as possible. Within a few days he arrived in Chapleau.

I immediately began flying him into the bush on day trips with two other experienced hunters from Michigan, Art Hutchings and Pete Madore. Around the 20th of December I flew them into King Lake (Mattanenda) where we had previously established a tent camp, so there was a clearing where they could cook their midday lunch. The morning I flew them into the bush the weather was beautiful. But by noon it was overcast and snow started to fall. I had three other groups of hunters in the bush that same day on day trips.

When the weather deteriorated quickly, I realized I wasn't going to have time to fly everyone out of the bush. I normally carry several extra sleeping bags and camping equipment with some food on board in case of emergency. Before I left Chapleau, I added some extra food and sleeping bags because I knew I was going to have to leave someone in the bush overnight. Since I had flown many of my guests into the bush on several occasions, I had a pretty good idea of who could survive a night in the bush.

Pete Madore had camped out on our winter moose hunt in previous years, so I knew that he was a good woodsman. I figured that he would make sure that Art and Howard were relatively comfortable. When I returned to King Lake and told them about my dilemma, I could see their hearts sink just a little. They were quite stoic about it; indeed I perceived that they all thought it would be an interesting chal-

Two winter moose hunters with guides Lloyd Morris and Leo Dumontelle

lenge. I showed them several poles that had already been cut and a location where they could build a lean-to for their unexpected night in the woods. We unloaded the food, camping equipment and sleeping bags, and I hurriedly took off in a snowstorm to pick up another party.

Howard had told me that they had seen a few moose in the area. I was hoping that when morning arrived, they would see one close enough to their camp to get a good shot at it. The temperature hit -25°F that night. I did feel a little apprehension about the three hunters I had left in the bush. When I arrived early the next day, they hadn't seen a moose, but they raved about the delicious T-Bone steaks I had given them for their evening meal. They had survived their winter ordeal like seasoned veterans and had a great story to take home.

Art and Pete had commitments which forced them to return to Michigan, but Howard stayed and we hunted another two days to get him his bull moose. On the second day we went out with an experienced guide, Ross Sawyer, to a small lake near a yard where I had just seen several moose. It was a perfect hunting day with a steady, east wind. Soon after we landed early in the morning, we sighted a small cow and a calf feeding. I knew Howard was looking for a bull, but he was ready to shoot the cow because it was his last day to hunt. We convinced him to wait. The conditions were so perfect that both Ross and I were sure there would be more moose in the area, if we were just patient.

We were slowly passing through a burnt-out area and getting a little tired from walking in the snow when I suggested that Ross climb up a small knoll to see what was in the next pasture. He quietly climbed to the top, stuck out his head to see what was there, and then motioned to us to approach the knoll. We crawled over as quietly as we could. Ross whispered to us that there were three bulls about 150 yards away. When I looked over the hill I could see them feeding about fifty feet apart. Fortunately, we were upwind from them. They seemed very intent on feeding.

Howard passed his camera to Ross so that he could film him shooting his moose. While Ross remained on top of the hill, we moved ahead thirty or forty feet. Howard found a little stump, cleared the

snow off it, and put his gun down. Ross was directly behind him shooting pictures, with a perfect view of Howard and the moose. Howard fired three shots at the bull standing in the middle of the group. After the third shot, the moose finally fell. When we measured the rack, it was 57 inches. The animal must have weighed about 1400 pounds.

Early the next morning we returned with a toboggan and hauled the butchered moose to the airplane. Since Howard wanted to have the whole head mounted, we skinned the animal up to the neck only. The head was so large that I couldn't fit it into the Cessna without removing all the seats. Once I managed to get the head into the aircraft, I could only put the pilot's seat back in. So I flew back to Chapleau by myself, with this monstrous moose head.

Howard had only one way to get his moose head back to Pontiac and that was on the roof of his station wagon. When he finally pulled out of Chapleau, with his car full of moose meat and the huge head on top, it was just a few days before Christmas. What a sight!

Howard Shelley with his moose

We ran our winter moose hunt for three years, until the Ontario government suspended the winter hunt once the herds leveled off. Each year we handled about a hundred hunters and took out about 25 moose per year. Considering the difficulty of hunting moose in winter, we thought a 25% kill was quite good. The local people in Chapleau, Timmins and Cochrane were in a much better position to hunt moose in the winter. They could wait for a windy day, then go out hunting on their snow machines.

IVANHOE LAKE: A NEW AIRBASE

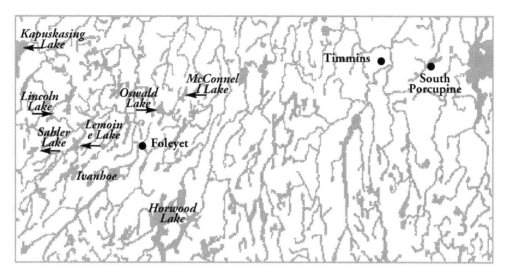

I was just a sixteen-year-old apprentice mechanic in South Porcupine when my boss, Ed Ahr, sent me by train from South Porcupine to North Bay with a cylinder for a Jacobs engine. I caught a northbound train from North Bay to Foleyet, arriving there the next morning.

Mr. Morin, who drove a team of horses for Pineland Timber, transported me from Foleyet to Ivanhoe Lake where the Custom Waco had been stranded for two days. The aircraft had been freighting ore from a small gold mine at the south end of Horwood Lake to Ivanhoe Lake. The ore was then hauled by teams of horses to the railway station at Foleyet. Eventually it reached the town of Cobalt where it was processed.

Since the Waco needed regular mechanical attention, the pilot was also a trained mechanic. However, this was a new type of cylinder that needed to be replaced. We worked together for a day and a half on the aircraft and when we had the engine running, we flew back to the South Porcupine air base. My twenty-hour trip by train and horse team seemed like

an ordeal by comparison to a flight that took less than an hour.

The mine at Horwood Lake continued to produce gold and I was sent back to Ivanhoe Lake for several weeks the following summer to assist the pilot. We stayed at the Merwins' fox farm, located on the present site of Red Pine Lodge. The Merwin brothers from Sudbury were the owners of Pineland Timber. Their summer home on Ivanhoe Lake was close to their sawmills at Foleyet and Shawmere.

During the afternoon, when the aircraft was on a flight to Horwood Lake, I used my casting rod from the dock and caught plenty of walleye, usually enough to feed the crew at the fox farm. If I caught a northern pike, I gave it to Mrs. Merwin who kept a pot of food cooking at the back of the house for the foxes.

All the seaplanes were based at the government dock near the fox farm. Another commercial pilot on the lake, Bob Landgeran, flew a Piper Cub with an 85-hp engine. Bob ran his own charter service and was always on call to locate the Waco if it was overdue. We became good

George Jr. with walleye and northern pike from one of the outpost camps

friends and continued our friendship for many years after he joined the Department of Lands and Forests in Foleyet.

Once I established my first airbase in Chapleau, I flew out of Ivanhoe Lake on several occasions fighting forest fires. Whenever I had the opportunity to fish in the area, I was impressed with the abundance of walleye and northern pike, as well as speckled trout. Since many of the lakes had never been fished they were prime fishing spots for an outfitter. In 1959 I bought a site on the lake from the Craig family to establish an airbase. The two cottages on the site had housed the gate keeper when I first visited Ivanhoe Lake in 1937. They continued to house our staff until they were destroyed to build modern accommodations in 1991.

The first season we built a floating dock and opened business for air charters. Dave McConnell flew a Cessna 180 out of the base the first summer. Then Tony Sahler and his family moved into the cot-

tage on the base the following year. Tony flew for a couple of seasons, first with a Cessna 180, then later with a Beaver.

One summer, when Tony and his family operated the base, the old log dam that regulated the water in the lake broke. As the water dropped twenty feet Tony had to keep adjusting the floating dock to accommodate the change. A new concrete dam was built that year.

Since there was a big demand for speckled trout fishing from the local fishermen in Timmins, we flew many trips into Dunrankin Lake. Octave Roy built a motel, North Miami Lodge, near our base. His guests frequently chartered the aircraft for day trips to Dunrankin. The lodges on Kapuskasing Lake, near Elsas, also kept the aircraft busy with charter flights. We picked up a considerable amount of mining charters from several companies from Timmins. They were staking claims south of Foleyet along the Old Woman River and into the old gold mining sites in Swayze Township.

In addition to the charter flights, we set up our own outpost camps for walleye and northern pike fishing. Several of the lakes that we chose for our camps were unnamed so we named them after our pilots: Moore Lake for Ross Moore, McConnell Lake for Dave McConnell and Sahler Lake for Tony Sahler. We also built cabins on Lemoine Lake and Oswald Lake and we bought a cabin at Lincoln Lake from Burr Vincent of West Branch, Michigan.

These new lakes were a walleye fisherman's paradise. Many of our guests who visited the Chapleau airbase made the trip to Ivanhoe Lake to try these new lakes. The fifty-mile trek on a dusty, gravel road didn't deter them from returning to Ivanhoe Lake year after year. Now the paved highway attracts visitors from all over the province and the northern states.

Ivanhoe Lake airbase with new log lodge, 1993

Once a provincial park opened on the lake in 1960, there was a flurry of activity in the summer. Many vacationers were attracted to the miles of sandy beaches which were perfect for swimming and boating. My family fell in love with the picturesque lake with its many islands. We built our own cottage at the airbase and spent many summers enjoying the surroundings.

George Jr., and his wife, Jeanne, now operate the base as Air Ivanhoe. They have made many additions and improvements to the outpost camps. In 1992 they com-pleted the construction of a beautiful two-story log lodge with a restaurant and a store at the airbase on Ivanhoe Lake.

The fishing for walleye and northern pike still attracts countless fishermen every year. George Jr. continues to fly in fishermen to some of my old outpost camps at Bonar Lake, Lemoine Lake and McConnell Lake, but he has upgraded the facilities with modern cabins. His new outpost camps on Kapuskasing Lake, Maariska Lake and Rush Lake offer excellent fishing for the novice as well as the seasoned fisherman.

ICE FISHING

By the month of March the intensely cold winter weather has subsided in northern Ontario and the idea of spending a day outside is appealing. Then my thoughts turn to ice fishing. There is nothing more invigorating than fishing through the ice on a clear winter day. Even when our children could barely walk, Joan and I loaded them into an aircraft on a sunny Sunday, and we flew off to one of our camps for a day of ice fishing. We lit a fire in the wood stove in the cabin to satisfy everyone's needs for warm drinks and shelter if the wind started blowing.

The kids loved fishing this way because they weren't forced to sit in a boat for hours. They could run around in the snow chasing each other and still catch a few fish—that is, if they were quick enough to get to the tip-up when the red flag signaled that there was one on the line. It always seemed that the girls hauled in more fish than the boys. They had the patience to keep a watch on the tip-ups. My sons often wandered off into the bush looking for animal tracks or whatever was of interest.

Our usual catch was walleye or northern pike. We switched to fishing for lake trout in the 1960s when the season opened year round. Matchy Lake, which is about thirty miles from Chapleau, soon became our favourite lake trout fishing spot. Even though we didn't have our own camp on the lake, there was a summer fishing lodge where people could stay overnight if the weather suddenly deteriorated.

We built a couple of huts on the lake and put them on runners so that we could move them around the lake with the Cessna. Since the fish weren't always biting in the same spot, it was worth our while to move the huts until we found the perfect locations. During the summer you can only find lake trout in the coldest, deepest parts of the lake. During the winter months they tend to inhabit the shallower parts of the lake. Finding which shallow part is the true test of the ice fisherman.

The legal limit of lake trout was five fish. On a good day, when we were fortunate to locate them, we could each catch that many, ranging from three to five pounds. The trout were quite fussy about what they would feed on. Only live minnows seemed to satisfy their palate. Finding live minnows in the winter was no small feat, but we managed to locate a source in Chapleau.

We set one tip-up for each person and then waited. Waiting was half the fun. If it was warm enough to sunbathe, we sat outside and chatted. But if there was a wind, we usually opted for the shelter of the hut. While we told stories or played cards and drank something warm, someone was supposed to keep an eye out for the red flag. As soon as a flag appeared, there was mayhem—everyone scrambled for the tip-up.

We usually relied on our speed to determine who was the one to pull up the fish; however, on one trip our friend Pete Debris decided it was time for other tactics because he was never the fastest. When a flag went up everyone bolted out of the hut. Just as Joan was about to claim her prize, Pete tackled her and left her sprawling in the snow while he hauled in the trophy. That led to an afternoon of hilarious high jinks but the ladies still ended up with the most fish.

Before we owned a Beaver, we usually put two aircraft on skis for winter travel—

a Cessna 180 and a J-3 Cub. I could only carry four adults in the Cessna and often there were more than four who wanted to go ice fishing for the day. So, on a few occasions, our friend, Dick Lapp, piloted the Cub while I flew the Cessna. One Sunday our friends, George and Gloria Collins, flew in the Cessna with Joan and I, while Dick flew the two-seater Cub with Mr. Soothern, a local business man.

We had fabulous fishing that day. As a result no one wanted to leave, but by 5:00 P.M. it began to get dark. I watched Dick and Mr. Soothern take off in the Cub to make sure they were headed in the right direction. Dick didn't have a lot of bush navigating experience. He had served with the RCAF as a pilot, but flying a light aircraft on skis was very different. The flight back to Chapleau was fairly simple. He could follow the railroad tracks once he was five miles from Matchy Lake. We took off about fifteen minutes later, expecting to find the Cub at the airbase when we arrived. Much to our surprise, it wasn't there.

Within minutes of our arrival, the sun had set, leaving me no opportunity to go in search of them. I had to admit I was having some anxious moments. Mr. Soothern was an elderly gentleman who would not fare well if he had to spend a night in the bush. Even with the emergency equipment and rations on board the Cub, his night would not be a very comfortable one.

We called Dick's wife and she came down to the airbase to discuss our strategy. Just as we were determining who was going to inform Mrs. Soothern about the missing airplane, the telephone rang. It was Dick, calling from a lumber camp in Dalton. He had turned in the wrong direction once he sighted the railroad tracks. The compass had frozen in the cold weather. When he finally realized he was heading west instead of east, he was running out of fuel and daylight. He and Mr. Soothern planned to spend the night at the lumber camp and fly back early the next morning. This news was a great relief to all of us. Now we could call Mrs. Soothern and at least tell her where her husband was spending the night.

Family and friends at Matchy Lake, 1966

Fortunately, not all our ice fishing trips ended so dramatically. They became such popular events with our friends that I often had to make a couple of trips to Matchy Lake to get everyone into the bush for a day of fishing. Nowadays, when March rolls around, the thought of ice fishing still crosses my mind, but it doesn't stay very long. The Florida sun has its ways of making even the hardiest of ice fishermen forget the joys of the exhilarating cold. My son John, who now operates the airbase in Chapleau, still carries on the tradition. He doesn't maintain an aircraft on skis for the winter, but he has a four-wheel drive that can take him just about anywhere.

THE PRIME MINISTER'S MOOSE

Some time after Lester Pearson became the Prime Minister of Canada, his secretary, Mary MacDonald, called me at our airbase in Chapleau and made a special request. The Prime Minister was hosting a VIP game dinner party. He wanted to serve moose meat as one of the main courses. He had specifically asked if I could provide him with a hundred pounds of meat for his party. Even though it was late in the moose hunting season, I was confident that I could find just the right moose to satisfy his desire, so I agreed.

I first became acquainted with the Prime Minister while I was stationed at RCAF base in Rockcliffe. At the time he was a high-ranking government official; then when he entered politics as a Liberal member of parliament in Algoma which included the town of Chapleau, we renewed our friendship.

A couple of days after Mary McDonald called, my good friend and long-time hunting buddy, Bill Clarke, and I flew out to Sahler Lake to dismantle the tent camp that we had used during the two busiest weeks of the moose hunt. Sahler Lake was one of our most popular hunting locations. It had already produced two moose that year, a bull and a cow.

We finished our chores quickly then paddled the canoe across the lake to a creek. We pulled the canoe onto the shore and walked up a trail along the side of the creek. About three quarters of a mile up the trail, we caught sight of a young cow feeding in the shallow water of the creek. Instantly Bill and I both had the same thought—there's the Prime Minister's moose. Without hesitating for one moment, I raised my gun and shot it.

While Bill hiked back down the trail to bring the canoe up the creek, I began the task of quartering it. The creek was so shallow that once we loaded the meat into the canoe, all we could do was push it. Bill and I spent the better part of an hour maneuvering the canoe into the deeper water. By then we were racing against the clock to get the meat loaded into the aircraft before darkness settled. Neither of us was keen to spend a night in the bush, particularly since we had just dismantled the tent camp and stowed it in the aircraft. Nature was on our side. The cloudless sky and partial moon allowed us to make it back to the base with our mission accomplished. I couldn't help but wonder how everything had fallen into place so neatly.

Within a few days, the meat was hung and butchered. I stored my share in our freezer at the airbase, while Bill headed home to Thessalon with his share to store in his home freezer. I planned to ship the meat to Ottawa on the CPR express, once I returned from a two-day fishing trip to Sylvanite Lake.

Upon my arrival at the airbase from my fishing trip, I entered the office and immediately noticed that someone had broken into the building through one of the windows. At first glance nothing appeared to be missing, but when I opened the freezer to pack up the moose meat, I realized what the culprits were after—the Prime Minister's moose! Then it was obvious to me that some missions are best kept secret until they are completed. A freezer full of moose meat can be an awful temptation to an unlucky hunter. I began to wonder who I had tempted.

I called the Ontario Provincial Police and reported the theft. Once I described whose moose meat was missing, they put their full attention on the case. Oddly enough, an OPP officer had stopped a car around midnight the night before on Hwy 101, at the Nemegosenda River. The officer reported that he distinctly remembered seeing some frozen meat in the back seat. He even inquired if the two men had enjoyed their hunting trip. Since he had recorded the license plate, it was a simple matter to trace the car to the owner who lived in southern Ontario. Two OPP officers in the area were dispatched to the owner's home to search for the missing meat. They came up with nothing, and the owner of the car denied any knowledge of frozen moose meat.

We speculated that the men had dumped the meat in the bush once they had been stopped by the OPP officer, so we drove out to the Nemegosenda River and searched along both sides of the highway for several miles. We never found any

trace of it. Who knows where it ended up? Hopefully, someone enjoyed it, even if it wasn't the Prime Minister's party guests.

This lack of moose meat left me in quite an odd predicament. It was too late to shoot another moose because there wasn't sufficient time to hang the meat and butcher it before it had to be sent. Fortunately, one of my good friends, Ross Sawyer, gave me a hind quarter of a moose that he had shot for his family, to send in place of the one that had been stolen. It may not have been as tasty as the young cow, but it was moose meat nonetheless. The dinner party turned out to be a success after all, and the Prime Minister conveyed his appreciation. But more importantly, I learned a valuable lesson: finish a mission before boasting about it.

Prime Minister and Mrs. Lester B. Pearson

BEARS IN CAMP

A young northern Ontario black bear looking for something to eat

Bear stories often remind me of my first encounter with a hungry bear when I was twelve years old. My brother Andy and I had trudged through bush and swamps for about ten hours before reaching a cabin which was situated about halfway between our camp at MacArthur Lake and our home in Timmins. At some very early hour of the morning we were awakened by the sound of someone banging at the door. Even though it was pitch black outside, we could see that it was a bear. Fortunately, we had secured the door with an iron bar.

I started talking to the bear, telling it that we didn't have any food and that it might as well stop banging because we weren't going to let it in. I must have been chatting just to soothe our frayed nerves. The bear didn't even acknowledge our presence. It made me wonder if the bear was after Andy and me as a tasty meal, or if it was interested in what it thought we had in our pack sacks.

While this was happening, the story of the little pig that built his house of sticks came to my mind. And there was the wolf, in the guise of a bear, trying to blow my house down. In the bedtime story, the house did get blown down. But this little cabin in the middle of the bush was originally built by a mining company that had given some thought to protecting the inhabitants.

The walls were made of solid logs, the windows had iron bars as well as glass, and the door was at least three inches thick with six-inch strapped hinges. None of this deterred the bear from trying to get at what it thought was an easy meal. The bear put its shoulder against the door and started shoving and shoving. When that didn't work, it rattled the bars in all four windows. At each window we shone our lamp in its eyes, hoping to scare it away. Instead, we could see that two smaller bears had come to join in the commotion.

At this point Andy and I backed off and fumbled to find our only weapon—an ax. Neither of us slept again that night. We just huddled together, ready to spring at a moment's notice. Eventually things quieted down outside. The bears must have wandered off to find a less challenging meal. At daybreak we gingerly stole out of the cabin and hurried home to the safety of our house in town.

My first encounter with a hungry bear may have been unnerving, but it left me with a deep appreciation for a well-built cabin. Later when I became a tourist outfitter, I had to build cabins for my guests that would protect them from the elements, including bears. I can't recall hearing that a bear successfully entered a cabin while the guests were inside. However, on many occasions bears have found a way in while the guests were out fishing or hunting.

In the summer of 1957 Ralph Stedman and his family were enjoying a week of fishing on Raney Lake. They returned from a day on the lake to find a bear inside the cabin, helping itself to their food. They tried to frighten the bear by yelling and banging gas cans, but it was so preoccupied with their provisions that it wasn't distracted in the least. After some deliberation, they decided that fire was the only way to scare away this nuisance bear.

Ralph's son Larry found a mop in the gas shed, soaked it in gasoline, lit it and then proceeded cautiously into the cabin with the torch. The bear was sufficiently startled to back out the doorway and take off into the bush. The Stedmans salvaged a few items of food and managed to eat a lot of fish for the remainder of their trip. They also learned to fasten the door tightly when they left the cabin.

During the summer of 1958 we flew a television crew from Green Bay, Wisconsin into our two cabins at Nemegosenda Lake to shoot some scenic film for an outdoor special. At the time, the camp at Nemegosenda was regularly visited by a bear; most likely it was attracted to a dump not far from the camp. Over the summer the bear had become rather tame. People would feed it the occasional fish when they returned from fishing.

Soon the bear was waiting on the beach for the guests and would go from one cabin door to the other, begging for food.

The television crew spent a considerable amount of time filming this bear's activities. They even managed to film an episode with the bear and one of their crew. The man, a former competitive wrestler, was sitting on the beach with the bear and put his arm around it. Then the bear put his arm around the man and the two of them began rolling around in the sand. Fortunately the camera was also rolling and they recorded this scene for their viewers back in Wisconsin. It was quite a hit! No one could believe that a wild bear had become so tame. After a couple of summers the bear just disappeared. No one knew for sure what happened to it, but I assume it was shot by a hunter. Its own lack of fear of humans was probably its demise in the end.

The Bishop brothers from Kingston had a rather unusual adventure with a bear that hung around the tent site at Kinniwabi Lake. They had seen the bear when they returned from fishing but they didn't mind its presence. On their last day in camp they went out fishing as usual. This time they kept their limit of fish to take out of the bush with them the next morning. They carefully cleaned their fish when they returned to the camp and stored them on ice in a cooler.

That night while they were sleeping, they were awakened by rattling noises outside. When they looked outside they spied the bear trying to get into the cooler. Since the bear couldn't open the cooler, it grabbed it and started dragging it into the woods. The Bishop brothers were not too happy about losing their fish to the bear, so they followed in pursuit. Finally the bear dropped the cooler and they reclaimed their fish. But the bear returned to their campsite looking for his booty.

The two men stayed up the rest of the night with their cooler so they wouldn't lose their fish. By the time the aircraft arrived in the morning, they were laughing about their night chase through the woods to rescue their fish.

Sometime later that summer, Bob Wells and his wife were camping at the same tent site at Kinniwabi Lake. They too had a night encounter with a bear. Bob's wife was awakened early one morning by what she thought was her husband stroking her leg through her sleeping bag. After about a half an hour she realized that this was not her husband touching her—she could hear him snoring. When she figured something wasn't right, she let out a scream, which woke up Bob, and they heard an animal running away. At the back of the tent they noticed that a bear's claws had ripped through the canvas. That was their last night sleeping in the tent. They had another three nights to spend in the bush before the aircraft returned to pick them up, so they packed their gear and moved over to the small cabin on Zola Lake.

We had a lot of bears hanging around the camps in the early days of our business because we allowed our guests to bury their garbage at nearby dump sites. Almost every week a bear would come into a camp. Sometimes they would get into a cabin and do a little damage. We put up with this nuisance for a few years, but by 1960 we decided to fly out most of the garbage. The guests burned their paper products and dumped their fish entrails on a small island in the lake. At the end of the week we flew out the rest of the garbage in large plastic bags. Today all operators must fly garbage out of the bush.

Usually when bears come out of hibernation in the spring, they eat plants, grasses and the shoots of young trees for a few weeks until their stomachs are ready for more substantial food, like meat or garbage. By the month of June there are often a few bears to contend with around the campsites. If they smell any garbage at all, they converge on it like buzzards. Even though we fly all the garbage out of the bush now, a bear might still come around a site looking for a fast meal before its favourite source of food, the berries, ripen. Unfortunately the berry crop has been exceptionally small the last few years. The bears have been even hungrier than usual.

At one time we weren't allowed to use guns to scare the bears, so we devised a few ways to deter them from developing a fondness for our camps. We tried throwing firecrackers or cherry bombs at them if they approached the site. Eventually some of the persistent bears learned our tricks and didn't leave when they heard the firecrackers. Now, on the rare occasion when a bear persistently frightens the guests and destroys the cabin, we have had to resort to shooting it.

In the spring of 1992 my son John had some problems with a nuisance bear that was regularly damaging the cabin at Rice Lake. Even when the bear managed to make its way into the cabin through the door, it often exited through a window, having destroyed furniture and camping supplies along the way. Every week John had to replace windows, screens, dishes or repair a door.

One day the guests returned from a day of fishing to find that the bear had broken into the refrigerator and consumed their meat and cheese. The next day they expected a check trip from my son, so they left him a note with a request for a gun. John was so frustrated repairing the cabin after each break-in, that he flew a rifle into the campsite that same day. While the guests were eating dinner in the evening, the bear arrived for his share of the repast. When the warning shots didn't scare the bear, they shot it. Since their food supply had been devoured by the bear, they decided it was only fair to devour the bear. The next night they dined on bear meat and left enough in the refrigerator for the in-coming guests to enjoy a few meals.

Whenever we build a cabin in the bush, we are assured that at some time a bear will visit it. It goes with the territory. Bears live in the bush. If we want to live there too, we have to live with them. Since we know they have a keen sense of smell and an eagerness to eat anything they can get their paws on, it's obviously up to us to keep our campsites clean of garbage and store our food in metal containers whenever possible.

However, the bears seem to have got-ten smarter over the years. Now they can open containers and refrigerators! It leaves us wondering how to coexist with an animal that learns our strategies faster than we can formulate new ones. The dilemma continues—every year we are faced with another bear that confounds us. No one who has ever had to destroy a nuisance bear feels happy about the situation. I can only hope that in the future someone will develop a safe and affordable instrument which emits an offensive smell or sound to deter bears from entering areas of human habitation. In the meantime, the bears are at a disadvantage because when humans and bears square off for the same territory, the bears are most often the losers.

WAWA AND HAWK JUNCTION

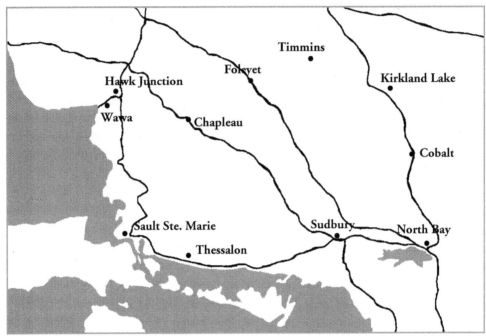

A section of northern Ontario showing railroads (grey) and highways (black)

Road access in northern Ontario has a tremendous impact on the fishing and hunting because it opens up vast areas of wilderness to sportsmen. When we arrived in Chapleau in 1954, there was just one gravel road into the town from Thessalon to the south, plus the Canadian Pacific Railroad from Sudbury; however, this relative isolation was short-lived.

Within ten years Hwy 101 connected Chapleau to Timmins in the east (officially opened 1962) and to Wawa in the west. Flying highway crews into the bush was one of our prime sources of income during the first ten years of operation in Chapleau. In fact, when I arrived in Chapleau in the winter of 1954, my first charter flights were to pick up a survey crew that had been working on the highway to Wawa. (It was finally completed in 1966.)

While Hwy 101 was under construction from Chapleau to Wawa, another highway was being constructed from Wawa to Sault Ste. Marie. When this highway along the shore of Lake Superior neared completion, we realized the potential of the tourist trade in the area. The new road would bring in a tremendous number of people from southern Ontario and the northern USA.

Since the area around Wawa had only been accessible by boat to Michipicoten Harbour or by railroad from Sault Ste. Marie, the fishing was virtually unspoiled. When we arrived and began operating an airbase, the number of tourists that passed through Wawa and stayed for a few nights was far beyond our expectations. During our first summer in Wawa, six new motels were constructed to handle the volume of people who visited the area. There were

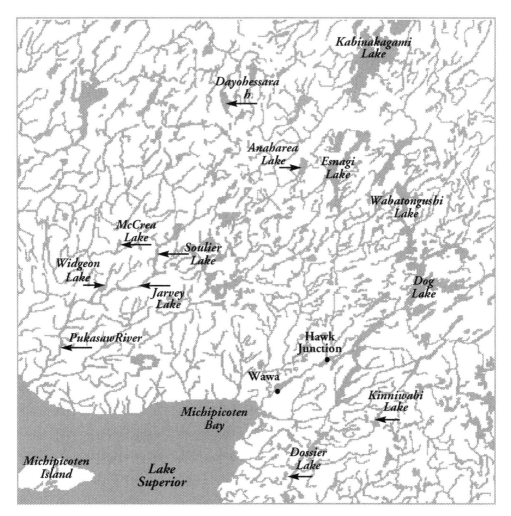

about a thousand tourists a day in Wawa, and most were looking for some outdoor activity. At first we started flying people on sightseeing flights. Then, when the demand increased, we began to fly fishermen on day trips.

Since we needed someone who was both enterprising and trustworthy to run the new airbase, we solicited the help of my wife's father, Captain John Watson, who had recently retired from the government taxation office in Belleville, Ontario. Captain Watson had served as an officer in the Royal Canadian Navy during World War I and subsequently became a captain on the Great Lakes. He had made several trips into Michipicoten Harbour during

his years of sailing on the Great Lakes and had discovered some interesting diversions in the area. When Captain Watson first arrived at the airbase on Wawa Lake, our pilot was out on a charter flight in the Cessna 180, but the office was open. A brief note on the desk outlined the pilot's itinerary for the trip.

Captain Watson sat down and waited for his return. In the meantime a black bear sauntered out of the bush and sat down about twenty feet from the door of the office. Captain Watson spied the bear and the bear spied him. They watched each other for several minutes. Captain Watson got up and started to walk out of the office, expecting that the bear would turn around and head back into the bush. It didn't—it just sat there waiting. Obviously someone had been feeding it, and it was going to wait for its customary meal before leaving.

We didn't have a telephone at the office, just a battery-operated radio which could be used to communicate with the aircraft or the airbase in Chapleau. Captain Watson began calling on the radio. He assumed that the Chapleau base would hear his message. My wife Joan was expecting her father to arrive in Wawa that day, but she wasn't quite prepared for his exasperated greeting over the radio. Actually he called for several minutes before she recognized his voice. She heard someone calling, "Joan, are you there?" over and over again.

She finally answered, "This is Chapleau, who is calling Joan?" The Captain responded, "This is your father and there is a big black bear sitting twenty feet from the office and he won't leave." Joan suggested that he make a lot of noise with the broom to scare it away. This new tactic worked and the bear grudgingly moved off the base in search of an easier dinner.

Captain Watson spent four months at the base in Wawa, but his reputation survived for several more seasons. He had a way of attracting all kinds of tourists into the office, and he always sold them a trip, even if it was just a fifteen-minute sightseeing flight. He visited the hotel and motel owners in town, was soon on a first-name basis with them and had them selling trips to their guests. When the tourists weren't interested in fishing, he sold them a trip to Quebec Harbour on Michipicoten Island to hunt for agates on the beaches. He started an agate club in town and soon the group was making excursions all around the Wawa area.

We weren't the only air service that established an airbase in Wawa to take advantage of the summer tourist trade. One of our local competitors, Leo Lamothe from Blind River, visited our base while Captain Watson was there. He wanted to meet this man who people claimed could sell a refrigerator to an Eskimo. Leo later told me that the Captain had maneuvered him into the office and was in the process of selling him a day trip to a fabulous trout fishing spot before he could tell him who he was. Shortly afterwards Leo closed his base and moved his aircraft back to Blind River.

The speckled trout fishing in the Wawa area quickly gained a reputation and attracted countless fishermen to our airbase. Most of the lakes west of Wawa abounded with trout but were too small for an aircraft to land on. We established outpost camps at a couple of larger lakes, such as Jarvey Lake, Soulier Lake, McCrea Lake and the Bremmer River where the trout ran to two pounds or more. Fishermen could access the Pukaskwa River from Jarvey Lake and Widgeon Lake and fish the rapids to the mouth at Lake Superior. After Ben East wrote an article about the four-pound speckles in the Pukaskwa for *Outdoor Life* magazine, trout fishermen clamored to make a canoe trip into the area in the spring and late summer.

In the spring we also flew fishermen into the mouth of the Pukaskwa River on Lake Superior for rainbow trout. In 1971 the federal government began proceedings with the provincial government to establish the area as a national park. At present, the park comprises approximately seven hundred square miles of forest and streams where fishing is allowed by permit only.

When we first established a base in Wawa many fishermen wanted us to fly them to Channel Lake on Michipicoten Island for lake trout. We obliged them for a

Beaver aircraft at the dock on Hawk Lake

few years; however, the strong winds on Lake Superior were quite hazardous to a single engine aircraft. We discontinued flying there on a regular basis.

Several lakes south of Wawa produced larger numbers of speckled trout all summer long, although the fish were considerably smaller than in the lakes west of Wawa. We bought two small cabins on Dossier Lake, a pretty spring-fed lake surrounded by high hills on the east and west sides. It became one of the favourites for day trips. Instead of flying guests into our outpost camp at Kinniwabi/Zola Lake from Chapleau, we began to fly them from the new airbase in Wawa because it was closer.

After two summers of operating the base in Wawa, we decided to move inland to Hawk Junction because the fog rolled into Wawa Lake from Lake Superior during the warm weather in the summer. Often we couldn't begin flying until noon or later, and this was not advantageous to flying day trips. The guests wanted to be in the bush by 9:00 A.M. so they had a

full day of fishing before we returned to pick them up in the late afternoon.

The Algoma Central Railroad (ACR) leased us a piece of land for a new airbase on Hawk Lake, adjacent to the newly paved highway. When I arrived in the spring to set up the base, the land needed to be cleared before we could begin flying. Fortunately a crew of workers that was constructing the highway between Hawk Junction and Chapleau agreed to help me in the evenings. Within two weeks they had moved the two small buildings from Wawa, dug a hole for a 2000-gallon fuel tank, constructed a 60-foot wooden staircase down the hill, built a 16 by 16-foot floating dock and erected a large office/reception space. By the middle of May we were ready for the first tourists that arrived.

We sent a Beaver aircraft to the new airbase with a very experienced pilot, Duke Perkins, who had been one of my students while I was stationed at the RCAF airbase in Rockcliffe. Duke had accompanied me to the northwestern Arctic in 1950 and had flown in Labrador and Newfoundland after he was released from the service. He had been flying Norsemen and DC-3s during the service and was looking for a change of scenery, so we hired him to fly a Beaver for the summer season out of Hawk Junction. He was an excellent airman, with superior navigation skills. We were confident that the base was in good hands.

As soon as the base was operational, we were overwhelmed with lodge operators who wanted to use our charter service to fly their guests because our base was at least eight miles closer to their lodges than the Wawa air bases. The traffic to the lodges on Dog Lake, Wabatongushi Lake, Esnagi Lake and Kabinakagami Lake was so heavy that we kept one aircraft busy with lodge charters alone. All the lodge guests could travel by train on the ACR to the lodges; however, a lot of them preferred the convenience of a twenty to thirty-minute flight. Since our airbase was located just two miles from the train station in Hawk Junction, many guests chose to fly one way and take the train the other.

By the third year of operation at

At the Hawk Junction airbase with a Northern pike

Hawk Junction, we stationed two or three aircraft at the base on weekends to fly guests to our outposts camps and the lodges. The traffic continued and the base was an excellent source of income until we sold it in 1972 to Dick Watson, the owner of Pine Portage Lodge on Kabinakagami Lake. Dick had built a second lodge and was in need of his own air service to fly his guests. I was ready to consolidate our operations.

EXPERT FISHERMEN AT BRUNSWICK LAKE

A few years after we built our camp at Brunswick Lake, we flew in a group of fishermen from Michigan that included eight men and their wives. As soon as the Beech 18 landed, the men unloaded their fishing equipment and raced to the boats to begin their fishing trip. The women were left on the dock with all the equipment to carry up to the cabins. Our caretaker, Emile Bouchard, tried to give the men some maps of the lake with the fishing spots marked, but they were in too much of a hurry to pay any attention.

It took the wives barely an hour to unload the equipment and supplies for the week. Then they too were ready for some activity. Since none of them had ever run an outboard motor, there wasn't much point in taking out the boats. Emile suggested that they fish from the docks which were in front of each cabin. He had to lend them some old fishing rods and tackle because the men had left with all their equipment. The women weren't fussy; a few of them were reluctant to put the night crawlers on their hooks, but again Emile was there to help them.

Within a few hours the women had caught about a hundred walleye from the docks. Once Emile taught them how to safely remove the hooks and return the fish to the water, they had the time of their lives catching and releasing small walleye and pike. They kept only the walleye that weighed about two pounds. By the time the men returned for a late lunch, they had enough big ones to feed the whole group.

When the women heard the boats arrive they ran down to the docks to show their husbands their catch and were greeted with angry faces. The men were furious because our brochure claimed that the lake

was full of walleye and they had only caught three fish that were worth keeping. They questioned Emile about the fishing but their wives answered by showing them their dozen fat walleye. It was a humiliating experience for the men to see all the fish their wives had caught off the docks in six feet of water, while they had burned ten gallons of gasoline in each of the four boats on their six-hour trip.

The men didn't live this experience down for the rest of the trip. When we flew them out of the bush at the end of the week, the women were still ribbing their husbands about their fishing skills. In one brief afternoon all the women had become expert fishermen and the men were probably sorry they had agreed to the trip.

Brunswick Lake was one of the easiest lakes to catch walleye. The men learned after their first experience that trolling for them was not necessarily the most productive way. Emile figured that the men must have covered most of the thirty square miles of lake on their first day, at a speed that would have scared any fish. After they settled down he showed the men where the fish were located and what types of bait they were feeding on. Soon they too began to enjoy the abundance of walleye at Brunswick Lake.

When we first built the camp on Brunswick Lake, the fish were incredibly numerous but they were all fairly small. The biggest walleye were about two-and-a-half pounds and the average was a pound and a half. We had learned from our experience on Nemegosenda Lake that we needed to remove some of the fish to allow more food for the remaining fish. The Department of Lands and Forests from Kapuskasing gave us some live boxes and our caretaker filled them with half-pound walleye, which were transported to restock other lakes. Over a two-year period the Department of Lands and Forests' aircraft made about a hundred trips into Brunswick Lake to take out walleye.

The northern pike fishing in Brunswick was excellent, especially in the early spring when there was still ice on the north end of the lake. It was common to catch northerns in the 20 to 25-pound range as they congregated at the mouths of the two rivers that flowed into the south end. As the season progressed the guests could boat up the rivers three or four miles and catch northerns and some bigger walleye.

When they were tired of fishing, the guests made the trip up the rivers just to photograph the game. From the beginning of June until September, they could sight from a half a dozen to a dozen moose on each trip. The rivers also abounded with beaver, muskrats and plenty of waterfowl—there was no trapping in the area at that time. Although we did operate a small moose hunt in the fall, we were very careful to take only a few moose. We realized that the abundance of moose during the fishing season was a major tourist attraction.

Even after the Department of Lands and Forests removed many of the small walleye from the lake, the fish were plentiful but still in the smaller range. We located other places where the ardent walleye fishermen could satisfy their desires for bigger fish. Omar Latour cut a three mile trail from the second bay on the southeast end of the lake to the Missinaibi River, and we left a boat and motor on the river so the guests could make day trips. Once they motored up the river about fifteen miles to the foot of a forty-foot waterfall, they could catch four and a half and five-pound walleye. The water in the river was

dark from minerals. For this reason the walleye were a very dark yellow colour.

Most of the guests visited the remains of the old Hudson's Bay Company post at the north end of the lake to search for arrowheads or whatever paraphernalia that was left at the site. At one time the post was a lively center of trade for the native people that lived and hunted in the area. My father, the late J.A. Theriault, made a canoe trip to this village in 1896 from his general store in Wawa. He and his partner paddled to Brunswick Lake, via the Hawk River, Manitowick Lake, Dog Lake, Crooked Lake, Missinaibi Lake and the Missinaibi River. This was the same route travelled by the early voyageurs who had canoed between Hudson Bay and Lake Superior.

In 1947 my dad and I flew to Brunswick Lake and Wawa. He pointed out each portage that he had made and the length of time it had taken him to carry the canoe and gear across. Their trip had taken two and a half weeks while our flight took just a couple of hours in my J-3 Cub. The year after his canoe trip to Brunswick Lake, a forest fire passed through Wawa and my dad was lured to the gold rush in Timmins.

My first flight to Brunswick Lake sparked the desire to build my own camp on one of the many beautiful islands. In 1957 we applied to the Department of Lands and Forests to purchase land on Brunswick Lake for our own camp—but our request was denied. Five years later we started to fly moose hunters from our base at Hawk Junction to an island at the south end of Brunswick Lake for an outfitter in the Kapuskasing area. When we heard that the Johnson Wax Company had received land to build a private camp at the north end of the lake, we lobbied our Member of the Provincial Parliament (MPP), Rene Brunelle, and J.W. Spooner, Minister of

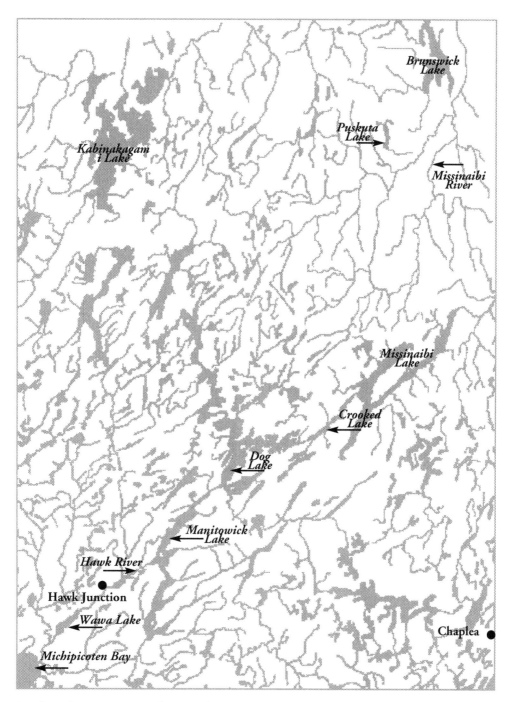

Lands and Forests, to see if our application could be reviewed. Eventually, with some persistence, the government agreed to sell us a piece of land on the lake to build our own camp. Since Brunswick Lake is twelve miles long I wanted to build near two rivers at the south end because the ice would melt sooner than at the north end.

In the fall of 1963 we transported forty loads of supplies on the Norseman to begin constructing five log cabins. We hired a skilled log builder from Wawa, Mickey Clement, and his team of helpers to erect the cabins over the winter. In February I flew two snowmobiles to the camp so the workers could haul the logs to the island. By the beginning of June they had completed the cabins and we were ready to fly in the first guests. Omar Latour, who had worked with Mickey constructing the cabins, stayed on as care-taker along with his wife Pat.

That summer Omar completed the construction of a floating dock in front of each cabin and began to build a sixth log cabin. By the end of the second season he had finished the cabin and during the fol-lowing year, the seventh cabin was built. Each cabin was set up for housekeeping for four to six guests. We provided two 14-foot boats on each floating dock. The cabins, which were placed in the woods about a hundred yards apart around the eleven-acre island, were connected by walking trails. Since the builders had used logs from the mainland to construct the cabins, the island still retained most of its beautiful pine trees.

The guests had the opportunity to experience life in the north woods in the comfort of a warm log cabin. There were usually twenty to thirty guests in the camp during the fishing season and half that many during the moose hunt. Omar and Pat were caretakers at the camp for three years. Then Emile Bouchard, Mike Henderson and my son, George Jr., took their turns helping the guests. Everyone at the camp appreciated having skilled woodsmen nearby to help them chop wood and to guide them to the best fishing spots.

When a lumber company from Hearst, Ontario began building roads into the area to haul out lumber, we immediate-ly felt concerned about the quality of the fishing in the lake. We petitioned various government offices to prevent the lumber company from cutting near the lake, but we received no support for our position. Then when a group from Hearst offered to buy the camp in 1971, we reluctantly agreed to sell it to them.

It was sad for us to sell such a beauti-ful camp, but we felt we had no option. We didn't feel it was fair to sell fly-in fishing trips to a camp that was accessible by road. The private camp owned by the Johnson Wax Company had been sold to another outfitter, so we were sharing the lake and that gave us another good reason to sell. I returned to Brunswick Lake just a few years ago and learned that the fishing has not been affected by the lumbering roads because access is limited to groups with permits.

NORTHERN CAMPS

At the Seal River camp

I was just a teen-ager working as an apprentice mechanic and dock boy at the South Porcupine airbase when I first heard about the trout fishing in the Sutton and Hawley Lakes area. The older bush pilots regularly flew a mail run to Fort Albany, Attawapiskat, Winisk and Lake River once a year on floats and once a year on skis. Most of them spent a night on Hawley Lake with a native family, the Chookomolins, who would take them up the Sutton River to fish for speckled trout. They came home with incredible stories of catching trout that weighed from five to eight pounds.

Their stories sparked my desire to make the trip myself, but it wasn't until after the war that I had my first opportunity. During the war the Ontario government declared the area north of the Albany River a hinterland. It was too remote to provide adequate services for private aircraft on fishing trips; however, mining exploration was still allowed. This eliminated all possible tourist operation and became a point of controversy for outfitters in northern Ontario. It wasn't a secret that the government had set up their own private fishing camps on Sutton and Hawley Lakes and regularly flew in dignitaries to enjoy the spectacular trout fishing.

SUTTON LAKE AND THE BRANDT RIVER

In the summer of 1947 Gordon Gauthier, Dr. Henry Hudson, and I finally managed to obtain a temporary permit from the Department of Lands and Forests in Cochrane to observe mineral outcrops at the gorge between Hawley and Sutton Lakes. In August the three of us took off from South Porcupine in our J-3 Cubs, each of us flying our own aircraft. We filled our long-range tanks, plus we carried twenty gallons of extra fuel in the cabin.

We flew north to Moosonee, and then headed northwest following the coast of James Bay. Since the Hudson's Bay Company Stores in Fort Albany and Attawapiskat had aviation fuel for sale, we were able to keep our tanks full. After two days of flying and exploring, we landed at the Chookomolin's camp on the northern shore of Hawley Lake. Sutton Lake in the south, and Hawley Lake in the north, are virtually the same twelve-mile lake divided by a gorge. At the northernmost point of Hawley Lake the Sutton River flows northwards sixty miles to Hudson Bay (forty air miles).

The Chookomolin family were most hospitable and escorted us to the gorge where they had observed a showing of minerals. After cursory examination we determined that it wasn't worth further exploration. We were more interested in the fishing anyway; mining was just an excuse to gain access to the area. I paddled up the Sutton River about ten miles to the first set of rapids with several members of the Chookomolin family, while Gordon and Henry used the only canoe with a 9-hp motor and managed to travel about twenty miles up the river.

Fortunately our arrival coincided with the migration of the speckled trout up the Sutton River. We were blessed with excellent fishing, catching trout that weighed four to five pounds. Both Hawley and Sutton Lakes also had tremendous lake trout fishing and the scenery was spectacular. Unlike the barren coast line, the area around the lake and the Sutton River is covered with spruce forest and thick, lush lichens hug the ground. It's a northern paradise! I left with the feeling that this place would be a perfect spot for an outpost camp.

I returned to the area in a Norseman two years later when I flew an RCAF survey crew east of the Sutton River, around Cape Henrietta Maria. We landed at the mouth of the Brandt River, set up a camp for our operations and soon discovered that the river was full of speckled trout. Unlike the Sutton River, the coastal area surrounding the Brandt River is treeless, although it is full of game. A herd of caribou and several colonies of snow geese and blue geese were rearing their young on the barren lands. As we flew further west, past the Sutton River, along the coast to Fort Severn, we sighted about fifty polar bear on the mainland and a large colony of walruses on an offshore island.

When the RCAF took on responsibility for search and rescue in the area, the Ontario government was forced to rescind its travel restriction; however, it responded by declaring the area a provincial park. The Chookomolin family were not happy about the continued restriction on tourism in their area. They lobbied for the right to an outfitters' license on Sutton/Hawley Lake—eventually, they were awarded one.

When the new Polar Bear Provincial Park was formally established by Order-in-Council in 1970, it contained 9300 square miles of territory. The park includes the area just south of Cape Henrietta Maria along the James Bay coast and west along the coast of Hudson Bay past Winisk. The mouth of the Sutton River is within the park boundaries, as is the Brandt River, but Sutton/Hawley Lake is outside the park.

In 1963 we began to fly tourists into Hawley Lake and the Chookomolins guided the guests up the Sutton River for speckled trout. There are about seventeen sets of rapids on the sixty-mile trip to the coast. The guides can usually float the eighteen-foot, square-stern canoes down the rapids once the fishermen have had their fill of fishing the pools below. Since there is no safe place to land a seaplane along the river from Hawley Lake to the coast, the guests have to spend a couple of days camping along the shore. Many choose to canoe down the entire sixty miles and have an aircraft pick them up near the mouth of the river, where the Chookomolins have built a goose hunting camp.

Once the Chookomolins became the exclusive outfitters on the Sutton River, the Department of Lands and Forests began using the Brandt River as their special fishing spot for their dignitaries. On one flight into the Brandt River, I counted eleven turbo Beavers that had transported VIPs from the south. A tourist outfitter from Cochrane, Lindy Loutitt, told me about his encounter with one of the government officials who had flown into the Brandt River with about twenty visitors on four aircraft. Even though Lindy was escorting just three tourists, this official told him that only native people could fish on the Brandt. Lindy, who was a Cree, born in Attawapiskat, laughed at him and responded that since he was the only native person there, he had more right to fish in the area than any of them. It was going to take more than just words to pre-

vent Lindy from taking tourists into the Brandt River to experience the tremendous speckled trout fishing.

We flew fishermen on charter flights into the Brandt River for a few seasons. The guests set up their tents along the river about ten miles from the coast. From there they could walk ten miles in either direction because there are no trees along the shoreline. In fact the guests could step out of the aircraft, walk a hundred yards to the first set of rapids, and be fishing speckled trout. The widest sections of the Brandt are barely a hundred feet, however it averages only about fifty feet in most spots. There are just three safe spots to land a seaplane along the first twenty miles of the river since there is a continuous flow of fast water, with rapids about every mile. The river flows about a hundred miles further south but only the first twenty miles from the coast produces enough trout to make a fishing trip worthwhile.

The fishing at the Brandt has its advantages over the Sutton River. The speckles run up the Brandt from the middle of June until the end of August. They are usually only found in sufficient numbers on the Sutton River during the month of August. There are more trout in the Brandt, but they average only about two pounds. In the Sutton River they will run to four or five pounds. You need a canoe to fish the length of the Sutton River; however, you can fish from the shore along the Brandt.

In the summer of 1971 Tommy Thompson and my youngest son, Richard, spent several weeks on the Brandt River enjoying the northern environment and assisting the guests. Tommy was an expert fly fisherman and a seasoned camper. It didn't take him long to find the best fishing spots along the river. By the time the first guests arrived, Tommy was a competent guide and Richard, who was always close behind, was picking up quite a few tips.

During their stay on the Brandt River, three turbo Beavers belonging to the Ministry of Natural Resources (formerly the Department of Lands and Forests) arrived with a group of politicians and civil servants, including the minister, Rene

Richard fishing on the Brandt

Brunelle. There were no other guests in the camp at the time so they set up their tents alongside ours.

A couple of the men immediately proceeded down the river with their fishing gear and returned a few hours later empty-handed. Since Tommy was busy at camp, he sent Richard to guide the disheartened men. Richard had taken his lessons very seriously. After two weeks of fly fishing on the Brandt with Tommy, he put on quite a display for the newly arrived fishermen. He showed them where to fish and what type of flies to use and even went so far as to cast their lines for them. The men returned to camp with their fill of trout and insisted that Richard was their chief guide for the remainder of their trip. Rene Brunelle, who I had grown up with in Timmins, later told me how impressed they all were with my young son's fishing and guiding skills.

Many of our guests enjoyed the novelty of fishing in the barren lands of the Brandt River. When they tired of fishing, the abundant wildlife along the shores entertained them for hours. There were usually mink and otter to observe, along with a herd of caribou and flocks of geese and ptarmigan nesting in the area. We encouraged our guests to travel in pairs up and down the river because it was not uncommon to meet a polar bear fishing on the other side.

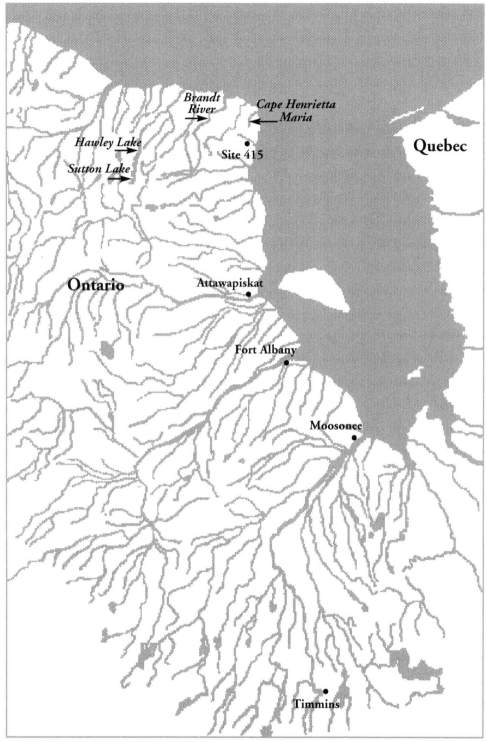

A section of northern Ontario showing rivers that flow into James and Hudson Bay

BACK TO THE SEAL RIVER

Bo Randall with a speckled trout on the Seal River, 1957

Bo Randall and I became friends because we shared a passion for speckled trout fishing. When I first started the air service in Chapleau, I flew Bo into Zola Lake and South Greenhill Lake to fish for speckled trout. Our friendship continued for many years afterwards. As soon as I discovered the incredible fishing at Foot Lake in the summer of 1956, I called Bo and he arrived in Chapleau in the spring of 1957 with his friends Al Cameron and Hank Beehler. They were one of the lucky groups that made a trip to Foot Lake while it was at its prime.

Bo and his friends from Michigan were true conservationists—they never took out a fish unless it was a trophy for mounting. They just ate a few fish and came out with photographs and memories. It was a real pleasure to fly sportsmen of this calibre.

Bo's interest was sparked when I told him my stories of fishing the Seal River. He managed to convince me to make preparations for a return trip. In August 1957, I picked up Bo and his two friends in Sault Ste. Marie, then we headed north in the Stinson Reliant. When I made my first trip to the Seal River in 1937, I flew in a Stinson Reliant CF-BGS that was owned by the McIntyre Mines. That aircraft was sold to the Ontario government, and later, when the government switched over to deHavilland Beavers, they sold their Stinson Reliants. I just happened to buy the same aircraft that I had flown with Harold Smith in 1937. Of course, it was completely reconditioned, but nonetheless, it was the same aircraft and there I was flying it again to the Seal River.

We took off from Sault Ste. Marie around noon, refueled at Remi Lake in Kapuskasing and arrived in Moosonee in the late afternoon. Since daylight lasts until well into the evening in the summer, we pressed on to Fort George. By morning it started to drizzle. However we had just enough ceiling and visibility to continue northward, arriving at the Seal River in the early afternoon.

We set up our camp at the same location where I had first fished in 1937. I couldn't help but reminisce about my first trip to the Seal River as a seventeen-year-old helping Harold Smith. It was on that trip that I met Ben East, who must have been twenty years older than me—now I was twenty years older and leading the trip in the same aircraft! On one hand, nothing had changed—the fishing was still fantastic and the country looked the same. On the other hand, everything had changed—there had been a war that claimed many lives, including the life of Harold Smith.

The fishing was just as I had remembered it—lots and lots of three- to four-pound speckles. Each of us could throw our lines in the water and have a fish on at the same time. Even though the drizzle remained with us the entire trip, it didn't affect the fishing. Our three days passed by so quickly that we hadn't finished telling all our stories. Bo and his friends were totally thrilled with their first trip to the Seal River. They had never before experienced speckled trout in such quantity.

The following summer, in 1958, Bo and I returned to the Seal River by ourselves. The two of us spent most of our time fishing the tributaries. Bo caught a seven-and-a-half pound trout in one of the upper rapids. That was an exception, since almost all of the fish we caught were under five pounds. These trout were magnificent specimens, with plenty of fight. A few years later I did see an eleven-pound trout taken out of the Seal River by one of my guests.

In the summer of 1959 I made five trips to the Seal River between mid-June and mid-August. My pilot, Peter Jansen, made another one. We flew four fishermen from the airbase at Chapleau on Sunday, spent three or four days at the Seal River, then returned by Thursday evening. Since we didn't have a license to operate a camp in Quebec until 1960, we flew the guests on a charter basis only. They brought their own camping equipment and food, and we hired an experienced cook for them. The guests were so pleased with the fishing that at least half of them returned the following year to repeat the experience—some of them returned year after year.

A trip to the Seal River was more than just an exceptional fishing experience. The guests had the opportunity to experience another culture that was still relatively unaffected by the modern ways of the world. On our way north, we stopped in Fort George where many of the native people were still living in their summer tents because their main camps were two or three hundred miles inland. The families would come together at places like Fort George, where they could trade and socialize while their children attended school.

The employees at the Hudson's Bay Company Store and the missionaries were storehouses of knowledge about the way of life in the north. They kept us informed of activities in the area. In the early spring I made arrangements with the Factor of the Hudson's Bay Company Store to hire a native family to help us at the Seal River camp. The family then travelled up the coast in their freighter canoe and set up their own camp just a short distance from ours.

When we hired a native guide, it was understood that he would arrive with his wife and his children. One of the first families we hired was the Naphash family from the Fort George area. Their son, Harry, began working at our Seal River camp with his father when he was just thirteen years old and spent several summers with us. During that time, he observed the ways of outfitting and later became a tourist liaison officer for the federal government, arranging fishing and hunting trips. When our northern camps in the Belchers and Long Island began operation, Harry was instrumental in finding guides to work at them.

The native guides arrived in our camp early every morning and escorted the guests on short trips to the upper rapids or out on the lake for lake trout fishing. The highlight of the week for most of the guests was an eight-mile trip to the coast in a freighter canoe to catch the trout as they began their migration up the river. There was also a shallow lake near the coast where we could land the aircraft, then our native guides would take the guests up the coast in their long canoes. The inter-coastal trip was a sight-seeing extravaganza as well as a wonderful new fishing experience.

In the summer of 1959 I flew a group from Kalamazoo, Michigan, headed by Clifford Willis, the Vice-President of Sales at the Shakespeare Company, to the Seal River camp. All the members of the group were expert fly fishermen who had fished for years in the prime trout streams in North America. They put on a demonstration of their fly fishing skill on several evenings. One of them would place a small plastic circle in a pool about sixty feet from shore and then they competed to see who could land a fly in the circle. The native guides from Fort George, who rarely fished with poles, were amazed at their accuracy and such incredible displays of skill.

One of the guests who was an accomplished archer brought along some of his modern archery equipment. None of the native guides had ever used bows, although one of them could remember watching his grandfather use one. The guest showed the native lads how to use

Cliff Willis fishing near the Seal River

the bow and set up a target for them. Without any practice, the first lad put three arrows close to the centre of the target. This was astonishing because several of us had tried to use the bow, but none of us could get anywhere near the target. The other native guides also tried the bow and in a short time they were all shooting nearly as well as the guest who had spent years perfecting his skill. Even though the native men had been using guns for years, they were still strong enough to easily put a hundred pounds of pressure on the bow.

The trips to the Seal River attracted all kinds of fishing enthusiasts and sportsmen. Joe Brooks, an outdoor writer, who had made the trip with Clifford Willis in 1959, wrote an article for *Outdoor Life* magazine about fishing the Seal River. This sparked many inquiries.

In 1960 we were officially recognized as tourist outfitters in Quebec, with a Land Use Permit at the Seal River. This allowed us to offer better services with our own camping equipment and staff. For ten weeks we flew guests on one-week trips from Sunday to Sunday; as one group flew up, another would fly out.

The summer of 1960 was a most unusual one for weather. Because the ice didn't completely melt in James Bay until August, there were all kinds of weather disturbances with the warm air over the cold ice. Ice packs moved down from Hudson Bay until the end of July and visibility was reduced to two miles with a five hundred-foot ceiling. We made many friends along the coast in Paint Hills and Eastmain because we had to stop so often to wait for the weather. It wasn't unusual that summer to spend a day and a half flying up and the same length of time flying back. Despite the weather, the fishing was tremendous and that was the most important thing for the guests.

THE EAST COAST VS. THE WEST COAST

Since I have fished extensively on the east coast of Hudson Bay in the province of Quebec, as well as the west coast in the province of Ontario, I am often asked to recommend a specific fishing location for speckled trout fishermen. This is a difficult request because of the variety of fishing and scenery on both sides. Some fishermen prefer to fish in the wooded areas of the Seal River in Quebec or the Sutton River in Ontario while others are willing to forgo the trees and camp on the barren lands, such as the Brandt River in Ontario.

Several members of the Yukon Club from Saginaw, Michigan had the good fortune to experience trout fishing on both the west and east coast of Hudson Bay. They made four trips with us, two to the east coast in northern Quebec and two to the west coast in northern Ontario.

In the summer of 1969 we flew eighteen of them north to Great Whale River in our DC-3 and then transported them in groups of six to three different locations. One group went to the Belcher Islands to fish for Arctic char, another group camped at Noname Lake (part of the Seal River), and the third group stayed at our goose camp on Long Island, and we flew them across to the fishing in the Seal River every day.

Everyone was happy with the fishing, but after one night of camping on the mainland and encountering an onslaught of bugs, the campers at Noname Lake elected to join their colleagues on Long Island where they had the comfort of cabins and relatively few insects to pester them. They dismantled their tents and stashed them in the bush, just in case the weather didn't permit a return flight to Long Island.

The main advantage of the trout fishing in areas such as the Seal River is that there are numerous deep lakes along the river systems where an aircraft can safely land. The lakes are often full of lake trout. The fishermen can usually walk a short distance to a set of rapids where they can fish for speckled trout. Most of the rivers have continuous fishing from the mouth up to a hundred miles or so inland, with places to land an aircraft every two or three miles.

The Seal River system is one of my favourite places to fish along the east coast. It offers a large number of trout in a variety of locations. From our camp at Ominuk Lake, the guests could fish the rapids where the lake discharged into the river. They could fish for lake trout and northern pike in the lake as well. Most of the guests also enjoyed the experience of travelling down to the coast to fish at the mouth of the river, where it empties into Hudson Bay. Once I found Noname Lake, we used this location regularly. Many guests opted to camp there in tents. There are quite a few little creeks and rivers within five or ten miles, and periodically to vary the fishing, we could fly over to other fishing holes.

One isolated hole, that I visited only once or twice a year, is an offshoot of the Little Salmon River. Very few people would dare to attempt a landing in this small lake since it has many rocks and sand bars. I've had to give explicit instructions to my pilots whenever I have asked them to land in this location. Because the pilot needs to secure the aircraft on a rocky beach, many inexperienced pilots are wary.

A large pool, about a hundred yards in diameter, with depths ranging from six to twelve feet, is created where the lake empties into the river. This is where I have seen the largest trout on the east coast. The pool is big enough to hold between twenty-five and forty big trout: speckled trout, lake trout and Arctic char. Everyone that I accompanied into the pool was amazed at the size of the trout cruising around in the crystal clear water. The fish were easily spooked so we encouraged fly fishing on barbless hooks. Most of the fishermen were happy just to catch and release them. A few took one big fish home.

The main disadvantage to trout fishing anywhere in northern Quebec or northern Ontario is the flies. When the warm weather brings out the flies, the trout will feed on them and the fishing can improve, but it can be a most annoying experience for the fishermen. Most ardent trout fishermen that I have known can withstand the bugs for quite a long time. Some will even succumb to wearing head nets while fishing. Eventually, however, the constant battle becomes tedious for all.

The same summer, 1969, that the Yukon Club were fishing on the east coast, we flew Howard Shelley north to the Brandt River with a TV crew. His subsequent show on "Michigan Outdoors" aroused the interest of some members of the Yukon Club who wrote to the Department of Lands and Forests inquiring about a trip to the Brandt River. The group received the information they needed to fly their own DC-3 aircraft to an old Mid-Canada Line site (Site 415). They arranged with me to transport them by floatplane from the landing strip to the Brandt River.

Twenty-three members of the group, accompanied by two native guides from Timmins, camped along the Brandt for several days. The weather was exceptionally warm at that time and the bugs came out. But the fishing was spectacular. One of the guides took a 16mm movie of twenty-three club members lined up on the shore of the Brandt. They all cast and each of them had

a trout on their line on the first cast. The movie was later shown on an outdoor television show in the Saginaw area. Even though the men all enjoyed the fishing on the Brandt, by the end of their week, they were all hoping for some cool northwest winds to blow away the flies.

The weather on the Brandt, like most of the rivers in the region, is quite changeable. If the wind is blowing from the northwest, the fog rolls in from Hudson Bay and temperatures hover around freezing. If the wind is blowing from the south west, the temperature is 80°F but then the flies come out and drive you crazy. There is no place to hide from them. The fishing is good regardless of the weather; however, it is far more pleasant to fish when there is a cool breeze to blow away the bugs.

For many members of the Yukon Club, it was their first experience trout fishing in the barren lands. When there are no trees along the river banks, it is much easier to get from one pool to another. The abundance of wildlife, especially the caribou and the geese, was a wonderful distraction and many of the fishermen spent hours photographing and hiking along the river bank to the mouth of the river at Hudson Bay.

The following year the group returned to the Quebec side and flew their DC-3 into Great Whale River (Kuujjuarapik). Our pilot, Bob Beaulac, then transported them in a Beech 18 on floats 150 miles inland to a small lake, Moulet Lake, near the Little Whale River. Marcel Vignault, who was an officer with the Quebec Provincial Police in Great Whale River and an avid fisherman, joined them as a guide.

The guests hiked about a half a mile on a trail to the Little Whale River and waded into the stream to catch speckled trout. There weren't as many trout as they had encountered along the Seal River and Noname Lake two years earlier. What they caught was in the four-to-five pound range, rather than the two-to-three pound range.

Before the Yukon Club arrived at Moulet Lake, we had flown in two 14-foot aluminum boats and two 9-hp motors so they could enjoy the lake trout fishing when they tired of fishing for the speckles in the stream. I had flown several trips into the area in the past, including Quebec government officials who were doing hydro surveys. In fact, they had built a small cabin for the crews and we took advantage of it as a cooking area for the Yukon Club.

The landscape in the Moulet Lake area is partially barren, with just a few low trees and bushes. Like the Brandt River, there was a herd of caribou that grazed near the river bank. Their curiosity nudged them closer and closer to the bank to get a glimpse of the fishermen.

This area, where the Yukon Club had delighted in such tremendous fishing, is now at the centre of a controversial proposal for a huge hydroelectric power facility. If the proposal gets the green light, the area will be completely underwater. A three-mile lake will need to be created as part of the project. The native people in the area, in particular, the Crees, have been lobbying against the construction of the project since it was proposed. They foresee it as the end of wildlife in the area.

On their last trip with us, we flew eight members of the Yukon Club from our airbase in Hawk Junction to the Chookomolin's camp on Sutton/Hawley Lake in northern Ontario. They canoed down the Sutton River with the Chookomolins as guides. Again they enjoyed the spectacular speckled trout fishing that is so famous in the Canadian north. The Chookomolin families (now there are two of them) run an excellent outfitting service. Their trips down the Sutton River have gained them a fine reputation. The only disadvantage is that their fishing season is restricted to the month of August, when the trout start their migration up the river. The guests also have to enjoy spending considerable time in a canoe because this is the only way to travel down the river. The landscape becomes barren just a few miles from the coast.

The next winter the building that housed the Yukon Club burned down and the group suspended their northern trips. Occasionally we hear from members of the group. In the summer of 1992 one of their children brought some of his father's old photographs to show my son, John, at his airbase in Chapleau.

Today the fishing on the Brandt River is restricted to those who have Aircraft Landing Permits. Just a few private individuals and air services make the flight regularly because of the limited number of safe landing places for a seaplane. In 1975, I made my last trip to Sutton/Hawley Lake and the Brandt River. Since then I have made yearly trips to fish the rivers along the east coast in the province of Quebec.

A HUDSON BAY SAFARI

In 1964, as members of the Fin, Fur and Feather Club (a group of outfitters that co-operated with Air Canada to offer packaged wilderness trips), we organized a Hudson Bay safari for four fishermen from New York. They flew on Air Canada to Timmins, Ontario where we picked them up and transported them to our airbase at Ivanhoe Lake.

After spending the night at the North Miami Lodge, Dave McConnell and I flew them north in the Norseman. Since the guests wanted a variety of fishing experiences, our only planned destination was our camp on the Seal River, where they had their initial taste of speckled trout fishing. From there we headed further north to sample what the other rivers had to offer.

Our sole limitation was the availability of fuel for the aircraft. While I was refueling the aircraft at Great Whale River (Kuujjuarapik), a Wheeler Airlines pilot described some incredible fishing in the Richmond Gulf area. Within a few hours we landed at Richmond Gulf and set up our camp on the north river.

The guests were experienced campers who brought along all their own camping equipment and food. In fact, their camping equipment was so modern and their skill at using it was so impressive that

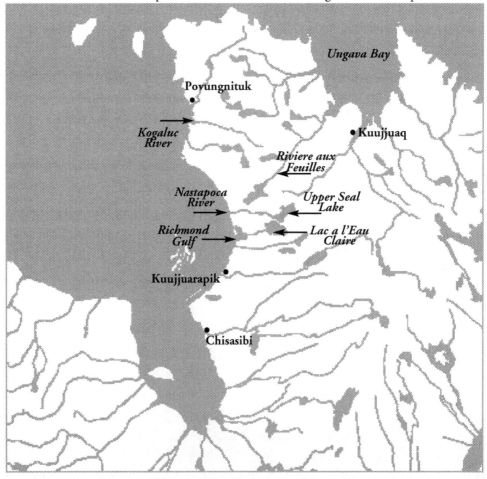

Dave and I learned a few lessons from them. We only caught about a dozen trout that weighed between three and six pounds. The following day we flew further north to the Nastapoca River. We caught a few fish in three or four sets of rapids, but we weren't satisfied—we knew there were more fish waiting for us somewhere.

As we were fishing the river, we met a survey group from Wheeler Airlines. The pilot, Gerry Deluce, told us that he had just returned from the Little Whale River where they had caught a tremendous number of speckled trout. We decided to head inland another hundred miles, towards Upper Seal Lake. Since we were able to purchase gasoline from the survey crew, we could prolong our exploration in the area.

Our trip inland proved worthwhile. The guests spent a day catching and releasing more three-pound speckles than they could imagine. Once they had their fill of trout fishing, they looked forward to the next fishing adventure.

We returned to the coast and landed at a widening of the Nastapoca River, about two miles from Hudson Bay, where there was a sandy beach. We camped there that night. The next morning we walked overland to fish in the salt water of the bay. A seven- or eight-foot tide usually flows into the river. Fortunately our arrival coincided with high tide so the fish were moving up the river.

When we arrived, there were about fifty beluga whales at the mouth of the river, feeding on cod. It was a good sign that there were plenty of fish. It turned out to be the most spectacular day of the entire trip. We caught Arctic char, speckled trout, lake trout and cod—all in the same waters. The guests were so enthralled with the variety of fishing, they had a hard time deciding which type of fish they wanted.

To catch the cod we took off our lures, put some bait fish on a hook, and cast out about twenty feet. They were just as delicious to eat as the speckles and the char. Late that day, we returned to Great Whale River where we took on more fuel. Then we headed south to spend the night in Fort George (Chisasibi).

This trip was a true northern adventure for everyone. I discovered a few new fishing spots and the guests had their first taste of trout fishing in the barren lands. Over the next winter, they continued to write to me, expressing their determination to have another taste of fishing in such wild settings. Two years later the same group of adventurers made another trip north to fish more of the rivers. This time Chuck Ellsworth and I headed north from Ivanhoe Lake with four fishermen in two aircraft, a Cessna 180 and a Beaver.

Over the many years of flying in the north, I had heard about the great fishing on the Kogaluc River, south of Povungnituk, where the Abitibi Pulp and Paper Company had established a camp. We flew to this area north of Great Whale River and set up our tent camp on the Kogaluc River, one set of rapids above the Abitibi camp.

The fishing for Arctic char and trout was even better than the stories that led me there. We spent two days catching speckles that averaged five pounds. We were so pleased with the fishing that we could hardly imagine that we would find anything that surpassed it. But our purpose was adventure, so we headed east. We fished several rivers that flow west into Ungava Bay, including Riviere aux Feuilles. We caught Atlantic salmon as well as all kinds of speckled trout in these rivers, sixty miles inland. We also flew into the Crater Lake area and fished for lake trout in the clear water. Wherever we set up a camp, we encountered herds of caribou that wandered into our site out of curiosity.

Wherever there are caribou, there are black flies. We encountered such an onslaught of flies that one of the guests developed an allergic reaction. His extremities swelled so much that we had to fly him back to Great Whale River for medical treatment. The hospital staff had become accustomed to treating this problem because there were many non-native people working nearby on the hydroelectric power plants that required the same attention. The native people must have an inherent immunity to fly bites. They never seem to be bothered by them.

Our journey was interrupted several times by deteriorating weather conditions, which forced us to land on a lake and wait. However, we always took advantage of the situation and explored the terrain for wildlife, including fish. Some of our best fishing experiences occurred when we landed because of bad weather.

Our eastbound trek took us as far as Fort Chimo (Kuujjuaq), where the guests delighted in photographing the native people and their village. We took on fuel, then headed southwest to Great Whale River (Kuujjuarapik) to rendezvous with our recovered guest.

As we passed over Lac a L'Eau Claire, we could see the landscape blackened by a huge colony of Canada geese that were nesting and feeding on the wild berries. It was just one of the many experiences that made the trip a totally northern encounter. The finale was a morning of trout fishing in the rapids at the Seal River before heading back to Timmins. The guests returned to New York with a few fish, some photographs and memories that would last a lifetime.

THE BELCHER ISLANDS, NWT

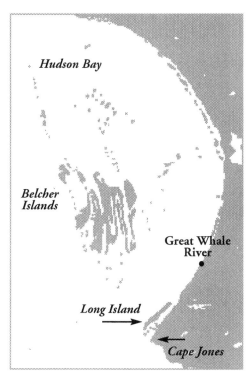

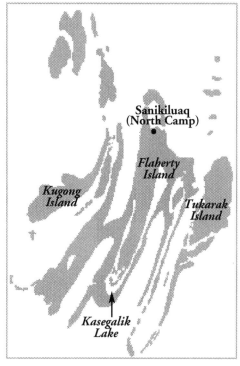

When I left the RCAF in 1953 and established an air service in Chapleau, Ontario, I immediately applied to the federal government to procure an outpost site on Great Bear Lake. While in the military, I had become acquainted with an Air Vice-Marshall, Hugh Campbell, who was one of my regular passengers. With the attention of Mr. Campbell, we received permission to build a lodge in 1961. However, that summer we were busy fighting fires and I wasn't able to fly to Great Bear Lake to choose a site. The governing agency was concerned about this, and the commissioner suggested that we choose a site that was closer to our airbase in Chapleau. He sent me a map of the Belcher Islands and a brief description of the Arctic char fishing.

The Belcher Islands are a group of long, thin volcanic islands which zig-zag over about five thousand square miles of sea in the southeastern portion of Hudson Bay. Even though they are located just sixty miles off the Quebec coast, they are part of the Northwest Territories.

The rolling rocky terrain is treeless, with only enough topsoil to support low-growing shrubs. The islands are dotted with many lakes and ponds which provide freshwater for the wildlife and the small community of native people. The largest fresh water lake, Kasegalik Lake, is nearly seventy miles long and forms a U-shape in the middle of Flaherty Island (named after Robert Flaherty, a British explorer who charted the islands in 1914). The native people called the lake "Kasegalik" after the rare, freshwater black seal that is found there.

I visited an Inuit village on Kasegalik Lake in the winter of 1962. The native

Kasegalik River on the Belcher Islands, NWT

people reassured me that the Arctic char fishing was spectacular. Before we built a lodge, I wanted to check out the fishing myself and choose an appropriate site. The following season I decided to fly in just two groups of fishermen with camping equipment.

In early July, I made a trip north to the Belcher Islands from the Seal River camp with Theo Paulishak, Bob Vandorick, his son, and two other fishermen from Scranton, Pennsylvania. Dave McConnell and I were piloting two aircraft, a Norseman and a Cessna 180. As soon as we approached the coast, we were stopped by fog. We turned around, but by then the fog had moved in to our Seal River camp as well. Good luck was with us. We found a lake that was clear, so we landed and taxied up to a beach.

It isn't uncommon to be grounded because of bad weather in the north country. The only way to enjoy the experience is to explore the countryside. I knew that the creek flowing into the lake had to have speckled trout in it because it was all part of the Seal River. Four of us walked a quarter of a mile to the creek. When we

arrived at a pool, we were dumbfounded by what we saw.

There were so many trout swimming in the small pool that it looked like a commercially stocked pond. We had hit upon a jackpot! We fished for a few hours and barely made a dent on the pool. We called it Noname Lake because it didn't have a name on any map. We managed to keep the location of the lake a secret for about four years—until the construction crews that were working on the hydroelectric power project, La Grande, found it. Then the fishing deteriorated.

The fog lifted around the middle of the afternoon at Noname Lake. The sun came out and there wasn't a cloud in the sky. We took off for the Belchers around 3:00 P.M. and landed on Kasegalik Lake, where the Kasegalik River flows out. We set up our tents, and then late that afternoon we took a walk up to the first rapids.

With light spinning tackle and three-inch red-and-white daredevils, we each caught several char that weighed between two and five pounds. The fish were not particularly shy. In fact, when we located them, the action was fast and furious. We found that a char would swim after a lure and snatch it, even as we lifted it from the water. Few other fish strike at a flashing lure with more enthusiasm.

The Arctic char, a member of the salmon family, is similar in appearance to a large brook trout, but without the wave-like marking on its back. The char has a forked tail and is more rounded than the brook trout. The char descend from the inland lakes to the sea during late spring. They begin their return trip in July. When they return to the rivers from the salt water, their colouring is almost entirely silver; it gradually changes to olive green on the dorsal surface, with bright orange spots on the sides, and a pinkish-red belly.

Even though we caught the greatest number of fish on spinning tackle, we found that the char spooked easily with lures. The pools needed to be rotated often. When we switched to streamer flies, which we weighed down and allowed to sink very close to the bottom, we caught some bigger fish in the eight- and-ten pound class. Since there are no trees to worry about, it is relatively easy to maneuver in such a way that the wind carries the fly to the fish, even in the high winds. The real worry is keeping your footing. The rocky river banks are quite slippery.

During our three days of fishing, we found that the fish form schools in the fast shallow water, near the mouths of tributaries or in the riffles near the gravel bars where the water is between four and eight feet deep. Even in the wildest of weather, the streams and rivers were crystal clear. We could usually see to the bottom of the stream and watch as the char approached the lure. If we didn't like the size of the char, we could jerk the lure away before it grabbed it. The water was so clear in the streams that it bubbled up like champagne and tasted as fresh and sparkling as spring rain.

The area around our campsite was full of wildlife—a flock of Canada geese were waddling around in their molting stage, eating the berries and caring for their young ones; some snowy owls were nesting up on the rocks which rise about a hundred feet above the gorge, where the river flows out of Kasegalik Lake.

I spent a lot of time hiking in the area in search of a good location to build our lodge. I finally settled on a site along the Kasegalik River, about a mile from the small Inuit village. Before I left I made arrangements with the native people to unload our building materials from the Hudson's Bay Company barge that would dock at their village in the fall.

Theo Paulishak with an Arctic char on the Belcher Islands

A SNOWMOBILE AND A POLAR BEAR CUB

When I was ready to make another trip north to the Belcher Islands in April 1963, I called my good friend Paul Pepoy in Cleveland and asked him if he was interested in a northern adventure. Paul, who was always up for something out of the ordinary, eagerly agreed to accompany me. He arrived in Chapleau within a week.

I wanted to bring a snowmobile to the Inuit on the Belcher Islands so they could transport our building materials from their camp to the site I had chosen to build the new fishing camp. The Inuit could have used their dog sleds to transport the materials, but that would have been a tedious process. Once the snowmobile was partly dismantled, I could fit it into the Cessna 180, along with some emergency equipment and one passenger.

The weather was very cold and clear on April 8th when we departed from Chapleau. But by the time we arrived in Kapuskasing, we were in the middle of a snowstorm. Two days later, we were still in Kapuskasing waiting for the weather to clear. On the third day we took off from Remi Lake and decided to see how far we could fly up the Kapuskasing River, even though visibility was less than half a mile. We were just about to turn around, when suddenly, it was as if a door had opened up. There we were in a new world of sunny blue skies. The glare seemed incredibly intense to us because we hadn't seen the sun in a few days. When we looked back, we could see the storm behind us, like a huge white wall. We couldn't believe our good fortune. We didn't question it; we just kept on flying north and we arrived in Moosonee two hours later.

The further north we flew, the warmer it got; as we flew over Paint Hills the temperature was 45°F at three thousand feet. This unusually warm weather was threatening to make landing difficult, since we were flying with skis only. When we arrived in Great Whale River, my concern was well founded. I could see about a foot of water on top of the ice. I circled the area and finally found a place near shore where I could land. Then I taxied through the water over the ice and maneuvered the aircraft up a big sand bar that was above the high tide.

We planned to spend just one night in Great Whale, but when we arrived, it was ptarmigan hunting season and many of the native men had just come in from a day of hunting. The flocks of ptarmigan passed through the village on their way north to their nesting areas, after spending the winter feeding in the forested regions further south as far as Val D'Or, Quebec. When the flocks fly north, they pass through Great Whale River in the thousands.

The native people call these white birds the "ghosts of the Arctic" because they quietly appear out of the white sky and then disappear just as quietly. I had hunted ptarmigan on a few occasions, in Manitoba and on Lac de la Hutte Sauvage in Northern Quebec, but I had never seen them in such great numbers. We couldn't resist the temptation to spend a day hunting in the hills around Great Whale River.

The next day, neither Paul nor I could conceal our amazement at the number of ptarmigan that the native men shot. In one blind, the empty shotgun shells were up over our ankles. Since the birds only pass through the village twice a year, the native people need to take advantage of the situation. They shoot as many as they can and salt them down in ten-gallon drums. That

Inspecting the new snowmobile on the Belchers

day both Paul and I had more than our fill of shooting ptarmigan; after a few hours, just holding the gun was tiring. In the evening we feasted on some of the tasty birds with our native friends. The dark meat was succulent and flavourfully seasoned with a little vegetable broth. Paul was an accomplished taxidermist so he took several birds home and mounted them; I kept one of the mounted birds in my Chapleau office for many years.

The following day the unusually warm weather continued as we flew to the Belcher Islands to unload the snowmobile. We hadn't come prepared for warm weather, but Paul and I stripped down to our undershirts in the 70°F weather. The Inuit were fascinated by this new machine. Within an hour we had it reassembled and they were experimenting with their new toy. Even though these machines are not part of their traditional culture, they helped us reassemble it as if they worked on them daily. In one sense they had a childlike attitude to the machine—they laughed and played with it like kids on Christmas day, but they also seemed to have a respect for it that superseded their fascination.

Our arrival in the Inuit village coincided with a visit from the crew of an RCAF aircraft. They had landed at the village to tag a polar bear which the native men had shot. When the Inuit shot the polar bear, they were unaware that it had two cubs. Shortly after the hunters brought the dead bear and the two cubs into the village, their Husky dogs killed one of the cubs. One of the RCMP officers asked us to fly out the remaining cub because they didn't have room on board their aircraft. They were on their way to Frobisher Bay and the officer knew the remaining cub would suffer the same demise if it was left at the Inuit camp. I agreed to take the bear cub because I figured we could get it on a scheduled flight south, where it would be taken care of and shipped to a zoo.

The Inuit rarely shoot a polar bear unless it poses some threat to their camp. They will shoot one if they have a market to buy the skin. They could trade a polar bear skin at the Hudson's Bay Company Store for any number of articles from clothing and blankets, to metal tools and canned food. When Paul and I expressed interest in the skin, the owner offered to sell it to us directly. We eagerly agreed and put the skin on board the aircraft with the

Polar bear cub on the Belchers

little cub.

One of the Inuit boys put a dog collar on the cub and we tied it down in the rear cabin of the aircraft with two chains to prevent it from coming forward into the cockpit. The cub wasn't fond of being confined in an airplane. It expressed its dissatisfaction by yelping and jumping around as far as the chains would allow it. The racket was so distracting that Paul spread out the mother bear's hide in the back of the plane to see if the little bear would find something familiar to distract it. The cub put its head on the mother's hide and finally settled down.

The bear was very frisky and behaved like a puppy, except that it was much stronger and could bite quite hard. We spent our first night with the cub in Great Whale River at the home of an Englishman who worked for the Department of Northern Affairs. His wife was an Inuit from the Belcher Islands. By a stroke of good luck, she knew how to handle a bear cub. Within minutes of removing the chains, she had the cub behaving like a trained house dog. It would follow her around the kitchen and jump up and sit with her on the sofa. When it misbehaved she would slap it and it would roll over. Paul and I couldn't believe this. Whenever we had tried to discipline it, it had growled at us or bitten us. We got so many nips and bites that we began to handle it with thick leather gloves.

It was our plan to leave the cub in Great Whale River, to be flown south by an Austin Airways DC-3. But when the aircraft was delayed, we were forced to take it further south to Moosonee. There was still no airplane or anyone willing to take the cub from us in Moosonee, so we continued south with our unusual cargo.

Soon after we arrived in Chapleau, I was desperate to find a home for the bear cub. Even though it looked cute and cuddly, it was not a typical house pet that you trusted. My children were enamoured with it, but we couldn't allow them to get too close to it. For a few days we kept it in a boathouse and fed it canned sardines. Then we decided to call for help.

Esher Ritchie and his sons, who ran their own bear hunting camp in the Chapleau area, were knowledgeable about the ways of bears. To my delight, they agreed to take the cub. When one of the sons came to our airbase to pick up the cub, he unchained it, threw it in the front of his half-ton truck and drove away—the bear cub was sitting on the seat with its two front paws on the dash board. That was the last I saw of the cub. The Ritchie family cared for it for a month or so before it was taken to a zoo in Barrie, Ontario.

Paul had the mother's hide tanned, and then he put a head mount on it. The shiny, white bearskin decorated the living room of our family home for twenty-five years before we gave it to our old friend, Fritz Slifcak.

Joan and our daughter Jane with the polar bear cub in Chapleau

SOAPSTONE CARVINGS AND SEAL HUNTS

Native soapstone carver on the Belcher Islands

The native people on the Belcher Islands were originally nomadic hunters who travelled around the islands in search of seals, walruses and whales. They hunted from kayaks, whaleboats and dog sleds. They lived in ice huts during the winter months and tents fashioned from animal hides during the brief summer. When the Hudson's Bay Company established a post on the islands, they traded their furs for food items, cloth and metal tools.

Once large quantities of iron-bearing rocks were discovered on the islands, several contingents of prospectors and engineers arrived to determine if it was worth mining. Nothing permanent came of these explorations. The native people had little use for the iron deposits, but they found a soft talc-serpentine stone on Tukarak Island that was easy to shape with tools.

This magnesium silicate stone was the product of hot silica-rich rock (from volcanic eruptions) forcing its way through magnesium-bearing limestone. The native sculptors discovered that they could take advantage of the variations of colour in the stone. Their sculptures of birds, seals and walruses became their most cherished trading item.

The year we built our camp on the Belchers, the Inuit began to bring their soapstone carvings to our camp to sell to the guests. At the time there were about a hundred native people living less than a mile away at the South Camp. Many of them were accomplished soapstone carvers. When a new group of guests arrived in camp, the carvers would arrive with their sculptures to begin bartering.

The Tukarak Island quarry, one of the

largest soapstone quarries in the Arctic, is about twenty miles from the South Camp. The Inuit could reach it by boat, although, if the ocean was rough, it could be a prolonged and sometimes treacherous journey. During our first summer at our new camp, I flew a couple of carvers to the quarry in the Beech 18. We picked up a whole ton of soapstone in about four hours. The Inuit men were so thrilled with their trip, they gave me half-a-dozen beautiful carvings for my services.

Some of the families worked as a team to create sculptures, each member having a specific role in the completion of a product. First the shape was roughly cut from a block of rock with an axe or saw. A rasp or knife was used to define the shape. Steel wool and sandpaper further refined the image. Then the sculpture was rubbed with an oiled cloth to bring out the natural luster and colouration of the stone. Sometimes small pieces of carved ivory or wood were attached to embellish a walrus or kayak.

The Inuit on the Belcher Islands are famous for their bird carvings. They carve seals and walruses as well, but mostly they carve Arctic birds. It was only natural that our guests would fall in love with these exquisite carvings. In the years before the Co-op, the Inuit sold them to our guests for the same price they would get from the Hudson's Bay Company, about ten dollars per carving. There were some bigger more expensive ones, but most of them were in that range. The first year the Inuit sold about $20,000 worth of carvings to our guests. The following two years, we advised our guests that they would be able to buy carvings and the Inuit sold between $20,000 and $30,000 worth of carvings.

By the fourth year the federal government decided to move the Inuit at the South Camp to the North Camp (Sanikiluaq), in the northern section of the Flaherty Island. The village was completely vacated; the school was dismantled and flown out, along with the generators. All the other buildings were left as they had been for years. It became an Arctic ghost town.

When the Inuit from the South Camp settled in the North Camp, the government appointed a manager to run a Co-op for them to sell their soapstone carvings to the public. The Inuit were still paid the same amount for their carvings that they had been getting from our guests, but the Co-op would sell them for four times the price. Now a ten dollar carving would cost forty dollars and the guests didn't have the pleasure of buying it directly from the carver. The Inuit didn't seem to like the new arrangement either. They would often wait for several months to get their share of the profits.

The first year after their move to the North Camp, some of the Inuit men made the four-day boat trip back to the South Camp to fish for char. They picked up some soapstone at the quarry along their way. Then they spent a few weeks carving in their old village. Again they came up to our camp in the evenings and sold their carvings directly to the guests. We suspect the Co-op put further restrictions on the sale of their carvings because we didn't see them much after that year. From then on, our guests could only buy carvings from the larger Co-ops in Great Whale River.

When the native people still lived at the South Camp, several groups of fishermen made arrangements with them for seal and whale hunting, as well as goose and duck hunting in early September. In the fall of 1966 one of these excursions became the subject of a story in the *Buffalo Courier-Express*. Outdoor writer Joe Glaser, and two other men in his group, accompanied Lucassie and Jonassie, two native hunters, on a tour of the outer islands. The guests had never seen geese and ducks in such numbers and easily brought home several for the cooking pot. But birds weren't their only quarry.

The native hunters gave them the thrill of a lifetime, as they chased a square-flipper seal for over an hour. These big-headed seals weigh about eight hundred pounds. The native people consider them a real challenge to hunt. They shoot the animal with a 12-gauge shotgun; then they spear it with a homemade harpoon made of whale hide. A float made of inflated seal skin is attached to the line to prevent the mammal from sinking once it is killed.

On the same trip they garnered another smaller seal and a 1200-pound white whale (beluga). The guests were put to work helping the native men haul the booty to shore where they cut up the mammals and reloaded them into the canoe. When they returned to the South Camp the Inuit began the arduous process of sorting out all the parts of the seals and whale. Both the Inuit and their dogs consume the edible meat, while the blubber is used in their oil lamps and cooking stoves. The pelts, which do not become articles of clothing, such as mukluks, gloves and skin pants, are sold to the Hudson's Bay Company Store.

Few sportsmen are rewarded with the opportunity to spend a day with native men who hunt as their livelihood. The simple lifestyle of the native people is now endangered as governments subsidize their very existence. It's no longer necessary for many of the native people to hunt the seals and whales when they are given food and clothing as part of their allowance. The power they once had as masters of their own destiny is quickly eroding. Many have substituted their own adventures on the open water with Hollywood adventures on satellite television.

Some guests watch as Inuit hunters clean a beluga

LONG ISLAND, NWT

I first witnessed the remarkable proliferation of geese on Long Island while I was in the RCAF, flying some government surveyors around Cape Jones. This island, just seven miles off the Quebec coast, is the nesting grounds for thousands of Canada geese (honkers). It is also the first landing area for huge flocks of blues and snows as they migrate south. The flocks begin to arrive in September to feed and rest before continuing their migration to their next resting area, at the southern end of James Bay.

After we built our fishing camp on the Belcher Islands, I frequently flew over the island on the way to our camp on the Seal River. Again and again, I marveled at the incredible geese population. When the federal government sold us a piece of property on Long Island, NWT in 1963, they had given us a time limit to build our lodge. By 1967 they were anxious to see some kind of progress on the camp.

The site I chose in the middle of the thirty-five-mile island is protected from the cold Arctic winds by a one-hundred-foot rock wall. It is as close to the hunting as possible; in fact, once the camp was built the geese would often wander right up to the cabins. A well-sheltered bay offers protection to the seaplanes and is regularly visited by seals, walruses and white whales. From the site, you can look across the sound to hills that rise to a height of five and six-hundred feet on the mainland of Quebec, five miles away. There is often a blue tinge on the hills that gives them a mystical appearance.

We purchased a DC-3 from the Hollinger Mines Iron Ore Company of Canada to fly the material up there as quickly as possible. We hired a construction crew from Timmins, as well as a crew

of workers from Great Whale River. Lumber companies in Chapleau and Timmins supplied us with enough lumber to construct three cabins. Each measured approximately twenty feet by thirty-six feet.

As soon as the ice melted in the sound in the spring of 1968, we flew in the first loads to Cape Jones, a 5000-foot gravel airstrip constructed during the Mid-Canada line project. The DC-3 could transport about six thousand pounds of material on each trip from the Timmins airport to Cape Jones. The materials were then hauled by a hand-pulled trailer to a nearby lake. Our pilot, Don Popert, and his crew loaded them into a Beech 18 on floats that was equipped with cargo doors. The materials were flown to the campsite at Long Island and another team of workers carried them up the hill.

The crews worked steadily from the beginning of July until the beginning of September to complete the three cabins. One cabin served as the kitchen and dining area, another served as staff accommodations, and the largest one accommodated eight to twelve guests. Over the summer we hired quite a few native people to work on the completion of the cabins. They arrived from Great Whale River in their own boats. Whenever there was a lull in the work, they went out in their boats to hunt the geese that nested on the island.

I was not present at the camp during the last month of construction so was unaware of their activity. The carpenters from Timmins, who were supervising the construction of the camp, also weren't aware that the native people were killing the geese while they couldn't fly in their molting stage. By September 1st, when the

Unloading the DC-3 at Cape Jones

first guests arrived, there were no geese left on the island. We had to wait about ten days until some new flocks arrived from the north to feed on their way south.

It was a first season to remember! After September 12th, a heat wave moved into the area. The temperature hovered around 80°F for about two weeks. Normally geese rest on the water where they are protected from the animals and move onto land once a day to feed. They rarely eat when it's hot. For days the geese just sat out on the ocean, about two or three miles from the camp. In an entire month of hunting, about fifty guests shot only a hundred geese. Quite a few of our guests were also avid fishermen, so we offered them the experience of speckled trout fishing on the Seal River and Noname Lake, and excellent sea trout fishing on the Burton River.

The Burton River widens into estuaries at its mouth on Hudson Bay. The river, which is about three hundred yards wide a mile inland, branches into two smaller rivers, each about fifty yards wide with a V-shaped island separating them. At low tide, when there is only about a foot of water, you can wade on the sand bars for a quarter of a mile. From the first week of

August until the middle of September, thousands of sea trout begin their migration with the tide. They swim up the river about a mile, and then drift back with the out-going tide. They are so plentiful as they move en masse into the river, you can stand on the sand bars with a landing net between your legs and catch three or four of them. But you can only net them when they run up the river. As they descend, the water is too high for wading.

The trout only run for about forty-five minutes so the timing is crucial. As soon as the tide started to rise at our camp on Long Island, we would jump into the boat and be over there in about twenty minutes, hopefully, just as these little silver fish were beginning to move up the river. We anchored the boat in the middle of the river and waded into the water. To increase the speed of our catch, we fished with barbless hooks and just flipped each fish into the waiting boat. In no time, we had enough for a fish fry. The trout are only between 10 and 14 inches long, but they were a perfect size for pan-frying. We cut out the innards and gills with a pair of scissors, rolled them in a little flour, and fried them whole.

Long Island is home to several species

Long Island goose hunting camp, 1975

of northern birds. The terrain is Arctic in nature, with promontories on the island that rise to about a hundred feet. These huge gravel eskers run eight to ten miles along the island. The winds constantly blow across the barren land so there are very few flies on the island to disturb birds or humans. Although there are fox on the island during the winter, most of them move across to the mainland before the ice goes out. Thus the birds have very few predators to disturb them while they are nesting and raising their young. Their only real predators are the humans that visit the island while they are molting.

There are about a dozen shore birds, including Wilson snipe, and many types of snow birds that nest on the island during the brief summer. Arctic grebes proliferate on Long Island. There are numerous flocks of lesser eider ducks, Canada geese and a few flocks of snows and blues that make Long Island their summer home. The birds choose the island for their nesting area because of the abundance of wild Arctic berries. From the first of August until the

15th of September, the berries are so thick, that no matter where you walk, you squash them under your feet. The birds get their fresh water from the countless small lakes that abound on the island. Many of the lakes are only five or six feet deep. Some lakes are deeper and some have only a foot of water. One lake is large enough to produce Arctic char. We built a small cabin on this lake to offer shelter when the high winds forced us to move the aircraft inland.

The blueberries on the island are sought after by both birds and humans. The native women are particularly fond of cooking with them because they have a low sugar content. Since the berries are quite dense, containing very little water, they can be stored easily and used throughout the winter. The same berries also grow along the coast as far south as Eastmain. And there is another sweeter, fatter blueberry that grows on the mainland. Goose berries, a moss-type cranberry, and a low brush blackberry are the favoured delicacies of the geese that visit

Long Island.

Millions of wild Arctic flowers grow on the slopes of the ridges behind the camp. When you fly along the ridges during the summer months, the masses of red, yellow, green and blue flowers form a rainbow of colour, extending for miles and miles along the island. The variety of flowers is phenomenal—from tiny, blue Arctic orchids to plants with five different colours of flowers on a two-foot stem.

One year, Vince Creighton, a retired game officer with the Ministry of Natural Resources, spent the summer on the island and identified many of the flowers. Some of them were so tiny that he needed a magnifying glass to verify their identification. The abundance and variety of flowers provide food for many of the birds that nest on the island. The geese also feed on a type of grain, a wild barley, that grows on some of the sand dunes during the summer months.

During the winter months, Long Island is home to many polar bears. When the winter winds blow snow west across Hudson Bay, it eventually arrives at Long Island. As the winds carry the snow over the ridges, it piles up in depths from one hundred to three hundred feet. Cornices are formed where the wind creates air spaces. Polar bears come from all over to den in these cornices, along the promontories at Long Island. They feed on fish and seals at the south end of Long Island, where a bay is open throughout the winter. Even though most of Hudson Bay is frozen solid seven months of the year, a current of warm water, that runs north-south, maintains a few miles of open water year-round. On occasion, I have flown native hunters from Fort George to a couple of islands just south of Long Island to hunt for polar bears. During the winter months the bear population is so concentrated in the area, hunting them is relatively easy.

By the summer most of the bears have moved off the island to forage in other locations, Only a few remain. The second year of operating the camp, we regularly observed a mother polar bear and her two cubs visit a dump site a quarter mile across the bay where we buried our garbage. Many of the guests enjoyed keeping track of their daily feeding ritual. Despite their value as a tourist attraction, the following year we cleaned up the dump and flew out the garbage. Even though the bears never came to our camp, we didn't want to risk the possibility in the future.

All our guests appreciated the comfort of our well-maintained camp. The sleeping cabin for guests was equipped with two single beds in each bedroom, indoor toilets and showers. The kitchen had a propane refrigerator and stove, as well as an electric refrigerator and a deep freezer that were fueled by a propane generator. We furnished the camp with some beautiful Thibault furniture that we purchased from the mission in Fort George. The first couple of years we were able to leave most of the furniture and supplies in the camp over the winter. Eventually people heard about our well-equipped camp, and we had to transport everything out for the winter. It was impossible for us to protect the camp from looting over the winter months. The law enforcement agencies along the coast were exasperated by the enormity of their territory.

One day at the beginning of the summer season, as I was flying over the camp on my way north to the Belcher Islands, I noticed some of our mattresses on the ground in front of the camp. When I landed, I discovered that someone had just been in the camp and had left quite a mess. They had taken a load of supplies, including our large deep freezer and had left another load outside, presumably to be picked up later.

I loaded the mattresses into the aircraft and whatever else I could find that was possible to move. As I took off over the strait, I noticed a freighter canoe heading out of our camp, loaded down with our deep freezer. What could I do? I didn't have a gun on board the aircraft. I knew whoever was stealing my deep freezer probably had one on his boat. My only consolation was that the freezer had stopped working the previous fall. I was going to have to fly it out for repair anyway. They saved me the trip.

We kept a 24-foot boat with a 50-hp motor at the camp for a few years before it too was spirited away. Then we replaced it with a 14-foot aluminum boat that we could fly in and out at the beginning and the end of the season.

When the native people in Fort George (Chisasibi) found out that I had received a license to build a goose camp on Long Island, they asked the federal government to help them establish their own goose hunting camps. In response to their request, the federal government sponsored four different goose camps at sites that had been used during the construction of the Mid-Canada line near Cape Jones. At the outset, the government hired tourist officers who worked for the Department of Northern Affairs to help the native people administer the camps. Once the native people became competent outfitters, they took over the administration of their own camps.

At first I experienced some tension in my relationship with the new camp owners. It appeared that we were competing for the same tourists. Over the years we all realized that we could help promote goose hunting in the area by sharing our knowledge and expertise. On a few occasions, I was able to help some of the camp owners by flying their guests when their regular flying service was interrupted.

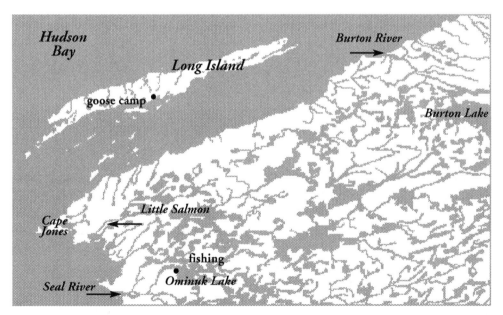

A LONG NIGHT ON LONG ISLAND

Fritz preparing a meal on Long Island

Fritz Slifcak, from Ft. Lauderdale, spent a good part of every September at our goose hunting camp on Long Island. He cooked for the guests and did a little hunting on his own. He mastered at least five different goose recipes and his fresh mussel soup was legendary. There were so many mussels on the island that when the tide went out, we could easily pick enough for a huge pot of soup.

One afternoon Fritz prepared a delicious meal and then informed us that he was going hunting by himself. He planned to leave the camp in a couple of days and wanted one last hunt to carry him over until the next season. He took his gun, a box of ammunition, his knife and a small packsack. We didn't think anything was unusual since he was just going over the hill a mile or so. But when night arrived, Fritz hadn't returned and we all started to wonder what happened to him. His close

friend, Paul Pepoy, began imagining all kinds of bizarre things: maybe he had met a polar bear or maybe he had fallen down the ridge. What we didn't realize was that Fritz didn't have a very keen sense of direction. Ten of us with flashlights attempted to search for Fritz. But the darkness was so heavy, it obscured the rough terrain and the numerous ponds that dot the island. After several mishaps, we were forced to return to the camp without Fritz.

Poor Paul was so worried. What was he going to tell Fritz's wife, Elly? He devised a scheme to help Fritz locate the camp. He wrapped a rag around a mop and soaked the rag in fuel oil. We helped him climb to the top of the hundred-foot rock wall behind the camp where he set the mop on fire. He made huge circles in the air with his torch, hoping that Fritz would be close enough to the camp to see it and use it as a beacon to find his way home. When one torch burned out, several new torches were made and passed up to Paul, who continued to signal for an hour. Despite our efforts, Fritz didn't make it home that night.

Morning arrived, after a sleepless night in camp. Snow squalls had moved in and we couldn't see more than a hundred feet in front of the camp. As soon as the weather cleared, just before noon, we mounted another search. While Paul and I took off in the Beech 18 and thoroughly searched from the air, the others fanned out on the island on foot. But no one found any clue of Fritz.

My concern was mounting. I knew that if we couldn't find Fritz soon, I was going to have to contact Fort George by radio and request help from the government Search and Rescue crew. They probably wouldn't arrive until the next morning though, and one more night outdoors would be very difficult for Fritz. Just as I was about to place the call, one of the hunters rushed into the camp with news that he had sighted someone walking along a ridge about a mile north of the camp. We confirmed with high-powered binoculars that it was Fritz. I knew he must be exhausted from his night alone on the tundra. I filled a thermos with hot coffee, grabbed a few cookies and ran out to meet him.

When we met, he was grinning sheepishly, more than a little embarrassed about his situation. We sat down while he drank the coffee and ate a few cookies to regain his strength before continuing the hike to the camp. By the time he arrived in camp, he was in good spirits and ready to tell us about his adventure.

Apparently he had only gone about half a mile from the camp, found a big boulder that was partially hidden by willows and admired the evening flight of geese. The sights and sounds of the honking geese mesmerized him and before he

knew it, darkness had fallen. When he tried to walk back to camp he couldn't see the familiar signposts in the landscape. He stumbled in one pothole of water after another, and then realized he was lost. He eventually reached the shoreline where he found some driftwood to built himself a fire. But he didn't sleep much because he was anxious to keep his fire going. When the weather cleared in the morning, he saw the aircraft fly over and watched where it landed. Once he had his bearings, he began to walk back to camp.

Paul asked Fritz if he had seen anything unusual in the night sky. Fritz acknowledged that he had seen some bizarre lights that whirled around like flying saucers, but he was afraid he was being tricked by illusions. He didn't want to mention it to us because he thought we would all think he had totally lost his senses out on the tundra. Howard Shelley, who was at the camp during Fritz's nighttime adventure, wrote a humorous story about it for *Outdoor Life* magazine.

WHERE O WHERE ARE THE GEESE?

Howard Shelley at Long Island goose camp

From 1968 until 1983, we had many years of fabulous hunting at our goose camp on Long Island. Our guests were a select group of hunters who had travelled all over America hunting birds. We specifically requested that all the hunters be prepared to walk to the hunting areas which were from two to seven miles from the camp. One year we transported an all-terrain vehicle to the island camp, but no one liked using it because the noise spooked the birds.

Generally the hunters went out at daybreak with an experienced guide who could call geese. They hunted until mid-morning and then returned to camp for a hearty brunch. They rested for a few hours or engaged in some light activity, such as skeet shooting. In mid-afternoon they went out hunting again—usually to a spot closer to the camp. Some travelled up the coast a few miles in the boat or went across to the mainland for either hunting or fishing. Most of our hunters were satisfied to shoot a couple of geese a day and then spend the rest of their time exploring the Arctic environment. Many hiked along the ridges in the afternoon with just a light

gun and a camera.

In September 1969 I had a memorable goose hunting trip with eight executives from the Upjohn Company in Kalamazoo, Michigan. We spent a night at Great Whale River before flying to Long Island. A storm whipped up during the night and the wind and waves washed the aircraft on shore. It took fifteen of us a whole day to push the Beech 18 back into the water. When we arrived at the camp on Long Island, the geese were in abundance and the guests enjoyed fabulous hunting for two days. Then, within a few hours, every bird flew away. There wasn't a honker, there wasn't a snow—there wasn't a goose in sight.

On Saturday morning, after three days of no hunting, I decided that more drastic measures were necessary to find some geese; the guests were scheduled to leave the next day and I wanted them to go home with a few birds. Six of the hunters agreed to accompany me to the mainland. As we got ourselves settled in the boat, to our dismay, the motor wouldn't start. We trudged back to camp and our guide, Emile Bouchard, worked on the motor until he finally got it working again. As I saw him walking up to the camp, I caught sight of a familiar sight in the sky: a big V. This was followed by another big V, and when I looked to the north I could see another big V.

I called the men out of the cabin and told them there would be no boating today—the geese had arrived. There must have been five thousand snows and blues flying over the camp at four hundred feet. They came in swarms; the Vs were each at least a mile long. They circled around the camp and some of them landed a mile beyond, some landed over the hill—they were everywhere. From our vantage point at the camp, the geese seemed to cover about fifteen miles of the island.

I walked over the hill with some of the hunters and we paired off in the brush where the guides had built some blinds. Each of them shot their limit of geese that morning. By early afternoon, the geese were so thick on the island, they came right up to the doorstep of the cabins. Wherever there were berries, the geese landed. They didn't care who was at the camp; they were so preoccupied with eating and so oblivious to us, we could have killed them with a broom. It was such an amazing sight. We had to immortalize it with photographs because we doubted that anyone would believe our story if we told them how many geese surrounded the camp.

By the time Howard Shelley arrived the next week to shoot a movie for "Michigan Outdoors," the geese had spread out on the island. Many flocks had left and been replaced by some bigger snows and blues and some honkers. When we closed the camp at the end of September, there were still many flocks feeding on the island.

After spending a few seasons at the camp, I came to realize that whenever there was an abundance of berries on the island, even more geese would land to fatten up on their way south. The snow geese that pass by Long Island on their way south have spent the summer nesting on Baffin Island, around Nettilling Lake, and then head south through Deception Bay and along the east coast of Hudson Bay. A group of snow geese also fly south from Southampton Island to Mansel Island and the Ottawa Islands. There is another flyway along the western coast of Hudson's Bay, through Severn and Winisk. Eventually most of the birds come together at Hannah Bay, on the southern tip of James Bay.

A week before the goose hunting sea-son opened in 1972, I flew my son, George Jr., and a native family, the Flemings from Great Whale River, to the camp on Long Island to get it ready for the first hunters. Just a few days before the season opened, my wife and Theo Paulishak and I landed at the camp. We were on our way to the Belcher Islands but decided to stay overnight because the weather had deteriorated. George Jr. told us there were some geese on the island and the little ones were just starting to fly.

We went to bed early but were awakened around 4:00 A.M. by the honking of geese. At daybreak I opened the window blinds; all I could see on the bay for half a mile was honkers (Canada geese)! There must have been ten or fifteen thousand in that flock. The noise was so deafening that we could barely talk to each other inside the cabin. Even when we opened the cabin door and started moving around the camp, they didn't leave. They were there to rest and eat and nothing was going to disturb them.

I almost stumbled over several geese as I walked down the path to the aircraft. When I climbed on the floats, a few of them swam away, but they weren't too concerned about my presence. Several hours later we were able to clear enough space on the water to taxi the aircraft out into the bay for take-off.

I began to notice that life was changing in the north when groups of native people began to hire aircraft (including our DC-3 and Beech 18) to freight thousands and thousands of pounds of geese from Cape Jones to Great Whale River (Kuujjuarapik) or Fort George (Chisasibi). Twenty-five years ago, I wrote an article in our local Chapleau paper about this situation and received feedback from a few outdoor writers in southern Ontario. They verified that this practice was indeed going on in the north and lobbied their politicians for change. They received the same response that I had received: the native people have been given the right to hunt geese whenever they want, whether the geese are flying north or south, and whether they are in the molting stage or not.

We sold our camp at Long Island to the Quebec government in 1984. They kept the camp open for a couple of seasons before abandoning it. The geese population had declined quickly. I returned to Long Island in 1988 with my brother, Andy and a friend, Al Latour. We stayed at the small cabin we had built on an inland lake. The hunting was disappointing because there were very few geese.

I left feeling that we would never again see the proliferation of geese that I had witnessed just twenty years before. As we flew south, the reason for the lack of geese became obvious. When we passed by the mouth of the Seal River, there were about a hundred tents with at least forty big boats along the shore line. As we progressed further south, there were more tents and boats every couple of miles for a hundred miles.

Joel and I with our geese and ducks at the Ivanhoe Lake airbase, 1992

When the hydroelectric plant at La Grande was under construction, a road was built from Matagami, Quebec to Chisasibi (Fort George). The government constructed a 200-foot cement landing dock that could handle 30-foot boats. Since then, the traffic has never stopped. Hunters from the south can now drive north from Matagami in about eight hours and be hunting late in the afternoon. Because only people who are familiar with the waters would dare hunt in this area, I must conclude that most of these hunters are young native people who arrive once or twice a year to ensure that they get what they feel is their birthright. I've talked to many of the older native people who actually live year-round in the James Bay area. They are not pleased with the situation. They too are aware of the depletion of the wildlife. But their concerns are not as loud as the young people's rally for their native rights.

I have given up goose hunting in the James Bay area, but I haven't given it up altogether. Now I wait for the few flocks that make their way down to the Chapleau area. Within the last two years, our quota of geese has been reduced from five per day to two per day. Fewer geese are flying south.

In the fall of 1992 my grandson, Joel (George Jr.'s son), and I hunted at Nemegosenda Lake. We shot two geese and a few ducks on the river. Joel's enthusiasm for hunting reminded me of my first trip to Hannah Bay. It made me sad to think that he would never have the opportunity to experience the kind of goose hunting that I had known.

PAUL PEPOY AND SHARK STORIES

I made a lot of good friends over the years of flying sportsmen into the bush. During my second year in business in Chapleau, in 1955, I met Paul Pepoy, a taxidermist from Cleveland, Ohio. While he was staying at Paquette's camp, he paid me a visit at my airbase and inquired about a fly-in fishing trip for walleye and northern pike. By then I had a boat at Nemegosenda Lake, so I flew him and his two friends there for the day. Well, they had such tremendous fishing that Paul was hooked on fly-in fishing for life.

From 1955 Paul flew into the bush with us at least once every season. He often made a couple of trips with friends from Cleveland. Eventually Paul took most of the summer months off work and spent his time guiding, fishing and enjoying life at one of our outpost camps.

Paul was willing to do just about anything to go on a hunting or fishing trip. On a very clear, cold day at the beginning of the winter moose hunt, I flew Paul and two other men into King Lake on a day trip. I knew the ice was thick enough to land the aircraft, but as I landed, I could feel a layer of slush over the ice. When the ice begins to form in November, the water freezes solid about two or three inches. This is often covered by a couple of inches of snow which acts as a blanket, insulating the ice. If a lot more snow falls, the ice will buckle and water will seep up through the ice. Slush emerges when the snow cover is disturbed by the weight of the aircraft. Once this happens, we need to make a runway with snowshoes and mark it with small pine boughs so we can find it again.

As I landed on King Lake to pick up Paul and the other two moose hunters, the skis started to freeze to the slush. With Paul's help pushing the aircraft, I was able

to fly out the two other passengers, but I had to leave Paul there to make a runway. Even though Paul had made a decent runway by tramping on the slush with his snowshoes, I was still concerned about stopping the aircraft. I made him jump on the skis while the aircraft was moving. It was not the last time that I made unusual demands on Paul.

A few years later on a trip to northern Quebec, I had to leave Paul alone for a few days on Noname Lake because we were overloaded heading to the Belcher Islands. The speckled trout, which were spawning at the time, were so plentiful that Paul could wade into the creek and the fish would swim between his legs. When I returned to pick him up, he told me how he could reach down into the water and pick up the fish with his hands, kiss them, and return them to the water. Fortunately there were lots of fish for Paul to eat because we hadn't left much food with him. Unfortunately we didn't leave him any matches. Poor Paul had to satisfy his hunger with sun-baked fish.

As a taxidermist, Paul was particularly fascinated with the behaviour of birds and small animals. He loved to sit outside the cabin on our Long Island camp and observe the wildlife as it passed by the doorstep. When the island was full of geese migrating south, they would come right up to the door and walk around like domestic fowl in a barnyard, providing that we didn't shoot near the camp. Harp seals often came up to the shore near the camp. Walruses and beluga whales swam in the bay.

On one occasion Paul was quietly sitting along the shore whittling on a piece of driftwood when he saw a lone seal swimming very quickly towards the shore. As

Paul Pepoy in Chapleau, 1990

soon as he stepped into the water to see if he could touch the seal, it turned around and headed back out to the bay. Within a few seconds, Paul saw half a seal fly into the air and the black-and-white body of a shark following close behind. As the water quickly turned dark red with the blood of the seal, Paul realized that he had scared it back into the mouth of its predator.

This was the only sighting of a shark in the waters around Long Island that I ever heard. And if I didn't know Paul so well, I might have doubted his story. I had had my own experience with sharks while hunting whales further north near Baffin Island. If they were in Hudson Strait, I knew that they could be found in Hudson Bay.

When I was stationed in Rockcliffe over the winter of 1949, I made several flights to Lake Harbour on Baffin Island. As I flew into the airstrip one day, I noticed some beluga whales in the strait, about two miles off a small island. After we landed, I told a couple of Inuit about the whales and they invited me to join

them on a whale hunt. As we neared the island in their 20-foot freighter canoe, we discovered that they weren't beluga whales—they were narwhals. The hunters chose the one they wanted and harpooned it. The whale was so long that we had to tie the tail to one end of the canoe and the head to the other end. With the added weight tied to the side of the boat, we could only travel at about 3 mph.

While we were smoking and chatting on the trip back to the village, I caught a glimpse of a fin coming through the water. I was very excited about this and told the men but they didn't pay any attention to it. The shark turned at the canoe and hit the whale at a 45° angle. The canoe shuddered and the shark swam away with a huge chunk of whale meat. Within a few minutes there were three sharks surrounding us, not big ones, but they must have weighed about twenty pounds each. They took turns swimming in and biting off a piece of whale flesh.

By the time we arrived in the village, about twenty minutes later, there was only half the whale left. The Inuit weren't perturbed by this in the least bit. A week later I returned to the village and the hunters gave me the 9-foot-long narwhal tusk. I carefully transported it back to Ottawa, cleaned it up with some jeweler's rouge, and hung it in my room as a memento of my narwhal hunting trip.

As an RCAF officer I was often invited to official government gatherings. Once in a while, I would recount this story about the narwhal and the sharks. One very refined lady, Mrs. Pearson, was so captivated by my story that I was inspired to give her the narwhal tusk. At the time, Mrs. Pearson's husband, Lester B. Pearson, was a high-ranking government official. When Mr. Pearson became the Prime Minister of Canada in 1963, I assumed that the narwhal tusk made it to the official residence.

WINTER ADVENTURES IN LABRADOR

When we moved the head office of our air service to the Dorval Airport in Montreal in 1966, we were authorized to become licensed outfitters in northern Quebec. The move also put us in close contact with several other air carriers and aircraft companies. In January 1968 the chief pilot from Field Aviation visited me in my office. He proposed a joint venture to recover a Cessna 172 that had made a forced landing on an esker south of Cape Chidley in Labrador.

Since I had flown extensively in the area while I was stationed at the RCAF base in Goose Bay, Labrador in 1950, I was quite familiar with the landscape and the weather patterns. The insurance company, British Aviation, was willing to pay us a reasonable sum just to attempt to recover their aircraft so we decided to take on the adventure. We both had our doubts about the likelihood of recovering it, however.

The aircraft we were to retrieve was owned by the Cessna Aircraft Company in Wichita, Kansas. It was being ferried to Europe when the two pilots landed on the esker. The skies were clear with unlimited visibility and a strong tail wind when they left Goose Bay and landed in Saglek Bay to take on fuel before proceeding to Frobisher Bay, two hundred miles further north. As they were crossing Resolution Island, they were informed by the control tower at Frobisher Bay that their strip was closed because the weather had deteriorated. The pilots turned around and headed back to Saglek Bay, but a strong head wind slowed their progress. They ran out of fuel about thirty-five miles short of the base.

Most of the mountains in northern Labrador have flat top eskers, so they were able to safely land the aircraft and send out a signal to the Saglek Bay tower. They secured the aircraft with some tie-down kits that they carried on board for emergencies and spent the night in the aircraft. The following day they were picked up by a helicopter from a Canadian Navy ship that was heading south to Goose Bay. For some reason, whether it was inexperience or bad weather, the two pilots didn't return to the esker with enough fuel to fly the plane back to Saglek Bay. Instead they returned to Kansas, and the Cessna Corporation called their insurance agent to reclaim their losses.

Two months had already passed, yet the insurance company was still willing to pay us to attempt a recovery. The weather in northern Labrador is notoriously bad in the winter and not suitable for flying light aircraft. We postponed our trip until March. Meanwhile, we had a pair of Cessna 172 skis rigged up so that we could fasten them in a hurry once we located the aircraft.

Finally on March 20th, I took off in one of my Beavers with wheel/skis from the Dorval Airport, with an aircraft engineer and a Cessna pilot from Field Aviation. The first leg of our flight took us to Labrador City, where we spent the night. We flew on to Schefferville and Saglek Bay the following day. The weather was sunny and clear but very cold, about minus 25°F at 3000 feet. When we landed at Saglek Bay, the wind was blowing at about 10 mph. The airport manager suggested that we park the aircraft in one of their hangars for the night because they were expecting strong winds.

Very few people visit Saglek Bay during the long winter months. We were treated very hospitably by the staff. Just before midnight, the first alarms went off

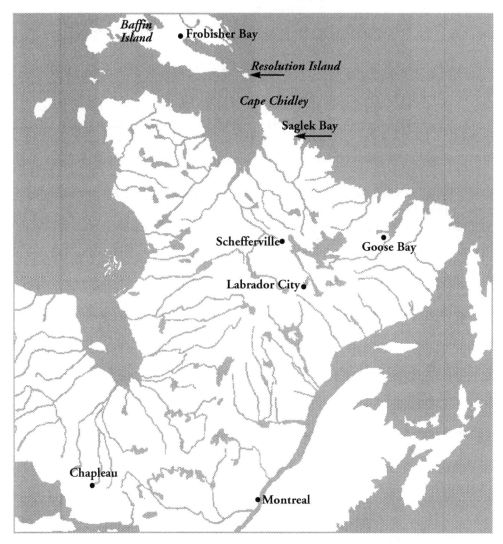

to signal that the wind had picked up to 60 mph. An hour later a second alarm went off, alerting us that the winds were now blowing at 100 mph. The manager at the base assured me that the hangars were well anchored into solid rock and cemented so that there was no way they were going to blow over, even with a 100-mph wind. This area is known to be the windiest section of the north Atlantic, so the local people are prepared for all possibilities. They also know that even when the wind is blowing at 50 mph at ground level, it could be blowing at 100 mph at 2000 feet and be calm at 6000 feet.

The following morning the skies were overcast and the wind was blowing at 40 mph. We decided to postpone the rescue attempt until the following day. As a diversion, I accompanied one of the mechanics in an all-terrain vehicle that resembled a small tank. Our mission was to set his three polar bear traps that were located several miles from the airbase.

The first trap we came to looked like a snowy mound but in reality was a twelve foot long plywood box with snow banks on three sides. My companion unlocked a winch at the front of the vehicle, ran the quarter-inch cable about 150 feet, and attached it to the top of a door on the open side of the box. I activated the winch from inside the vehicle and the door pulled up. He locked it in place and returned for bait—fifty pounds of frozen cod—which he threw into the opened trap. Once the trap was set, he unhooked the cable, retracted it and we drove to the next trap. We followed the same procedure at the next two locations, and then returned to the base to wait.

Early the next morning we went out to check his traps. The door was still open at the first trap so we moved on to the second trap, where we found that the door had closed. The bear must have heard the vehicle arrive. When we disembarked and walked closer to the trap, we could hear it snarling and pushing against the door. We unhooked the cable from the vehicle and hooked it up to the door; then returned to the vehicle and activated the winch.

As soon as the door was half-way up, the bear began its exit towards us. It rushed at the vehicle, but stopped short about fifty yards and veered off into the whiteness. My friend was ready with his camera and took a picture of it as it approached. The last trap we checked was empty. We returned to the second trap and rebaited it with more frozen cod.

Routinely, once a week during the winter months my friend catches a bear in one of his traps and photographs it as it exits. He estimated that there were about ten bears that lived close to the base. He had caught each one of them several times. This is certainly one way to get to know your neighbours.

By midday the wind subsided and the temperature was a warm 20°F, with bright sun and just a hint of a wind. We took off in the Beaver and headed towards the location of the Cessna; the radar tower directed us to the exact spot where the aircraft had landed on the esker. When we arrived, the aircraft was gone. After an hour of searching, we found it about two-and-a-half miles from its original position. The wings had sheared off and landed about a hundred feet from the fuselage.

We took pictures of the wreckage for the insurance company and returned to Saglek Bay. No one was surprised that the aircraft was completely destroyed. In fact, most people thought it would have been a miracle if it was salvageable. We spent another night at Saglek Bay, a night at Schefferville and three nights in Labrador City, waiting for the weather to clear, before we arrived back in Montreal. Winter flying in northern Canada tests your patience, as well as your survival skills. I told an awful lot of fish stories on that trip, and returned with some polar bear photographs to remind me of my adventure.

TRAVELS ABROAD

Joan with her marlin in New Zealand

When you are in the business of tourism, it helps to sit in the back seat once in a while and be a witness to how others do it. Once our business was established and we could afford to take a vacation, Joan and I began to travel to other parts of the world as tourists ourselves. Our trips, which took us to Europe, South America, Central America, the Caribbean and New Zealand, were always a source of inspiration, as well as a relaxing way to unwind from our hectic seven-month tourist season. Even though we were exposed to some spectacular scenery in places like the mountains of New Zealand, our thoughts always returned to Canada. We came home with a much deeper appreciation for our country and what it had to offer.

We had the opportunity to fish on many of these trips. It often turned out that Joan had the best catches, probably because she took the whole thing much less seriously than I did. Catching trophies didn't interest us; just fishing and having a good time was our goal.

THE RAIN FOREST OF SURINAM

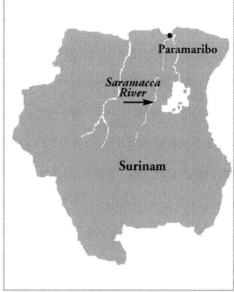

Bill Gallagher of Fenton, Michigan had booked trips to our northern camps on the Belchers and Long Island for several years before he sold Joan and I on a wilderness trip in another part of the world. Bill was quite an outdoorsman. He traveled around the globe looking for new and unusual adventures.

On one of his excursions, he discovered the tropical rivers in the small South American country of Surinam, which had just been opened for tourism. He assembled a group of sportsmen and adventurers for a canoe trip into the jungle. The selling point was jaguar hunting in the interior and tarpon fishing on the coast. Neither interested Joan or me, but we decided to make the trip just for the experience of travelling in the rain forest.

We left Toronto on March 8, 1974 and rendezvoused with our travelling companions in New York City. We spent our first two days in the beautiful port city of Paramaribo, acclimatizing ourselves to the weather and the new taste of Dutch food.

(The country of Surinam belonged to the Netherlands; however, a year later, in 1975, it gained its independence.) We basked in the sun and warmth of Paramaribo where the weather was quite favourable, averaging 80°F, even though the city is just 6° north of the equator.

Early in the morning of our third day in Paramaribo, our group travelled by bus to the Saramacca River where we met our guides. Two guides who spoke reasonable English were with us the entire trip, while the two guides who operated the forty-foot dugout canoes, changed at the major villages along our route. One driver ran the two 40-hp outboard motors at the back, while another maintained a position at the front, with a twenty-foot-long pole. We travelled at about 10 mph with the motors running. When we passed through rapids, the drivers maneuvered with the long pole.

The experience of travelling into the rain forest was breathtaking; life along the river was so vibrant that we got exhausted from the stimulation. The first day we covered eighty miles, but because of a late start, it was dark before we came to the village where we were to spend our first night. Even though our guides were familiar with the waters, the darkness descended rapidly and we were completely engulfed. Joan pulled out two flashlights from her handbag. The guides, who were at the front of the two canoes, used them to survey for rocks.

Once we arrived at our destination, we had to wait for our luggage to be transferred to smaller canoes. We sat in the darkness, listening to the night sounds of the jungle. As we flashed the light of our two flashlights on the shore, the beams caught the reflection of hundreds of caimans; their eyes shone like flashing Christmas lights. We were concerned about making a transfer with these crocodile-like reptiles waiting to see if anything fell into the water. Our guides assured us that these reptiles weren't the man-eating variety. They were the size of a Florida alligator, about five to eight feet long, and fed mainly on fish and water fowl.

The guest lodgings in the village were small huts made of straw with thatched roofs. Ours was quite cozy and clean. We were thankful for the comfortable beds—the only hint of civilization. As we were eating breakfast the next day, one of our guides noted that he had seen our lantern turned off during the night. He warned us that blood-sucking bats will fly in through the open windows at night and land on humans. They won't approach if a lantern is burning. From then on we burned our lantern all night.

While our companions went jaguar hunting, Joan and I had a guided three-mile walk into the rain forest. We paddled up the river to an area where one of the native families had cleared a trail into the forest; each family of hunters had a specific trail assigned to them by the village council. As we walked deep into the jungle, our ears rang with bird calls, but we could only see an occasional blur of colour against the dark green vegetation. Every once in a while we caught sight of a macaw or a turkey. We saw monkeys everywhere—up in the trees and swinging on the branches. The native people hunt monkeys, but on this day we just watched and admired their agility.

Along the trail we met a native man who was using a stick, with an old pop can at the end, to clear a small area of the forest to plant banana trees. After a week of cutting and burning, he had cleared only half an acre. Our guide explained that there was very little timber harvesting because the people had no tools and no way to transport the lumber to the markets. The primary hardwoods that were suitable for harvesting—a type of maple and purple heart—were too heavy to float down the rivers. In time, this would surely change when the demand for hardwood increased.

As we continued our journey up the river in the long dugout canoes, the water became clearer and we could see the piranha swarming in the main currents in the fast water; they rarely stray into the slower water of the side streams. Just as we caught sight of a small wild pig swimming near the shore, it got caught in the current and was dragged near a school of piranha. The eight-inch carnivores grabbed onto the pig and devoured it in a few minutes. The water boiled with piranhas and that was the end of the pig. The big piranhas, which are the prized game fish, are more difficult to find. They only feed in the deepest parts of the river.

Joan and I had our first fishing adventure while the hunters made their second excursion. The guides escorted us to a rocky beach along the river where it was possible to cast into the fast waters.

When we disembarked from our canoe, we saw jaguar footprints leading into the jungle. That was more than the hunters saw that day.

My first cast yielded a fish, but before I could get it to shore, it crunched through the hook like it was a corn flake. I was undaunted; I fitted my line with a stainless steel hook on a red-and-white daredevil and cast into the current where they were feeding. I hooked into one that weighed about three-and-a-half pounds. This time the hook held. As I landed it, two guides rushed over to help me remove it from the hook. This was no small feat because the teeth are deadly.

When Joan saw that the daredevil with the stainless steel hook was doing its job, she chose her place along the river bank and began to fish too. It wasn't long before she hooked into a four-pound piranha. She landed her fish on the rocks and signaled to the guides to help her take it off the hook. They all saw that she had caught a fish, but none of them moved to help her. She struggled with her fish, took out her pliers, and managed to get it free of the hook. Each time she caught a fish, she had to wrestle with it herself. Yet, whenever I caught one, the guides rushed over to help me. It was a rather unusual twist of the norm.

As the morning progressed and the heat increased, I felt compelled to go swimming. One of the guides showed me a safe place along the beach and the two of us took a little dip. We tried to convince Joan that it was safe but the memory of the little pig and the piranha was too close. Later in the trip, several members of the group, including Joan, did swim in a set of rapids.

That afternoon we caught about twenty fish for our supper. We had been served fish at almost every meal, but not piranha. The guides watched in amazement as I filleted the piranha. They had never seen anyone clean a fish in this manner. When I was finished, they asked for the razor-sharp teeth to use as arrowheads. Cooking the fillets in a frying pan was another novelty for them as the native people usually boil their fish or grill it. Our pan-fried piranha were firm and flavourful, much like a walleye.

The native people ate fish regularly; however, the men weren't the fishermen, the women were. The native women fished at night in the still waters, using a short line with a bamboo pole. They caught a large fleshy fish, called "dorado" because of its golden color. It looked like a sucker with heavy scales and weighed up to twenty-five pounds.

Our communication with our village

Fishing for piranha on the Saramacca

167

guides was quite limited. They spoke only rudimentary English. I was able to communicate in French with one that had been to school in nearby French Guiana. I convinced him to take me on a hunting trip for wild pigs (peccaries). Since he could only keep track of his route by blazing a trail with a machete, he was reluctant to travel far into the jungle. I showed him my compass and described how easy it was to travel anywhere and return to the same place.

We paddled down the river several miles and stopped at an unmarked spot. I took out my compass and we began walking into the bush. We had only travelled half a mile into the jungle when he stopped and crouched down. He had picked up the scent that the peccaries use to mark their territory. I couldn't smell anything distinct; the smell of the rain forest was still so new to my senses.

We crept into their area, as the peccaries have a very keen sense of hearing. When we were within a hundred feet of them, he began to call. In a few minutes, several of them approached us. He pointed out which ones I should shoot with my 12-gauge shotgun. I shot four small ones, each weighing about twelve pounds. That was all the two of us could carry out of the bush.

I taught him how to use the old prospector's compass that I carried in my tackle box and gave it to him as a gift. I wanted to give him my gun also but he wouldn't take it. He reminded me that I had registered it as I entered the country, and I would be asked to present it again when I departed. The punishment for selling a gun to a native was imprisonment. In 1974 the native people were only allowed to hunt with traditional weapons: a bow, a spear or blow darts. All

of these work, but they certainly aren't as efficient as a gun. Using traditional weapons, an animal is most often wounded. The hunter needs to track it for miles before it dies.

Our canoe trip took us a total of 250 miles into the interior, about two hundred air miles from the capital of Paramaribo. The return trip was much faster since we were travelling down the rapids instead of up them. We had many opportunities to see wildlife along the river, as we often sat in the canoes for eight hours a day. In some sections of the river, we saw hundreds of caimans lying on the banks or partially submerged in the water. The native people didn't have much use for them. Without guns they were awfully difficult to kill.

Joan was the only non-native woman on our trip and the village guides who had never encountered women outside their territory treated her like one of their own. Not only wouldn't they assist her when we were fishing, they also wouldn't carry her luggage. She travelled quite well, considering these handicaps.

A few years after our trip to Surinam, we saw a documentary on television in which an American woman claimed to be the first white woman to travel in the same area of the Saramacca River that we had visited. This woman made it sound like it was the most dangerous country in the world. She had flown up the river in a twin Otter and was accompanied by a guide and biologist. To us, the trip was no more dangerous that a canoe trip in the Chapleau area. In fact, it was a little easier since we didn't have to make the portages ourselves. Even though the wildlife in Surinam was different, and may have been hazardous without a knowledgeable guide, we never felt that the trip was risky.

FISHING IN NEW ZEALAND

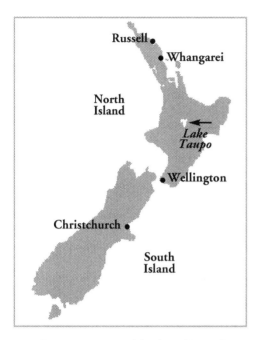

I was six years old when Zane Grey made his first fishing trip to New Zealand in 1926. He set new standards for angling by landing the first broadbill swordfish ever caught in New Zealand waters, a record 450-pound striped marlin, a 111-pound yellowtail and a 784-pound black marlin. Zane Grey didn't stop there. He went inland to fish for the famous rainbows and landed an 11 3/4-pound female trout and an 11 1/2-pound male in the Tongariro River. His book, *Tales of an Angler's Eldorado*, published the same year, elevated the New Zealand tourist industry to its highest level.

By the time Zane Grey returned the following year with his own boat, he was such a celebrity that even royalty vied for a chance to fish with him. I remember reading Zane Grey's book about fishing in New Zealand when I was fourteen years old. From then on, I was determined that one day I, too, would fish New Zealand.

In the winter of 1981, I finally did get my chance to spend a few months fishing in New Zealand with my wife Joan. Our first stop was the city of Taupo which is situated on Lake Taupo, the largest inland lake in New Zealand. The lake is known in fishing circles as one of the best spots for large rainbow trout in the world. The Tongariro River, where Zane Grey caught his rainbow trout, flows into Lake Taupo.

Rainbow trout aren't native to New Zealand; they were introduced to Lake Taupo in 1883. The original stock was imported from the Pacific northwest, perhaps Oregon or British Columbia. Now New Zealand runs its own very successful restocking program.

Joan and I rented an apartment on Lake Taupo, about a mile or so from the town. Our place was just seventy-five yards from the shore and came equipped with a 12-foot boat and an outboard motor. From our window, we could observe the conditions on the lake and choose a time to fish when the winds weren't too high. We soon discovered that it didn't seem to make any difference whether the barometer was rising or falling. We could catch fish just about any time of the day.

For our first trip onto Lake Taupo, we hired a local guide to take advantage of his experience at locating the shoals. The preferred bait is a four-inch flat fish with an orange body and black spots. These lures are made in America, especially for the New Zealand market. All the hardware and sporting goods stores handled a variety of sizes. Since only single hooks are allowed in New Zealand, no treble hooks, the flat fish is balanced with the single hook at the rear. Our guide preferred a wire monel line on a large reel. This type of equipment didn't appeal to me, so I bought a light down rigger along with twelve-pound test monofilm line to get into the deeper water.

During the warmer months—January and February—the rainbows feed about forty feet from the surface. I employed the same method that I use to fish for lake trout in the summer months in northern Ontario. I obtained a depth chart and trolled at 3 mph to keep the lure agitated enough to attract fish. The average rainbow at Lake Taupo went to six pounds, although at the mouths of the rivers, the fly fishermen were catching trout in the ten-pound class.

Even though I relished every moment spent on Lake Taupo, my favourite trips were into the mountains to fish in the streams. Soon after we arrived at Taupo, we chartered a flight into a government-operated outpost camp. The combination of scenery and rainbow fishing was breathtaking. The pilot landed on a 2000-foot gravel strip on the side of a mountain, and we hiked from there to the camp at the top of a hill, about 3000 feet above sea level. The mountain streams were so clear that from two hundred feet in the air, we could see large rainbow in the pools below. With that sight in mind, I could hardly contain my enthusiasm.

Fly fishing in the pools for the huge trout was a lot more difficult than I had imagined. The trout were rising to the surface and grabbing a real fly, but whenever I casted out, it was ignored. In preparation for this trip, I had purchased a dozen streamer flies, tied by an expert New Zealand trout fisherman. When the fish didn't bite these local flies, I began to wonder if my choice was well made.

After an hour or so of watching trout surface then quickly swim away, I realized

that the rainbows were spooked by the leader. These trout had obviously seen a considerable amount of fishing tackle. I never did catch one of the really big ones, but I did enjoy catching many that weighed between five and six pounds. What I needed to find were streams that hadn't been fished regularly.

Much of the best rainbow fishing is located in isolated mountainous country. Unfortunately, this area is impossible to reach, except by helicopter. The local people use helicopters to hunt deer in the mountains. The deer population has grown to such an extent that the animals interfere with the reforestation by eating the new plants. The foresters lasso a deer from the air and haul it up on a winch into the helicopter.

I made friends with a couple of pilots in Lake Taupo who flew into the mountains weekly to round up some of the deer. They offered to drop me off near one of the mountain streams and pick me up a few hours later, when they had finished their hunting. All the narrow, fast-flowing rivers had pools at the bottom that were full of trout. These fish weren't quite so wary and I could catch them with fly equipment. They were such a delight to catch, especially when they exhibited their legendary prowess of leaping into the air once hooked. In a couple of hours, I caught and a released as many as twenty rainbows. I only kept enough to repay my hosts for their generosity in transporting me.

Once I had satisfied myself with fishing in the Taupo area, Joan and I travelled to the South Island to see the territory. While I was enjoying a game of golf on a course south of Christchurch, one of the locals told me about the rainbow fishing on a nearby river. The next day I followed his directions and found that what he had described was absolutely true. Within an hour or two, I caught nine rainbows, weighing about four pounds each. The river seemed full of fish, but where were the fishermen? I was the only one fishing that day. And when I drove by a day later, there wasn't a soul fishing. This would never happen in North America. I could only assume that when you live on a small island with salt water all around and plenty of freshwater lakes and streams in the interior, fishing loses some of its allure.

When all the inland fishing was done and the sights were seen, our attention turned to the ultimate in angling—deep sea fishing. We travelled to the northernmost point of the North Island and the small community of Russell, where Zane Grey had made his base in the Bay of Islands. The community was still a bustling deep sea fishing port, but the atmosphere didn't suit my fancy.

We travelled all over the tip of the island looking for the right place to settle into some fine fishing. I eventually met a Maori fisherman in a gas station and described the kind of fishing spot I was looking for. He suggested a small village called Tutukaka, near the town of Whangarei. When we arrived, we knew it was our paradise.

Joan and I were awe-struck by the beauty of half a dozen long rocky fingers, or peninsulas, which extended into the ocean. Everywhere else we had seen black or brown beaches but here, between each finger, were beautiful, white sandy beaches. Walking trails along the top of the peninsulas made each finger a perfect location for surf fishing. Along the leeward side the catch was snapper.

The New Zealand snapper are very similar to the red snapper that are caught in the warmer parts of the Atlantic. Like their American counterpart, they are usually taken on bait, rather than artificial lures. The locals were catching them with just a little spinner and an earthworm. They are an excellent eating fish, whether baked, broiled or filleted and pan-fried. Just about every restaurant in Tutukaka served them in a variety of ways.

At the end of the peninsula where the ocean currents were strong, I fished for a type of sea trout. The locals called them Kahawai. I rented a heavy nine-foot rod with twenty-pound test line and tied a six-inch heavy lure to the end. These Kahawai were good strong fighters, much stronger than Atlantic salmon. Even the small ones put up the most incredible fight, with quick turns, leaps into the air and wild rushes. Catching one just to enjoy the sheer excitement of landing it, was the object of the game.

The native people didn't like the taste of them—snapper was their preference. They just caught and released them, or sold them to the charter boats for bait. If the winds weren't too strong, it was easy to catch one of these fish on every cast. Most of them were around five pounds but there were a few bigger ones. One day I kept a couple of them and we cooked them for our dinner. They were quite acceptable, but definitely didn't have the flavor or delicacy of the snapper.

After a few days of exploring and surf fishing, I was ready for deep sea fishing. We took a liking to a charter boat owner whom we had met at the local town hall, where everyone seemed to congregate in the evening. Early one morning, we set out from Tutukaka in his 30-foot diesel boat with his mate. We didn't have far to go. The continental shelf is just four or five miles off the coast. We had been out on the ocean for less than an hour when we started to set up the lines. Each line was baited with a two-pound sea trout.

Within half an hour, Joan's line hooked into a striped marlin. It became obvious very soon that this fish was a monster. Even though Joan was strapped into her chair, she had to put her feet up on the stern to brace herself. I was afraid she was going to be pulled into the water. The captain wouldn't let me touch her to hold her back in the chair because then the fish wouldn't be considered a legal catch.

Since neither Joan nor I were experienced deep sea fishermen, we had to completely rely on our captain's ingenuity to help her land the fish. He was well versed in the proper technique of when to let the line out and when to reel in. It took Joan the better part of an hour of hard labour to land the marlin. As we hauled it into the boat, we realized that it had been foul hooked on the side. That's why it proved to be such a difficult one to land. The marlin had undoubtedly gone for the bait, missed it, and then got hooked.

We rebaited the lines and hooked into two more big ones that day, but we lost them both. As we sailed into the harbour, the captain proudly flew the marlin flag to show everyone what we had caught. It turned out to be the only marlin caught that day. The captain was more excited than we were when it weighed in at 97.2 kilograms (approx. 214 pounds). It was the biggest fish caught on his boat that season. We declined the option of taking the fish home to mount or eat. The captain and his mate enthusiastically agreed to keep it for themselves. It was the experience we both treasured. Joan still has the certificate as a souvenir of her marlin.

We spent three months in New Zealand. I left with all my boyhood dreams satisfied. Before departing, I paid homage to the great outdoorsman, Zane Grey, at a museum near his old fishing grounds in Russell, New Zealand.

Non Member   Tag No. ....

WHANGAREI DEEP SEA ANGLERS' CLUB
(INCORPORATED)
Base: TUTUKAKA, P.O. Box 401, WHANGAREI, New Zealand.

CAPTURE AND WEIGHT RECORDING CERTIFICATE

Length .... Girth .... Nº 207

Date of Birth Junior Angler ....

Angler Mrs J. Theriault Species S/Marlin Weight 97.20 Kgs

Address Chapleau Ontario Canada

Where Caught Off Taihururu Date 26-3.81 Line Class 37 Kgs

Time Hooked 11.00 Time Boated 12.00 Name of Launch Marco Polo

Catch confirmed by .... Launchman.

I, the undersigned, do hereby declare that I am a Financial Member of the Whangarei Deep Sea Anglers' Club Inc. and that the above named fish was brought to gaff by me in full accordance with Club and I.G.F.A. Rules.

Signature of Angler ....

Signature of Weighmaster b. M. Franks Date Weighed 26. 3. 81

A CARIBBEAN ADVENTURE

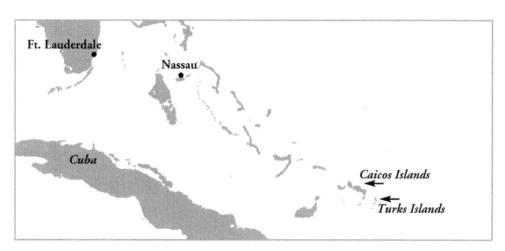

When Joan and I began to make our winter home in Florida, I had many opportunities to fish in the Caribbean. During the winter of 1983 we accompanied our old friends, Ed and Bonnie Erickson, on their Hatteras twin diesel from Ft. Lauderdale to their winter home on North Caicos Island. Ed had been a guest at our northern camps on the Belchers and Long Island on several occasions. He had hunted moose with us in Chapleau for twenty years. He was a seasoned sportsman, having travelled all over North and South America, as well as Africa, on fishing and hunting excursions. He convinced me that I would experience some of the best sea fishing in my life on this trip.

We were also accompanied by another old friend, Fritz Slifcak from Ft. Lauderdale, who was a skilled mechanic and a great chef. Even though Ed's boat had just been repaired in Ft. Lauderdale, I wanted to make sure that if anything went wrong, we had a technician on board— even the thought of being stranded on the open seas didn't make me feel comfortable.

We didn't begin our serious fishing until we were south of Nassau. When the

seas were calm, we trolled leisurely as we made our way southeast towards the Turks and Caicos Islands. Our journey took us to Norman Cay, Staniel Cay and Lee Stocking Island. We took on fuel and supplies in George Town. When the waters got rough, we found shelter in a cove and fished or snorkeled. We passed many small islands along the route, so there were always opportunities to hide in comfort on the leeward side. Once past George Town we crossed over to Hog Cay on Long Island, followed the island south then headed east to Crooked Island. We passed Salina Point on Acklins Island before heading southeast to Little Inagua Island.

Ed's boat was well-equipped with an aft fishing deck, about twenty feet long and eighteen feet wide. There was also a lower platform where someone could stand to assist in landing a large fish. The boat carried several seven-foot-long rods, four of which had large Penn reels with 60- to 80-pound-test lines with preset drag.

We fished with three rods at a time. Joan occupied the middle deck chair, holding a long rod with about thirty-five yards out behind. We set two rigger lines out about seventy-five yards each. Usually the lines were staggered to present baits over a wider area and to create an illusion of a small shoal of frantically swimming bait fish. For some reason, the baits closest to the boats produced the most fish and Joan was the busiest of us all.

Although some fish can be taken from a drifting boat, the more active predators like marlins, wahoo and tuna, prefer moving baits. I like to fish these species by trailing baits behind a moving boat so that the baits resemble the living food on which they prey. Ed had purchased several dozen small ballyhoo and kept them frozen for use as bait.

The fishing was just as spectacular as Ed had promised. In one afternoon Joan caught and released about eight hundred pounds of fish, mostly kings and wahoo. The fishing was usually prime until the sharks found us. Once they located our boat, the fish we caught on our lines were chewed up or eaten before we reeled them in. The sharks would come right along the side of the boat and cut the fish in half. If it was a small fish, they would take the entire body and leave us just the head with the lure. One afternoon we hit upon a school of barracuda, catching several small ones that weighed about six pounds. Before we could release them though, the sharks came along and ripped the entire fish off the line.

Every night Fritz cooked a new fish recipe which we supplemented with lobsters that we found in the coves. Ed and I took turns diving for lobsters in about eight feet of water. While one of us dove, the other was on the lookout for sharks. Fritz had the gun ready just in case one came along.

It wasn't just the sharks of the swimming variety that we had to be aware of; we had to be on the lookout for sharks of the human variety. Pirates had been known to board unsuspecting boats, or boats that were stranded and in need of repairs. Ed had brought along an arsenal that included an automatic weapon which was stored on the top deck. If we saw another boat as we were trolling, we gave it wide berth. Most of the other boats were just as cautious as we were. They in turn gave us wide berth. We never had to take any kind of evasive action, but we were prepared nonetheless. Night was the most dangerous time—one of us was always awake on watch with the automatic weapon ready.

As we approached North Caicos Island, Ed directed us towards a submerged pinnacle a few miles southeast of Little Inagua Island. This underwater island that rose up in the ocean abounded with an indescribable amount of sea life. I counted three or four schools with five hundred or more fish in each school. We caught tuna and king mackerel that were in the forty and fifty-pound range as well as thirty-pound wahoo.

The sharks were everywhere. I ran the boat from the top mast for a couple of hours and had a bird's eye view of their size and number. There must have been two dozen 15-foot sharks swimming in the area. Joan was so nervous that she retreated to the lower cabin. I was more in awe of them than frightened; the graceful twists and turns of their sleek bodies were mesmerizing. Ed and Fritz and I took turns fishing and running the boat. Eventually, high waves forced us to seek shelter at Little Inagua Island.

Our ten-day trip was one big adventure from the moment we left port. The fishing couldn't have been better! There were always more fish than time to catch them. But it was the sharks that were undoubtedly the most memorable spectacle. I had never seen so many and at such close range.

REFLECTIONS

Jack Kuiper and G. Theriault at Kasegalik Lake on the Belchers

I have lived a very fortunate life because I have made a living doing what I enjoy the most—flying and being outdoors. Even though I didn't have much time to reflect on life while I was busy building and maintaining the air service, I still managed to write the odd article for the local newspaper and send letters to our members of parliament.

The environmental issues were just as prevalent then as they are now. Today they get more publicity because nature has become fashionable. I applaud the media and the action groups that are protecting our wildlife today. But I would caution them to think clearly about the issues. Their vision may not allow them to perceive the broader picture—because that picture is not static.

Nature itself is always evolving, that's the nature of life. Even without us human beings, living at this moment in time, on this planet, nature would be evolving. We just need to tune into that ongoing change and live according to its fluctuations. And the only way to do that, is to really live in nature, to listen to the vibrations, to be aware of our presence here.

THE NORTHERN LANDSCAPE

The flight from Sault Ste. Marie north, to the Belchers and Long Island, has left such a deep impression in my memory, that even now, I could fly it without a map. As I think about the flight, I can visualize the terrain below the aircraft as if I was in the cockpit. The land has its own personality that I have come to recognize after countless years of flying over it. Its appearance changes with the seasons but its essential character is always the same.

As you fly north from Sault Ste. Marie, the northern forests of spruce, pine, poplar and birch prevail. The forested landscape is punctuated with hundreds of irregularly shaped lakes containing little islands encircled by sand beaches and flat limestone. As you travel ever northwards, the trees gradually begin to diminish in size. By the time you arrive in Chapleau, the trees average sixty feet in height. They continue to decrease in size as you fly north of the Kapuskasing area, where they are perceptively smaller and less dense.

The flight takes us along the Abitibi River, where the land is quite flat. We see just a few spruce and poplar growing near the river. From the air, the land looks swampy but I know from experience that the ground isn't wet—what predominates are grasses and mosses. At one time, the area was covered by the sea. As you approach James Bay at the community of Moosonee, the trees have dwindled to twenty or thirty feet in height.

We often stop in Moosonee to take on fuel, and then continue the journey further north into James and Hudson Bay. As we travel east from Moosonee to Rupert House (Waskaganish), we cross a fifteen-mile stretch of open water; then continue northeast along the coastline. The land is relatively flat, except for one hill which is exactly eighty miles from Moosonee, between Rupert House and Eastmain. We call it Sherrick Hill. You can see it from quite a distance. At 500 feet above sea level, it stands out like a mountain.

North of Eastmain, the country changes again. Just inland from the coast of James Bay, there are hundreds of lakes and rivers, with trees along the shorelines. Past Fort George (Chisasibi) and the hydroelectric plant on La Grande River, the landscape begins to stretch out for miles as there are very few settlements anywhere. Reindeer moss begins to cover the ground. When you land on any of the lakes or rivers, you immediately feel the silence of a land that has not been developed, not been intruded upon. The water is so clean that you can dip your hand over the side and drink it. Even during the winter, the snow is absolutely pure white; no soot from a passing train or fallout from a nearby factory.

When you breathe this pure air, you feel that this land is your home. This is where you start to remember that you are inseparable from all other life. If you take time to listen, you can begin to hear the earth breathe. Then you realize that you are breathing in the same rhythm. As you peer up at the night sky, filled with stars and galaxies and streaked by the endless, shifting cloud formations, you can imagine how all of life must be connected, like each strand in a spider's web.

To be totally at one with life in this part of the world, you have to be aware of the constant shifting, the endless cycles of nature. Nothing is static; change is expected and respected. Within minutes or even seconds, the weather can turn on the unsuspecting traveller. The lakes in the

Northern Ontario landscape

James Bay area are so flat, that in a few minutes, a 40-mph gale can whip up. The waves turn into a massive fury that can easily flip a canoe, or even a float plane that is not well-secured.

As you pass into Hudson Bay from James Bay, the islands are treeless. The quietness of the barren landscape is unnerving to the new traveller. Some lives are so accustomed to the constant buzz of machines and electrical wires, that the sounds of nature can disturb a de-sensitized nervous system. Some people feel uncomfortable for days, because they resist the experience and hold on to their old way of functioning. Others allow the silent functioning of nature to penetrate into their physiology, and soon their way of thinking becomes quieter. Yet, they are aware of every little fluctuation in the environment. When this begins to happen, you understand that the earth we live on has a spiritual life, as full as any individual soul.

Very few people have had the opportunity to experience nature in such an undisturbed state. How long this part of the country will remain isolated, is not something I care to think about often. The demands for power in the south have already scarred the area northwest of Ft. George. The threat of more power plants is a nightmare for the native people who live there year-round.

The old native people had visions about this land. They never claimed to own it. No one can own this land. They told me that they were its caretakers; they were responsible to protect the land for future generations. I know their visions didn't include dams and roads that would forever alter their simple way of life.

THE DEMISE OF OUR FORESTS

From the time I was a very young lad, the lumber companies in northern Ontario and northern Quebec employed environmentally safe lumbering methods. The jack pine was cut from early December until the end of March. However, after 1960, pressure was put on the government to allow clear-cutting. The demand for paper was rising and the lumber companies couldn't operate efficiently using small tractors and horses during the winter months. They wanted to do most of their cutting in the summer. As a result of this new, faster method of harvesting the trees, we began to see some of the most beautiful forests clear-cut and completely destroyed.

Before clear-cutting was allowed, I could hardly notice from the air when an area of forest had been harvested. I was flying at least a hundred hours a month over the forests of northern Ontario, from Sault Ste. Marie to Moosonee, so I had a bird's-eye view of the situation. After 1960 when clear-cutting became the common practice of the lumber companies, what I saw from the air began to change.

At first I saw small areas of half a mile by a quarter a mile stripped of trees; then it increased to even larger and larger tracts of land. Soon I could see huge areas of denuded land—it was an eyesore even from 2000 feet above the ground. Many of my passengers began to take notice of this, since the devastation was very difficult to miss. I could only shake my head and wonder at the effect of political lobbying. Even though I did lodge my protests, a tourist outfitter's cry is not as loud as the paper industry's professional lobbyists.

When the lumber companies cut the trees during the winter months, they didn't need to make permanent roads, so much of the land remained isolated and secure from the onslaught of vehicles. But once they began clear-cutting during the summer months, they needed to build more permanent roads that could be travelled by anyone with an all-terrain vehicle or a four-wheel drive. It wasn't long before the lakes near these roads were overrun with fishermen who had no concern for maintaining the integrity of the lake. It was each man for himself and the race was on to see who could despoil a lake first. During the summer months, these poachers would take as many fish as they could fit in their deep freezer. And during the winter months, they would arrive in their snowmobiles and set gill nets under the ice. Within one season, a lake was looted.

The arrival of a logging road was a very sad situation, especially for those of us who had spent years caring for the fish population of a particular lake. Once a logging road went anywhere near it, we had to abandon a lake. Sometimes it felt like losing an old friend. I quickly learned how easily man's intervention affects the balance of nature. When men don't think of the future, but only think about their selfish concerns in the present, nature responds by shriveling up. We are nature's gardeners. If we treat the land and lakes like friends, they will always provide for us. But if we forget to nurture them, they die, just like children will die if we starve them.

The forestry program developed by the Ontario government has had some very positive effects on the continued growth of our forests. The use of controlled burns in clear-cut areas and old forests renews the soil with potash and forces the pine cones to open for new growth. Years ago, the native people who lived on the prairies used this method to manage their land. It works on the principle that when you destroy it, it comes back stronger and healthier. You need fires to regenerate a forest. Today, the foresters are burning up to a thousand acres at a time. Ten years ago in the Chapleau area, they burned about four square miles. Foresters from around the world came to learn from the experiment. Today the area is completely reforested.

In some areas, small sections of clear-cutting may not be totally devastating. But there are certain areas, which I call the sand flats, where clear-cutting should never be allowed because of the subsequent problem with erosion. These are the areas where only selective cutting must be allowed. Otherwise it may take several replantings before a new tree will grow. If a newly replanted forest in the sand flats doesn't receive a lot of moisture during its first year, the new trees won't survive.

We have seen a number of areas north and northeast of Ivanhoe Lake, where the land is still barren thirty years after it was clear-cut: the replantings have never been successful. Right now, none of the larger lumber companies is willing to spend the extra time and money to practice selective cutting in these areas. Smaller operators should be allowed to bid on the contracts in these areas. Without the overhead of the larger companies, the smaller operators can work during the winter using the older, more environmentally safe methods, and still generate a profit.

As if the logging roads and the clear-cutting weren't enough to destroy our forests, aerial spraying has taken care of the rest. Anyone who believes that the chemicals used to kill the broad leaf plants and trees in the forest are safe, is totally deluded. These chemicals, like 2-4-D, are basically the same as the defoliant, Agent Orange, that was used during the Vietnam

A controlled burn in the Chapleau area

War. I watched an aircraft spray the forest around the Chapleau airport many years ago. Prior to this spraying, the area was one of the most popular spots for blueberry picking. After that one application, there wasn't a blueberry to be seen for years. The chemical doesn't just affect the broad leaf, it affects everything that lives in the ecosystem: the birds, the squirrels and chipmunks; even the mushrooms and the moss.

Between the clear-cutting and the aerial spraying, the wildlife has very little chance of escaping unharmed. When the timber jacks and harvesters arrive in the forest to cut the trees, they strip the land as fast as the machinery can advance. Any animals that were nesting in or around the trees, perish or are left homeless. If they manage to dodge the machinery, then the chemical spraying finishes them off. I'm no expert biologist, but even a novice can notice that there are fewer and fewer birds and small mammals around the camps. Today, when I visit my cottage on a secluded lake north of Chapleau, I rarely see a squirrel or a rabbit anymore.

While flying over the forest in northern Ontario, I have witnessed many things that have been hidden from the public. To me, one of the most disgusting cover-ups was the covert airstrips that were used by aircraft to spray the forests. I found them concealed just a few miles off the highways. No one who is fishing on lakes in the area is warned that spraying is taking place. I once had the misfortune to be on the ground near an area that was being sprayed. I can honestly say that the effect is harmful. My eyes watered and my breathing became laboured. It wasn't a pleasant experience. Small wonder that the game has been affected.

When I visited New Zealand in the winter of 1981, I asked a forester how they controlled the growth of broad leaf in their forests. He told me their big secret— they used sheep! When a forest needed to be cleaned up, they let several hundred sheep loose in it. Within a few months,

A clear-cut area in the sand flats of Northern Ontario

the broad leaf was gone. Such a simple ecological method of weeding the garden! Where did we go wrong? When I returned to Canada, I told this story to a deputy minister in the Ontario government. He just laughed at me. Fifteen years later, the Ontario government began experimenting with sheep to control the broad leaf in the forests. It's amazing how long it takes for some people to wake up to the pitiable way our forests have been treated for the past thirty years.

In my estimation, the destruction that has been allowed in our forests in northern Ontario and northern Quebec is no different than what is being allowed in the tropical rain forests. I witnessed the destruction of the Amazon River valley when I flew as a photographic consultant on a Lear jet in Brazil in 1967. What is happening here in Canada isn't much different. If the amount of lumber harvested does not decrease, then I predict that within ten years all the lakes south of the Albany River will be accessible by road. Once the lakes and rivers are open to regular traffic, the wildlife is severely threatened.

I'm sure there are many people who believe that, in all fairness, everyone should have access to Canada's natural resources. Roads open up the country so that even those who cannot take the time for a canoe trip, or those who cannot afford an airplane trip, will be able to appreciate the land. I cannot argue that the land is only for a privileged few. It does belong to all of us. It is our heritage. It is our pride and joy that we offer to all mankind. *But—it must be respected.* If it is violated, it will suffer. A wise man once said that the wealth of a nation is dependent on the number of trees in the country. I believe him. If we disrespect our trees and our wildlife, all of us are impoverished and our children will bear the consequences.

CONVERSATIONS WITH FISHERMEN

I have been escorting fishermen to northern Canada for over thirty years. During that time, I have had some tremendous conversations about nature, and fishing in particular. Most of my guests have been expert fishermen who have fished trout streams all over North America. Many have fished in Europe as well. They usually knew a lot more about fishing equipment and technique than I did, so I listened very carefully and tried to pick up some pointers.

Of course there were disputes to settle. There seems to be a class distinction amongst fishermen: the dry-fly devotee holds himself superior to the wet-fly fisherman; all fly fishermen hold themselves above those who use spinners; and naturally the spinners hold themselves above the bait fishermen. It has always seemed a little foolish to me, because I think of myself as a fisherman who uses whatever method works best to catch a fish. Sometimes a wet fly is better to use than a dry fly, and sometimes spinning equipment is superior. And there are occasions when bait fishing is the only way to catch a walleye. So much depends on the situation, that if you restrict your method of fishing, you are likely to go home empty-handed.

Fishing in the far north does require some skill in fly fishing. It is the only method of fishing that will keep the fish feeding. If you use spin tackle in most northern rivers, whether it is for char, lake trout or speckled trout, the noise will eventually deter the fish from eating. I've watched a spin fisherman catch three fish in a pool and then no more. The fish had been spooked. Once the fish are rattled by the splashes of the spinners hitting the water, they move on to another pool. It may be days before they return. This spoils the fishing for everyone else. A fly fisherman, who keeps himself in the shadows along the shore, can fish from morning till night and the fish will feed most of the time. I have always recommended that my guests who accompany me to the north have some basic skills in fly fishing.

On one trip to the Seal River with Joe Brooks, a writer for *Outdoor Life* magazine, and his gang from the Shakespeare Co., I had a firsthand opportunity to watch an expert fisherman be put to the test against a novice. Joe and his companion were fishing in a canoe along the Seal River, halfway between Ominuk Lake and the coast of James Bay. While Joe was able to cast a perfect fly, landing it within an inch or so of his target, his companion was whipping it across the mark and letting the line touch the water first.

Tommy Godfrey and I were in another canoe nearby and witnessed the result of this display. It turned out that the novice, who wasn't casting so well, landed the biggest trout that afternoon. It was the topic of conversation in camp over our evening meal. While the amateur caught the four-pound trout, the expert had to be satisfied with a few smaller ones. Sometimes luck wins over skill even in fishing.

Conversations with fly fishermen always lead to the topic of drag. If your leader or the line falls into the water before the fly, this drag signals to the rising trout that what you are offering him isn't real. However, some consider that drag on a wet fly is acceptable. Since I have never had the time and patience to perfect my casting skills, I have never been able to cast within three to six inches of my target. Basically, I'm a drift fisherman—I use streamer flies and don't worry too much about casting precisely. I follow some basic rules like casting upstream rather than downstream when using dry flies. And I try to use flies that simulate the type of insects the fish seem to be feeding on. In the end, I usually catch as many fish as the experts around me, so my technique must be effective.

One family of ardent fishermen, the Vandoricks, from Scranton, Pennsylvania, made at least fifteen trips with me to the Seal River and the Belcher Islands. Bobby Vandorick and his sons were in a class of fly fishermen that far surpassed any that I have known. They could expertly tie any fly. They knew exactly when to use a dry fly, a wet fly or a nymph. It was no wonder that they caught more fish than everyone else. In the evening, we would sit together and they would explain their techniques. It was a privilege to listen to these experts.

Most of the fishermen who accompanied me to the Arctic, came on these northern adventures to experience a new, fresh world, where nature was supreme. Fishing was their excuse, but appreciating nature was their purpose. Once the thrill of catching so many fish wore off, their attention usually turned to the greater environment. After a morning of fishing, they would return to camp with their quota of fish, and then spend the rest of the day hiking and photographing. Their fascination with the surroundings grew as they began to value all the small details that nature has to offer.

Often our evening discussions centered on the local flora and fauna. I carried some field books which identified the vegetation and small mammals and shared these with my camp mates. During one season on Long Island, Vince Creighton, a retired official from the Ontario Ministry of Natural Resources, spent many nights with the guests identifying the Arctic flowers and grasses. His discussions about the interrelationship of the various types of vegetation enlightened us all. Even that small amount of knowledge about the environment led us to a deeper appreciation of the delicate balance of nature.

Refueling the Beech 18 at Moosonee

FISHING DREAMS COME TRUE

Occasionally, the topic of fishing comes up when I'm playing golf. When it does, the fishing tales get taller and the shots get wider. Soon we are enjoying a few cold ones in the club house and the topic is still fishing. When two avid fishermen recognize each other, there's no way to stop the flow of stories. Ultimately, you end up on a fishing trip together because that's what drives you both.

I met a real fisherman in Jack Kuiper. We first played golf together in Florida in 1984. Soon our golfing friendship evolved into a fishing friendship when we fished for bass on Lake Placid. The following summer, Jack and his wife, Bernie, joined us at our Nemegosenda camp for a few days of walleye fishing.

Once Jack had his taste of fly-in fishing, he was hooked. On his first trip to the far north with me in 1986, he wanted to fulfill all his fishing desires in one trip. I assured him that he could do so in ten days—or less. Since he wanted to fish for speckled trout, northern pike and walleye, we headed north from Chapleau in my Beaver aircraft. We made our first stop for fuel at Moosonee, a small native community at the southern end of James Bay.

There isn't a whole lot to do in Moosonee, especially when the black flies are out in full force, as they are in mid-July. The few places to visit are the souvenir shops that sell mementos to the tourists who arrive daily from Cochrane. The transportation costs are so high in Moosonee that everything is expensive, especially aviation fuel, which costs about five dollars per gallon. Within an hour, Jack and I had the aircraft refueled and set off for our first fishing spot, the Kapisaouis River.

We left Moosonee in perfect weather, managed to skirt a front near Eastmain, then landed on the Kapisaouis under sunny skies, about three hours later. Since fishing was foremost in our minds, it didn't take us long to secure the aircraft and get our gear ready for some speckled trout fishing. We climbed down to the foot of the last rapids and waded into a small pool. The water was so clear we could see the trout as they hit our Mepp spinners. What a thrill to watch a beautiful speckled trout grab your lure! Within a couple of hours, we had exhausted ourselves with the sheer excitement of the experience. When hunger overcame us, we set up our camp about a hundred feet from the river bank and pan-fried a couple of our trout. It was the finest of feasts, fit for true fishermen only.

While we were fishing, a slight breeze on the river kept the black flies away from us, but once the wind died down, the flies found us and pestered us most of the night. We woke up very early the next morning, ready to fish for a few hours before heading further north to the Seal River. Just as the day before, the trout never failed us; they rose and struck on almost every cast. We saturated ourselves for a couple of hours, then headed back to our little camp and again feasted on fresh trout before flying off to the Seal River. I knew we were going to have more incredible trout fishing, and I hoped there would be fewer black flies. The area around the Seal River is more open, with fewer trees and bushes to harbour insects.

When we arrived on the Seal River in the early afternoon, Jack elected to sleep in the old cabin rather than pitch a tent. Since we had sold our camp in 1970, the Ft. George Band had given me permission to use the cabin for non-commercial use when it was not already occupied. It had suffered greatly over time though, and not much remained of the beautiful little log cabin that we had built overlooking Ominuk Lake. The glass had disappeared from the windows and much of the caulking had eroded between the logs. But, it was a roof over our heads and a haven from the bugs.

The Seal River has rarely disappointed me in all the many years that I have fished it. Sometimes I need a few minutes to figure out what the fish are biting on; however, I always arrive well prepared for all possibilities. I carry both fly and spinning equipment with me. Once we waded into the rocky stream, we could see the trout rising all around us, and they were feeding only on flies. Jack and I caught and released so many we stopped counting. We kept just a few fine specimens for our evening meal. A cool breeze kept the black flies away from our camp, so we enjoyed our feast outside with a big bonfire to keep us warm.

We arose early the next morning to try our luck again. I like to fish the streams in the early morning, just as the new day is dawning. The trout seem to have such voracious appetites from their nighttime fast that they seize the lure like real bulldogs. Once they're on, they fight right to the finish. For several hours, we engaged in the contest, not minding the hunger that was lingering in our bellies. When we both felt satisfied, we headed back to camp for a well-deserved breakfast.

Jack was itching for some northern pike fishing, so I set him up in a section of the lake that had produced a 35-pound northern several years previous—W.D. Harrison of Houston, Texas had caught that one. Since I still had the taste for speckled trout, I hiked a little further up the river to another set of rapids and another pool. I returned from my little excursion with a few stories to tell Jack about the fish I had caught, but it was Jack who had the most exciting one to tell.

Jack was beaming with pride as he displayed a 50-inch northern pike that weighed about 25 pounds. He had been fishing near a weed bed with a light spinning rod, eight-pound test line and a red-and-white daredevil. After landing a couple of smaller northerns, he hooked into this big one that gave him the fight of a lifetime. It played all the tricks that northern pike are supposed to play. It made several long runs, taking a hundred feet of line with it, then dove to the bottom to brood, always keeping the pressure on. Jack's patience and perseverance won in the end and the pike surrendered after a long and arduous battle.

Jack had fulfilled two of his desires so far, and this was day four of our trip. Walleye fishing was the only item left on his list. I knew we could easily fulfill that desire near the airbase in Chapleau. On our way south, we stopped for fuel in Eastmain, then spent a night in Moosonee. By late afternoon the next day, we landed on a small narrow lake east of Sahler Lake. Earlier that spring I had hidden a 12-foot boat near the shore. Within two hours we had a string of ten walleye that weighed about three to four pounds each.

Even though I prize walleye as a great game fish, compared to our recent experiences with speckles, I felt slightly unsatisfied with the contest. We spent the night at my son John's cabin on Sahler Lake and supped on some of our walleye fillets. These fillets were so light and tasty that I erased all my doubts about walleye fishing.

On our last night together, we reminisced about all the wonderful fishing we had experienced that week. Jack had fulfilled all his desires so effortlessly that he wondered if it had been a dream. But it wasn't—he had the 25-pound northern pike to take home as proof.

1988: ANOTHER NORTHERN EXCURSION

Fishing in the far north has a way of getting into your bones. Once you have had the experience, even when you feel completely fulfilled by it, the desire comes back in a year or so. I knew Jack Kuiper had been infected with the fishing disease and he would have to give in again. In 1988 we made our second trip north together in my Beaver C-GPUS. We were accompanied by another Beaver aircraft flown by Russ Bannock, a former president of deHavilland Aircraft of Canada. Russ brought along two friends who were avid trout fishermen, Doug Woolings and Bruce Mullen.

Russ is a well-seasoned flyer who knows his aircraft like the back of his hand. He should have—he was one of the developers of the Beaver at the deHavilland. He got involved in flying in the late 1930s, in Edmonton, Alberta, and flew with some of the pioneering bush pilots in northern Alberta and the Northwest Territories. He joined the RCAF in 1940 and was decorated with a Distinguished Flying Cross and a Distinguished Service Order before the end of the war. Even though he was offered a permanent commission with the RCAF, he chose to work for deHavilland. He not only helped develop the Beaver, he tested it and took charge of its sales program. He was instrumental in selling over a thousand Beavers to the US Air Force and the US Army, as well as over four hundred Otters and Caribous. These aircraft were used domestically and in Vietnam during the war. Now that Russ has retired, he has the opportunity to make fishing his priority.

Our first stop was the Seal River where we all relished the sensational speckled trout fishing that we have come to expect at this location. We managed to contain our enthusiasm though, because we knew we were headed for more variety. Our final destination was the Belcher Islands, which are situated in Hudson Bay, ninety miles further north. We chose a beautiful sunny day to make the flight from the Seal River. As we crossed Hudson Bay at 3000 feet, we all marveled at the beluga whales swimming amidst the ice packs. It was a sight to be seen!

We landed effortlessly at the Belchers on Kasegalik Lake under a clear blue sky. The Arctic tundra was a new experience for Jack and the others. Unlike the Seal River, which is covered with small coniferous trees, the Belcher Islands are barren; rocks, mosses, and wild flowers are the only ground cover. I have spent many seasons in the Arctic so the barrenness is no longer startling, but for the others, it was a novelty. At first, you can only see the tundra as a cold desert; however, after a few days, you notice the subtlety of the colours. Only then can you begin to appreciate the stark beauty of the landscape. Now, whenever I am on the tundra, I find solace in the emptiness and experience a sense of expansion. Nothing is hidden from view: there's just the sky, the water and the barren land.

We tied up the aircraft along the rocky shore and quickly prepared our camp. Once the chores were completed, the group was itching to catch their evening meal. They were all keen to have their first experience with this fish that I had talked about so much. I led them down to the first set of rapids where I was quite confident that we could catch enough Arctic char for supper.

What amazed them most was the clarity of the water. The water in Kasegalik Lake is so crystal clear that you can see down thirty or forty feet. When they start-

Two Beavers at Kasegalik Lake on the Belcher Islands

ed fishing they were lost in the revelry of catching char. The fish were hungry for our mepp-type spinners, and we fished like men who had been starved for days. It was only the approaching darkness that made us aware of the lateness of the hour.

We cooked up our booty, and then recounted our experiences of the day. Each of us had our own version of how we had caught the perfect fish. Just as I was preparing for bed, I noticed that a south wind was picking up. Russ and I were both wary of this change and decided to move the two aircraft further apart. The wind continued to rise and that's exactly what Russ and I also had to do. During the night, we spent many hours tying and retying the two aircraft to keep them apart and facing the wind. When I am fishing in an isolated location, with no radio communication to an airbase, I am apprehensive if there is any threat to my only method of transportation. I usually sleep in the aircraft so I can be constantly on guard.

By the next morning, the wind had abated and the weather was perfect for fishing. The char greedily took our lures in the morning, but as the afternoon wore on, they began to ignore them. At that point, we decided to get out our fly rods and wade into the rapids. The char responded well to our flies. We all caught as many fish as we wanted.

The Arctic char in Kasegalik Lake migrate from Hudson Bay to spawn. While in the sea, these migratory char are mostly silver, with a steely blue-green back, pale pink spots on the sides, and a pale orange tinge to the belly. Once they enter the Kasegalik River, they gradually take on a predominantly orange or red colour. I've encountered the same Arctic char all over the Canadian Arctic—their patterns vary only slightly. The only fish that comes close to the char in appearance and taste is the Dolly Varden, which I found in the rivers and lakes bordering the northern rim of the Pacific during the RCAF survey trips in 1949 and 1950.

The Arctic char has become such a treasured fish all over the northern hemisphere that a new, non-migrating variety has been introduced to inland lakes in England and Ireland, as well as France, Germany, Scandinavia and Switzerland. In 1969, my air service flew a biologist into the Ungava Bay area to complete research on the Arctic char that were later transplanted into some of these lakes in Europe. Since the non-migratory variety doesn't move from saltwater to freshwater, its colouring doesn't undergo the same dramatic transformation. It maintains a greenish-brown colour with an orange/red belly and reddish spots on the sides.

Arctic char taste best when they come from the cold northern waters. As the water temperature rises, their flesh becomes softer. One of the great joys of fishing in the Arctic is that the fish are fresh when you eat them. I simply fillet them, roll them in flour and fry them in a little oil. There's nothing tastier after a day of fishing!

As we were enjoying our evening meal of fresh char, the wind started to pick up again. During the day the direction of the wind had varied, but as the evening progressed, the wind started to blow from the west and increased to 40 mph. Since the aircraft were parked into the wind, it didn't seem to be an immediate problem. However, as the wind increased, it shifted to the northwest, and we had to put additional lines on the aircraft. Russ and I had brought along some old automobile tires to act as bumpers so the aircraft wouldn't rub up on the rocks. Even a small puncture in a float can ground a seaplane for days. Our nighttime efforts paid off and the aircraft weathered the storm.

The following morning, the wind subsided enough to allow us to enjoy a morning of fishing. By midday everyone was ready for a change of scenery. We packed up our gear and prepared to return to the Seal River for more speckled trout fishing. We left Kasegalik Lake with quite a strong north wind and arrived on the Seal River in a record time of thirty-five minutes. Russ and I were delighted to secure the two aircraft on a nice sandy beach where they were well-protected from

the wind. I looked forward to sleeping through the night.

When we arrived back at the Seal River the weather had cooled down to 50°F, just about normal for July. The big fly hatches were over and the trout had moved from the lower pools. Our challenge was to find them again.

Russ and I hiked down the river but found very little action. We were both using fly rods and spin equipment interchangeably, but we only managed to catch a few small trout. While Jack put his attention on fishing for northern pike from the sand beach, Russ and Doug and I hiked to the upper section where Ominuk Lake empties into the river.

Doug started to work his fly rod with a small nymph on a #16 hook. He let it drift very tightly to the shore; within seconds he had a strike and landed a beautiful two-pound trout. At the time I was fishing with a small mepps spinner, but when I saw Doug catch his second fish, I dropped the spinning outfit and made a quick switch to the fly rod. The fish were feeding on black fly larvae, no rises, just gobbling as much of them as possible.

Russ was also spin fishing further downstream, but when he saw the action Doug was getting on the fly rod, he came bounding towards us and took out his fly rod. We were all anxious for some action. The three of us took turns allowing the small fly to drift along the shore line. Once we hooked a fish, we walked downstream to land it, while another fisherman was setting up his fly further upstream.

The next morning, when we returned to the same place to fish, we could see hundreds of trout rising. Each of us landed and released at least thirty fish before we broke camp. Our biggest challenge was to pull ourselves away from the stream and head back to civilization.

SUMMERS ON THE SEAL RIVER

Jack Kuiper and I prepared for a return trip to the Seal River in July 1992. It had been a cold wet spring in northern Ontario, but I never really expected that by mid-July we would still find ice on James Bay. Once we refueled in Painthills (Windminji), we barely managed to fly at 300 feet because of the rain and cloud cover. We arrived at Noname Lake, along the Seal River, in fog and drizzle. The weather didn't improve the entire trip.

I wasn't quite sure what to expect from the fishing at Noname Lake. At one time, it was my favourite spot along the Seal River, but once it was discovered by a construction crew that was working on a hydroelectric power plant at La Grande, the fishing deteriorated.

A forest fire had passed through the area the summer before and I wondered how this was going to affect the fishing. When we arrived in the fog and drizzle, the area looked like the aftermath of a war— everything was black. The trees that remained standing were charred and bare of any new growth. We set up our camp and in no time all our gear was covered with soot. Despite the depressing conditions, we felt undaunted and quickly headed off to the rapids, ready for the trout.

Walking was quite slow going. The fire had burned all the moss and ground cover. Eventually we arrived at my favourite old pool and set ourselves up with our spinning equipment. On my first cast, I was compensated for my efforts with a strike. Immediately the trout burst out of the water, flashing its colours, then took off downstream. After it had made a couple of hard runs, I managed to get the trout into the shallow water where I could land it. It was a beautiful specimen, with pink and black

spots along its silver flanks. By the time I released the trout, Jack had one on his line. These trout were hungry! We fished for several hours, totally absorbed in the experience; it was just the fish and us, nothing else mattered.

The next morning when we woke up, we could see our breath in the cold air. I peeked out of the tent and the black charred world had turned white. To take away the chill, I pulled the gas stove into the tent and made a pot of coffee. Only those obsessed with trout fishing would get out of a nice warm sleeping bag and hike to a pool in the snow. We must have been obsessed, because that's exactly what we did. We put on our winter jackets, and our wool gloves, and headed out knowing what was out there waiting for us. We didn't even mind the arduous walk over the slippery boulders.

In the early morning hours, the trout are very sensitive to the sound of casting lures. I've discovered that they usually hit flies at this time. We were ready for them. Jack had brought a floating line that was an orange colour but it spooked the trout. Once I equipped him with a dark green sinking line with streamer flies, he had the time of his life. I had four different fly reels with me, so we could take advantage of the changing conditions. The following day, we had to switch to floating lines and dry flies. Every day that we were in the pools, the fish were feeding on another fly hatch. We had to adjust our flies to whichever mayfly or sedge fly was prevalent that day.

Over the few days we spent at Noname Lake, Jack and I must have caught and released about a hundred trout that weighed between two and three pounds each. I would never have believed that the fishing could be so abundant after a fire had devastated the area. Actually, I think it may have improved the fishing because as the trees burned, insects were released from the bark. Trout love to eat bugs of any kind.

I'm quite sure we were the only non-natives who fished this part of the Seal River all summer. Most people would have been deterred by the desolation of the landscape. Jack and I managed to ignore all the minor details of imperfect weather and soot, to find an oasis of fishing pleasure. We feasted on fresh trout at every meal and brought a few fillets home for our families. When we arrived at the airbase in Chapleau, my son John cooked up a veritable feast with our trout fillets and his moose burgers. It was a trip to remember for many years—one we will talk about on the golf course for many seasons. Even before Jack left Canada, he made plans with me to return in 1993.

Jack and I talked about our future trip to the Seal River on several occasions in Florida, but by the spring, he reluctantly had to cancel for business reasons. As soon as Jack changed his plans, I had another person in mind who had been wanting to return to the Seal River. George Griffith, founder of *Trout Unlimited*, had made his first trip to the Seal River with me back in the 1960s and was anxious to make another trip at ninety-three years of age. I was a little apprehensive about his ability to walk the rough trails from the camp to the river, but he assured me that he was willing to do anything to fish again on those streams. I hired a

guide from Timmins, Larry Yusik, and George brought up a friend from Grayling, Ed Parks, to help him drive his car to Ivanhoe Lake.

We met up with Russ Bannock, his son, John, and friends, Doug Woolings and Bruce Mullen, in Cochrane. We flew straight through to Noname Lake in the two deHavilland Beavers. Before we set up our camp, a couple of us hiked back to the rapids to check out the pools. We found that they were full of trout, just waiting for our lures. Our two aggressive young men, John and Larry, worked with their chain saws and had a trail blazed to the rapids and the camp set up by the time Russ returned with our first feed of fresh speckled trout.

Ed and Larry slept in a comfortable 10-by-12 canvas tent with George. I had brought along a camp cot for George, just in case the weather turned cold. Naturally, it did by the second day. The wind turned to the northwest. As the weather cooled, we lost all the black flies and mosquitoes.

George Griffith on the Seal River in 1962

When George was ready for his first day of trout fishing, Larry preceded him to the river, and cut the brambles along the shore so that George could sit on a chair and fly cast. Once we had him settled, George announced that he would be satisfied to catch just six trout. The river was boiling with trout that weighed between one-and-a-half and two-and-a-half pounds. As George caught each trout, he admired it and returned it to the river. Within an hour or so he had caught his six trout and put his fly rod away. We escorted him back to our camp and again dined on some fine trout. He declined our invitation to return to the rapids for more fishing. George had satisfied all his fishing desires in a couple of hours on the Seal River. He never did return to the pools. He was happy to sit around the camp and entertain us with his fishing stories.

Everyone else went fishing and came back to camp to tell George about the trout they had caught. Ed and Larry chose to fish the upper rapids and caught several fish that weighed over five pounds. On one of their excursions, Ed returned to the camp for lunch before Larry could tear himself away from the fishing. While he was fishing, a black bear appeared on the other side of the stream. Larry had asked me about the chances of encountering a bear on the Seal River while we were flying north. I assured him that I had never seen a bear this far inland. I think that Larry's concern stemmed from an incident the previous year when a young man was mauled to death by a black bear in the Cochrane area.

Larry was very cool about the presence of the bear just a hundred yards across the stream. He gradually moved further downstream, but the bear followed him, maintaining its position on the other side. It was only when the bear began to cross the stream that Larry took more evasive action; he climbed a tree along the shore. Even he can't figure out how he did so wearing his hip waders. About an hour later, we were wondering what happened to Larry. John took a hike up the stream to find him.

Larry heard John coming and yelled to him to return to camp to get something to scare the bear that was still sitting under the tree. By the time Ed and John returned with frying pans, the bear had wandered off, but Larry was still in his perch.

We spent an evening discussing the likelihood of meeting a bear and what to do when the bear gets curious. I have travelled in the Seal River area for forty years and this was the first time I heard of a bear so far from the coast. However, in the future I will warn everyone about the possibility.

Each day the weather got worse. By the third day the temperature was just a few degrees above freezing. Fortunately the weather cleared on the fourth day and we dismantled the camp. We had to divert thirty miles to refuel at LG2 (La Grande) because there was no aviation fuel available at Paint Hills. As we approached the coast, the ceiling dropped. Even though the visibility was fifteen miles, we had to fly at 200 feet until we passed Rupert House. The weather lifted just east of Hannah Bay and we had 1000 feet to Cochrane. After refueling, Russ and his friends flew south to Huntsville, while we continued our trek to Ivanhoe Lake.

Everyone returned with at least one new story to tell. Larry had his bear episode and Ed had his five-pound trout. George had another Seal River trip to add to his repertoire. Not many trout fishermen at ninety-three years of age have either the desire or the ability to endure a camping trip in such cold, windy weather. George certainly proved that his devotion to trout fishing goes beyond the norm.

TIME TO WATCH NATURE AT WORK

Fishing at Sahler Lake outpost camp, 1992

I can honestly say that I haven't spent very many days in the bush without catching my share of fish. For the past few years, I've enlisted the aid of an electronic depth finder to determine the depth and the movement beneath the boat, but it still takes some skill to master the other factors which have a say in whether or not the fish bite—that is, choosing the right bait and the right time to fish. Once all these are accounted for, I usually expect that a fish will be unable to resist the temptation. However, with regard to fishing, anyway, nature seems to have its own ways of supporting or ignoring my desires. Just when I think I have mastered the workings of Mother Nature, I'm foiled, and left wondering where I went wrong.

In July 1992, I spent a few days fishing at Sahler Lake with my wife Joan. Prior to our trip, my son, John, provided me with a detailed map of Sahler Lake, outlining the best fishing spots. Our air service had established an outpost camp on the lake in the 1960s to take advantage of the excellent moose hunting. The hunters discovered that the lake produced some good-sized northern pike, as well as lots of moose, so we stocked the lake with walleye. Within a few years, we were able to use the lake as a regular fishing location during the spring and summer season.

With map in hand, Joan and I headed out for some solitude and fishing. We unloaded the aircraft, and then hiked to a nearby pond to pick up some minnows from a trap that had been set by the previous guests. It was my first fishing trip of the season. I was a little anxious to taste fresh walleye. But it wasn't to be. In our search for walleye, only two northern pike liked the looks of our lures. Even though both northerns were about two feet long, one was rather thin so we released it and kept the fatter one for breakfast. When a northern is large enough, I can fillet it so that there are very few bones to pick out. And when caught in the cold, northern

Ontario waters, they are quite tasty. Even the most ardent walleye fisherman can be fooled with a well-filleted northern pike.

Early the next morning, as the light was just beginning to appear, I snuck out of the cabin, hoping to attract a few walleye during their traditional feeding time. Fishing all by yourself, as the world begins to wake up, is one of the most sublime experiences. I have to admit that it's as close as I ever get to morning meditation. The silence of the night gradually gives way to a few chirps. Then before I know it, a symphony of sounds completely envelopes me. About this time, the mist that had hugged the lake completely disappeared, with hardly a trace.

I fished in earnest, but to no avail. I arrived back at the cabin without a fish but with a feeling of satisfaction, nonetheless. The serious fishing had not yet begun and I was anticipating a hearty breakfast to prepare me for the long-awaited contest. I don't really think of my fishing trips as a contest between myself and the fish, or even between myself and other fishermen. It's more of a test of my own intuition—whether or not I can read the signs of nature well enough to harvest some of her fruits.

Joan and I feasted on the pike, listened to the news on our battery-operated radio, and then set out for a day of fishing. The weather was quite cool for the first week in July. It was the kind of unpredictable weather you expect in May or September. Fortunately, the sun came out for what looked like a rather pleasant day. We crossed the lake and trolled along a rocky shoal where I was sure the walleye would be hiding. On our first pass, we could see a few movements on the depth finder, but nothing went for our lures.

I hadn't spent much time fishing on Sahler Lake and wondered what we would find in a little bay just off the rocky shoal.

As we approached the bay, we saw a loon with two chicks on her back, swimming near a large rock that stood directly in front of the entrance to the bay. Even though I slowed down, the loons continued to get more and more agitated as we approached. When we were within fifty feet, the adult loon quickly dove under the water. The young ones weren't able to follow. The adult loon surfaced fifty feet behind us and then raced towards us shrieking and beating its wings on the water. We weren't quite sure whether it was a warning for us or the chicks. Within a few seconds, another adult loon arrived on the scene. Meanwhile, the chicks were paddling in circles, trying unsuccessfully to scramble up the slippery rock.

We felt like helpless intruders in the situation, but decided that our only course of action was to proceed through the narrow entrance to the bay. Turning around might have been even more confusing, because then we would have been heading directly towards the adult loons. Once our boat passed by the chicks, the parent loons arrived to collect their offspring. The shrieking stopped and some sense of calmness was restored as they all swam off towards the shoreline.

The bay turned out to be quite shallow with too many reeds for walleye fishing. We made a quick turn around and headed back into the lake. As we passed by the rock at the entrance, the adult loons and the chicks were huddling close together along the shore. Both the adults kept watch of our activities until we were far away from their territory.

We trolled over the rocky shoals once again. This time I got a strike in front of a beaver lodge which was hugging the shore. The walleye hit on a yellow-silver Shyster lure in about twelve feet of water. Landing it was quite a tricky procedure. Since I had neglected to bring a landing net, I brought the fish in close enough to reach out, grab the line, and hoist it into the boat.

The four-pound walleye was a beauty! Just looking at the fish made me shiver as its shiny golden skin sparkled in the sun. I was quite sure that there were more walleye down there waiting for our lures. Joan switched to a spoon and we drifted in the area for another hour until hunger got the better of us.

The walleye, which was large enough to feed both of us, satisfied our hunger but not our desire for more fishing. We unanimously agreed to return to the beaver lodge to see if the walleye had developed an appetite. While I put on another spoon, Joan rigged up a walleye harness with two minnows. She casually remarked that perhaps the beavers might object to strangers setting up shop at their front door.

Within fifteen minutes, her prediction came true as an adult beaver surfaced right next to our boat, rolled over and slapped its tail on the water when it dove under. We were both stunned by the beaver's speed and the racket it created. It was obvious that this was not a happy greeting. Sometimes, when nature gives you these signs that it's time to move on, you just can't help but wonder what would happen if you didn't. So we stayed and continued to fish.

We began to wonder about the beaver's activities when we heard some cooing noises coming from the lodge. About ten minutes later, the beaver surfaced suddenly and repeated his demonstration on the other side of the boat. This time the splash was enough to spray Joan.

Even though we were still determined to stand our ground, or our water, we began to feel that our intrusion was stifling the beaver's daily routine. Reluctantly, we lifted our anchor and drifted along the shore. As soon as we had moved about twenty yards from the front of the lodge,

the adult surfaced, followed by two younger ones. While the young ones frolicked with each other in the water, the adult kept surfacing nearby to check out the situation. Now it was obvious to us that we had been trespassing in their territory during one of their evening rituals.

We continued to monitor the beavers' activities from our new vantage point until Joan got a strike. It was only our second walleye of the day, but it was worth the wait. It was another good-sized fish, perfect for eating. Just when the fishing action was picking up, darkness began to descend over the lake. As we started up the motor to head back to the camp, the beavers were still swimming around in front of their lodge, but the adult seemed to be the only one at work.

The next morning I tried my luck again along the rocky shoal but nothing was biting, not even the northerns. Once it started to drizzle, the serenity of the morning dissolved and I realized it was time for breakfast. I returned to the cabin, lit a fire to take off the chill of the damp air, and turned on the radio to listen for the forecast. It sounded like it was going to be a wet day in camp.

The weather never did improve, nor did the fishing. I've discovered over the years, that in these situations, the only sane approach is to just enjoy every moment, even if it's not what I expected. Joan and I wiled away a few hours listening to a Blue Jay baseball game on the radio. Then, when the urge came upon us, we tidied up the camp and flew back to the airbase, dodging a few rain showers along the way.

Even though we left Sahler Lake without completely satisfying our desire for the taste of walleye, we took some fond memories of loons and beavers and a more settled feeling of being closer to nature. There was always the next trip to look forward to and more fish to be caught.

LOOKING BACK AND LOOKING FORWARD

When I was a young lad paddling down the Mattagami river and hiking along the trail to MacArthur Lake, I never thought there would ever be a time when life in the woods would change. There seemed to be so much forest and so many lakes that I could never imagine that this precious gift could be in danger. But then, I never considered a population explosion that would put heavy demands on all of nature's investment.

In northern Ontario many of our natural resources have been pushed to their limit by the industrial giants of the south—in particular, our minerals and our trees. But the one resource that we all took for granted was the wildlife, the game fishing and hunting.

How could I foresee that the waters in northern Ontario would be fished out? In those days it wasn't easy to get to most of the lakes, unless you hiked for several days through the woods, or canoed down a river, or, if you were very lucky, flew in a seaplane. There weren't many roads through the forests because they were expensive to build and maintain. The railroads offered some access to remote areas. A few tourist outfitters took advantage of this and built lodges on the lakes with railroad access.

As I grew up fishing the lakes and rivers around my hometown of Timmins, I quickly learned that fish don't stay fresh long after they have been taken out of the water. I was taught how to wrap a fish in moss to preserve its freshness, until I returned it home for my mother to cook. And as I got older, I began to cook fish over a camp fire to savour the delicate fish at its freshest. The thought of taking more fish than I could eat or safely carry home never occurred to me. What was the point? At a very young age, I had to satisfy my passion for fishing by catching and releasing the fish I couldn't keep.

The native women in the Timmins area prepared fish for the winter season by smoking it in a small smoke tent or drying it on lines. Of course, it never tasted quite the same as fresh fish, but it certainly filled the belly on a winter day. They usually cooked it in stews along with potatoes and carrots, which helped mask the strong flavour. The fish tended to acquire a sharp taste once it was preserved for any length of time.

The idea of taking large quantities of fish only became widespread when modern methods of deep freezing were available. I was already living away from home by the time my parents bought an electric refrigerator in 1945. The first time I tasted fish that had been frozen, I was surprised at how closely it resembled fresh fish. It was only when I tasted fresh fish again that I realized that the resemblance wasn't that close. Fresh fish have a subtle flavour; it is never sharp or flat. The aftertaste is clean and odorless. Fish that has been frozen doesn't melt in your mouth.

When I became a tourist outfitter in the Chapleau area, my staff and I made our guests aware of their limit of fish and encouraged them to abide by those restrictions. To ensure that this was done, we often had game wardens from the Department of Lands and Forest on our docks when the aircraft landed. If a guest took too many fish, he was fined immediately so there was no reward for abusing nature's harvest.

I had both ecological and business-related reasons for encouraging our guests to be moderate in the amount of fish they took out of the lakes. If I condoned over-fishing then the lake would soon produce fewer and fewer fish. We controlled the number of guests at our outpost camps each season to be sure that the fishing never deteriorated. My sons continue to use many of the lakes where I first established outpost camps in the 1950s. The only lakes which they can no longer use are ones that now have road access.

Roads were built into many of the remote fishing spots when the lumber companies were allowed to begin clearcutting in the 1960s. Then I began to notice the devastation that access roads can have on the fishing. Once people can load up their truck or all-terrain vehicle with pounds and pounds of fish, they do so. There simply aren't enough game wardens to police all the new roads that the lumber companies have built. While it is very difficult for a canoeist or a hiker to carry out more than his limit of fish, it is very easy for a person with an automobile to carry out as many fish as he can store in coolers in his vehicle.

We have learned by bitter experience that no waters can stand unrestricted fishing year after year. Even though the supply may stand up well, eventually a danger point is reached and the balance is destroyed. Once the fish have disappeared from a lake, it takes constant attention and thousands of tax payers' dollars to restock a lake and bring it back to its original levels.

It seems wiser now to put our attention on preserving what we have, rather than trying to reconstruct nature's perfect environment. I think we have all learned the hard way that we cannot squander what was our birthright. We need to pass on what we have to the future generations so they too can appreciate nature's beauty.

When I began my career as an outfitter in Chapeau, the majority of our guests were true sportsmen who respected the art of fishing. For them, the true pleasure was to catch and release fish. I'm sure there were instances of immense catches from our lakes. However, this kind of activity is becoming rare. Modern anglers seem to be more interested in perfecting their skill at releasing fish than killing them. If this trend continues, we can look forward to endless years of superb fishing on our Canadian lakes and rivers.

Today John and George Jr. are so determined to promote this type of sport fishing that they offer a discount to their guests who opt for a trip to a lake that they have designated as "catch and release only." The guests are allowed to eat fish while at the outpost camp and take out only one fish per person. John and George could only afford to develop smaller, more isolated lakes by offering them on a "catch and release" basis. It ensures their investment and protects the fishing for future generations.

Even though this "catch and release" system is officially used in other provinces, including Manitoba, the government of Ontario doesn't yet sponsor these programs. What this means is that the outfitters who ensure that their guests practice "catch and release" have no protection from others who drop in to the lake and take out as many fish as they catch. I can only hope that our own government soon sees the value of enforcing a program whereby all the lakes in Ontario have the protection of some type of "catch and release" system.

LIKE FATHER, LIKE SONS

My three sons—John, George Jr. and Richard, 1993

My life has revolved around airplanes since I was fourteen years old. It didn't come as a surprise to me when my three sons all decided to become commercial pilots. I never remember encouraging any of them to pursue a flying career. In fact, I may have suggested alternatives, but that didn't stop them from doing the one thing that was completely natural to them.

All my children, including my three daughters, grew up reading maps. Each took their turn sitting in the co-pilot seat acting as the navigator. Their navigation skills were superior to many of the pilots that I hired. On one occasion, my oldest son, John, had to map read for a pilot who got lost when he decided to fly over a fog bank. When the fog finally cleared, they were about twenty miles beyond their destination, Raney Lake. There were no recognizable lakes in sight. John spotted a village on a lake and they landed to ascertain their whereabouts. Once they had established their location, John easily navigated them back to Raney Lake. That same pilot never did learn to read a map and eventually got stranded for several days on a lake near James Bay.

When John completed his commercial license in the spring of 1972, he hadn't yet trained on the Beaver and we needed another Beaver pilot immediately. I had confidence that he could learn the skills quickly, so I took him with me on a fire patrol in Biscotasing, twenty miles south of Chapleau. We were stationed there for about four days when I was called back to the base in Chapleau for some other emergency. I had an aircraft fly down to pick me up and left John with the Beaver to continue by himself. The weather was still very dry and the fire danger was extreme.

Two days later, it began raining to the west and the Beaver was no longer needed for fire patrol. By the time John arrived back in Chapleau, the storm was very close and the winds were blowing down the river at over 30 mph. He landed the Beaver in front of the airbase. Then his difficulties began because he couldn't get the aircraft turned downwind to taxi it back to the dock.

Unlike the smaller Cessna aircraft, a Beaver doesn't naturally turn downwind. As soon as it gets broadside to the wind, the force of the wind on the tail pushes the nose of the aircraft into the wind again. Each time John tried to turn the aircraft around, it wouldn't complete the turn. His efforts took him to the other side of the river. In desperation to avoid hitting one of the boathouses on the shore, he gave the aircraft full power in the turn and this pulled it around. He came within ten feet of knocking a wing off the aircraft but learned how to turn downwind. Today, the Beaver is equipped with a different set of floats, with larger water rudders so that the pilot no longer needs to apply full power to turn it downwind.

John went on to perfect his skills flying the Beaver as well as the twin-engine Beech 18. He flew for a couple of other air services to hone his skills before becoming an outfitter and settling down to his business in Chapleau. In the summer of 1978, he flew for Simpson Air out of Yellowknife on a contract with the Geological Survey of Canada. He had the opportunity to fly into many of the places that I had visited while I worked on the RCAF surveys in 1949 and 1950, including Bathurst Inlet, Coppermine, Point Lake and Great Bear Lake. He also spent two years based in Fort Chimo, Quebec (Kuujjuaq), flying a twin Otter for Air Inuit.

George Jr. followed in his older brother's footsteps and took to a flying career early in life. He combined his skills as a pilot with the skills of an aircraft mechanic/engineer, and subsequently operated as our chief engineer. He and his wife, Jeanne, now own a much expanded airbase at Ivanhoe Lake. They have perfected their skills as outfitters and now offer sportsmen the opportunity to fish/hunt in first class motel accommodations, as well as fly-in and boat-in outpost camps.

My youngest son Richard, like his older brothers, began his flying career at a young age. His path has taken him out of northern Ontario and into the international airports around the world. Now as a captain on a 757, he flies to Europe and Asia, as well as North and South America. He still comes home in the summer for a fishing trip to our family camp.

Every year in early August, John reserves his outpost camp at Nemegosenda for the exclusive use of our children and grandchildren. Joan and I began taking our six children on these annual vacations in 1958. Now they are giving their children the opportunity to experience life in the outdoors.

That's the most amazing thing: life just goes on—with us and without us. None of us are permanent fixtures on this landscape; we are all trespassers in God's country.

Three Beavers at the Nemegosenda camp, 1993

CPSIA information can be obtained
at www.ICGtesting.com
Printed in the USA
BVHW012009020222
627941BV00011B/219

9 781887 472463